AF718729

Shaping Tradition

African Social Studies Series

VOLUME 14

Shaping Tradition

Civil Society, Community and Development in Colonial Northern Ghana, 1899–1957

by

Jeff D. Grischow

TUTA SUB AEGIDE PALLAS · 1683 ·

BRILL

LEIDEN • BOSTON
2006

This book is printed on acid-free paper.

Library of Congress Cataloging-in-Publication Data

A C.I.P. record for this book is available from the Library of Congress.

ISSN 1568-1203
ISBN-13: 978 90 04 15243 4
ISBN-10: 90 04 15243 1

PRINTED IN THE NETHERLANDS

For Joanne, Doug, Yvette and Sydney

CONTENTS

LIST OF MAPS AND FIGURES

ACKNOWLEDGEMENTS

This book is based on my doctoral dissertation entitled "A History of Development in the Northern Territories of the Gold Coast, 1899–1957." Many people have supported the project, but I owe a particular debt of gratitude to my thesis supervisor, Robert Shenton, for his insights, criticisms and moral support. Alan Jeeves, David Eltis, Barry Riddell and Gavin Williams also provided valuable feedback. At Queen's University I enjoyed the company of a strong group of African studies colleagues, including Glenn McKnight, Louis Awanyo, Kobena Hanson, Simon Rutabajuuka, the late Bazaara Nyangabyaki, Amir H. Idris, Mike O'Brien, and the late Lewis Mtonga. Also at Queen's, I could not have survived this project without the support of Mike Dawson, Russell Johnston, Martina Hardwick and Ross Fair. Research funding was provided by the Social Sciences and Humanities Research Council of Canada, the Ontario Graduate Scholarship Program and the School of Graduate Studies and Research at Queen's University.

Many other people have been with me along the way, through the good times and the bad. My colleagues at Wilfrid Laurier University, both faculty and staff, have provided a welcome academic home for the past five years. Beyond the academy, many friends have provided constant encouragment and support. In Ontario: Michael Alemu, Arun Pal, Pat Skinner, Mark Spielmacher and Scott Davis. In Britain: Joanna, Aurora and Isolde Peberdy, Phyllis Ferguson, and the late S.W.D.K. Gandah. Also in Britain, I had the good fortune to meet and interview a wide range of people. In England, I would like to thank B.J. Silk, Basil Hoare, and Sylvia Lynn-Meaden. In Wales, the Peberdys were instrumental in establishing research contacts. In Scotland, John and Betty Hinds, A.F. Kerr and Ian and Sheila Baillie kindly took me in and shared their memories. Many people in Ghana made my stay both enjoyable and productive, especially Edward and Comfort Narh Tawiah and Sigrid Ann Snitzer. No less important were T. Sayibu and Samata Imoro, Albert and Eugenia Tenga, Amadu Mahama, Alhaji Mustapha Ali and B.S.T. Gandah, as well as Dr. Nana Brempon Arhin and Dr. K. Kwabia at the Institute of African Studies, University of Ghana. I would also like to thank the staff of the National Archives of Ghana in Accra and Tamale, the Public Record Office in London and the Rhodes House Library at Oxford University. More recently, Carola Lentz read the entire manuscript and offered many valuable comments and criticisms. Cheryl Lemmens expertly prepared the index and offered very helpful editorial comments. At Brill, Sasha Goldstein and Renee Otto patiently and expertly guided me through the production process.

Most importantly, my parents Joanne and Doug Grischow, and my wife Yvette Waterman-Scott and step-daughter Sydney, have been by my side during an intensive and challenging revision process. This book is dedicated to them. Of course, as is always the case, I bear sole responsibility for any errors of omissions.

CHAPTER ONE

CIVIL SOCIETY, COMMUNITY AND DEVELOPMENT IN COLONIAL NORTHERN GHANA, 1899–1957

In an important recent book, Michael Edwards recommends building African civil society on the foundation of "associations based on primordial attachments," which "are a natural consequence of the ways in which African societies have been structured in the past."[1] Edwards' view typifies much writing on African development, in which community—preferably in its "natural" form—is invoked as a tool for building civil society in the name of better development. Much of this literature equates civil society with community on the basis of associational life. In particular, governance scholars privilege voluntary associations, which are called upon to act collectively for the good of all citizens by exerting pressure on the state. For example, Michael Bratton defines civil society as a "public sphere of collective action," which provides a political space for communities to develop rules of legitimate governance.[2] Hyden echoes Bratton, emphasising the role of civil society in the "conscious management of regime structures with a view to enhancing the legitimacy of the public realm."[3] In a recent study of Northern Ghana, Mohan defines civil society as a "pluralistic space whereby associations act as transmission belts between the individual and the state".[4] In this literature, the balance of interests between competing associations leads to national policies that benefit the community of citizens. Good governance thus requires the strengthening of local, community-based organisations.[5] Lest we think that this idea is confined to the ivory

---

[1] Michael Edwards, *Civil Society* (Cambridge: Polity Press, 2004), 31.

[2] Michael Bratton, "Civil Society and Political Transitions in Africa," in John W. Harbeson, Donald Rothchild and Naomi Chazan (eds), *Civil Society and the State in Africa* (Boulder: Lynne Rienner Publishers, Inc., 1994), 75.

[3] Goran Hyden, "Governance and the Study of Politics," in *Governance and Politics in Africa*, ed. Goran Hyden and Michael Bratton, 7–8 (Boulder: Lynne Rienner Publishers, 1992).

[4] Giles Mohan, "The Disappointments of Civil Society: the Politics of NGO Intervention in Northern Ghana," *Political Geography* 21(2002):127.

[5] Goran Hyden, "Civil Society, Social Capital, and Development: Dissection of

tower, it also has emerged at the World Bank in the guise of Community Driven Development (CDD). Under CDD, local communities define their own priorities and express them to development agencies through community organisations. According to the Bank, CDD will replace corruption with transparency and good governance, vulnerability with security, and a lack of trust with social capital.[6]

The equation of community and civil society in this literature contrasts sharply with the colonial experience in Northern Ghana (the Northern Territories of the Gold Coast), where colonial officials invoked community *against* civil society in an attempt to preserve African social structures while extracting resources and labour for the colonial economy. In this manner, colonial development policy sought both economic transformation and social changelessness, or, in the language of Governor Sir F.G. Guggisberg, development without "denationalisation." Guggisberg equated denationalisation with individualism and westernisation, which had emerged in southern Ghana (the Colony and Ashanti) during the uncontrolled development of trade and cash crop agriculture. These developments produced a vibrant African educated elite as well as a growing number of unemployed school leavers, both of which posed an economic and political threat to the colonial administration. Economically, a prosperous African population threatened to undermine colonial control over trade and access to cheap labour, while the concurrent development of unemployment fed into labour unrest. Politically, the educated elite challenged the legitimacy of colonial rule through campaigns of anticolonial resistance, which by the 1940s were strongly supported by unemployed youth in the cities. These trends reinforced earlier colonial beliefs that the emergent African elite had to be reined in because their development was "premature," in that it had not unfolded naturally from within their traditional social structures. The disintegration of tradition produced social chaos, which challenged colonial rule, rather than a smooth transition to modernity within the bounds of colonialism. In other words, the development of African civil society was a danger to the colonial state, a realm of conflict rather than co-operation. In response, the colonial administration

a Complex Discourse," *Studies in Comparative and International Development* 32, No. 1 (Spring, 1997): 8–9.

[6] http://www.worldbank.org/participation/CDD.htm.

invoked community as a hedge against civil society in order to maintain state power while exploiting the resources of the colonies.

The Idea of Civil Society

Underlying this argument is a specific interpretation of civil society, which I identify as a realm between the family and the state associated with economic development, the rise of the market and the appearance of the middle class. This interpretation differs from most advocates of governance and social capital who tend to describe civil society simply as a constellation of voluntary associations. The difference is significant, and it reflects different conceptual strands of the civil society debate. Whereas the "associationalists" draw on Alexis de Tocqueville, my interpretation of civil society leans more heavily on the lineage stretching back to Adam Ferguson and the Enlightenment. For reasons discussed below, I believe the latter to be more useful for assessing the colonial development project in Northern Ghana.

It is significant that the associational school of civil society draws on Tocqueville rather than Adam Ferguson because it leads to the assumption that voluntary associations are rooted in a natural form of community, which reinforces the conflation of community and civil society. In his analysis of nineteenth century American democracy, Tocqueville offered an inclusive vision of *political* society, which privileged voluntary associations and included virtually all citizens of a state.[7] Tocqueville's idea of political society drew on the pre-Enlightenment theory of traditional natural law, which equated civil society with political society and contrasted the civil realm to the state of nature. This notion revolved around the idea of a natural community, "grounded in history and place," which privileged community co-operation over conflict. Rooted in Tocqueville, the associationalists thus tend to emphasise the cohesive side of voluntary association and community.[8] In contrast, Adam Ferguson separated civil society from political society and the state and emphasised its connections to commercial activity rather than natural bonds of community. Ferguson argued that civil society developed out of economic

[7] Laurence Whitehead, "Bowling in the Bronx: The Uncivil Interstices Between Civil and Political Society," *Democratization* 4, No. 1 (Spring, 1997): 94, 99.

[8] Robert Fine, "Civil Society Theory, Enlightenment and Critique," *Democratization* 4, No. 1 (Spring, 1997): 8, 12, 15.

progress, with the development of capitalism as a necessary condition for its growth.[9] Hegel and Marx carried this idea further by linking civil society not only to the division of labour but also more specifically to the development of the bourgeoisie.[10] For Ferguson, Hegel and Marx, therefore, the development of civil society was associated with the emergence of the commercial sphere during the development of capitalism in the eighteenth and nineteenth centuries. In other words, it represented "a network of distinctively economic relations, the sphere of the market place, the arena of production, distribution and exchange."[11] As such, civil society was not rooted in any form of natural community; instead it developed out of associations of property owners in capitalist society.[12]

As a realm of individuals pursuing individual interests, civil society was contradictory and full of conflict. "In Enlightenment thought," writes Fine, "civil society denoted a sphere of contradiction," rooted in the material inequality produced by the early development of capitalism in Britain.[13] For Hegel, civil society was not a harmonious sphere; rather, it was "a restless battlefield" where private, individual interests clashed with one another between the family and the state.[14] For Marx, civil society was a realm of conflict, reflecting the interests of the middle class to establish its dominance and capture the power of the state.[15] In the process, the production of inequality through the market threatened to destroy previous forms of community through the atomisation of society.[16] For Enlightenment thinkers, in other words, the emergence of civil society posed a political problem associated with the breakdown of community.[17]

[9] John Keane, "Despotism and Democracy," in *Civil Society and the State: New European Perspectives*, ed. John Keane, 40–1, 44 (London: Verso, 1988). Ellen Meiksins Wood, *Democracy Against Capitalism: Renewing Historical Materialism* (Cambridge: Cambridge University Press, 1995), 239–40.

[10] Whitehead, 97; Eboe Hutchful, "The Civil Society Debate in Africa," *International Journal* 51 (Winter, 1995–6): 63.

[11] Meiksins Wood, 241.

[12] Whitehead, 97.

[13] Fine, 17.

[14] Keane, 51, 54–5.

[15] Noberto Bobbio, "Gramsci and the Concept of Civil Society," in *Civil Society and the State: New European Perspectives*, ed. John Keane (London: Verso, 1988): 75.

[16] Jack Lively and Andrew Reeve, "The Emergence of the Idea of Civil Society: the Artificial Political Order and Natural Social Orders," *Democratization* 4, No. 1 (Spring, 1997): 68.

[17] Fine, 19.

In anchoring their analyses in Tocqueville, present-day civil society theorists—especially the governance advocates—tend to conflate the Enlightenment conception of civil society with Tocqueville's idea of political society. This is significant for our purposes because it diverts attention away from civil society as a potential realm of conflict associated with the breakdown of previous forms of community. As we shall see below, colonial officials were well aware of this possibility, and for this reason the idea of civil society rooted in the Enlightenment provides a more appropriate starting point for this study than Tocqueville's conception of political society and voluntary association.

Colonialism, Development and Power

Wary of the potential for civil society to produce disorder and conflict, colonial officials tried to block its growth as they brought African societies under the power of the colonial state. That this project invoked community against civil society is demonstrated very effectively in Mahmood Mamdani's influential book *Citizen and Subject*. Mamdani argues that colonial states perceived civil society as a threat and invoked community to exclude rural Africans from its sphere in the cities, attempting to block them from the very public sphere that the governance advocates call the civic public realm. Drawing on Gramsci, Habermas and Eley, Mamdani argues that the public sphere was an antagonistic sphere, "a sphere of conflicting interests." More importantly, the institutions of civil society could be used either in support of or against the will of the state.[18] On the one hand, the dominant class can use civil society to achieve control over the citizens of a state. On the other hand, civil society can provoke political mobilisation and strife which challenge the state's hegemony.[19] These challenges unfold in the realm of the public sphere, which according to Habermas developed first in Europe, where the emerging bourgeoisie "shaped 'an associational life' along voluntary and democratic principles". For Eley, associational life within the public sphere produces exclusion as well as inclusion. Civil society, that is, includes competing "publics," where one group in the public sphere

[18] See Hutchful, 73.
[19] See Hyden, "Governance and the Study of Politics," 7.

takes over public life and excludes other publics from its realm (women, ethnic minorities, peasants, et cetera).[20]

Drawing on the idea of competing publics, Mamdani moves beyond exclusion to assess the structures of power through which the excluded groups were incorporated into the sphere of colonial power. Exclusion from civil society was based on the exercise of "another form of power," which Mamdani identifies with indirect rule. Colonial states imposed indirect rule on the African peasantry by formulating and enforcing customary law, based on tradition. In urban areas, by contrast, colonial states imposed civil law, based on the rights of citizens. Colonial power in Africa thus worked itself out through a bifurcated state, where "urban power spoke the language of civil society and civil rights, rural power of community and culture. Civil power claimed to protect rights, customary power pledged to enforce tradition." In rural areas, excluded from civil society, enforcing tradition necessitated the preservation of African community. Colonial states in Africa therefore turned community against civil society in the construction of customary rule in the African countryside. Put another way, colonial states tried to shore up traditional community through indirect rule in order to *exclude* African peasants from civil society. Based on this project, colonial officials fused political power (legislative, executive, judicial, administrative and coercive) in the hands of the chiefs under the system of indirect rule. Mamdani calls indirect rule "decentralised despotism" and he notes that it used customary law and land tenure to maintain peasant communities as subjects rather than citizens, answerable to custom rather than rights. In contrast to the associationalists, therefore, Mamdani argues that the colonial state in Africa used community *against* civil society in constructing indirect rule in the countryside. In Mamdani's words, "more than anywhere else, there was in the African colonial experience a one-sided opposition between the individual and the group, civil society and community, rights and tradition."[21]

Mamdani's allusions to language and power naturally lead into the debate over the relationship between European discourses and colonial rule. For some scholars, colonial discourses of African custom and tradition constituted a "knowledge-power base" that defined

[20] Mahmood Mamdani *Citizen and Subject: Contemporary Africa and the Legacy of Late Colonialism* (Princeton: Princeton University Press, 1996), 15–16.
[21] Ibid., 15–22.

Africans as being in need of colonial intervention and forced them to submit to a universalising Western project.[22] In this formulation, discourses themselves have social consequences, forcing local people to operate within their terms. "The production and circulation of discourses," writes Artruro Escobar, "is an integral component of the exercise of power."[23] James Ferguson has applied this idea to development discourse in Africa. As the central organising concept of our time, "development" constitutes the "dominant interpretative grid" through which we view the non-western world. Drawing on Foucault, Ferguson argues that this dominant grid functions as a "conceptual apparatus . . . an elaborate contraption that *does* something." But what does development achieve and how is it accomplished? Studying a project in Lesotho, which unfolded between 1975 and 1984, Ferguson concludes that development discourse contributed to the expansion of bureaucratic state power over isolated areas of the country. This was not the intended result of the project, which was supposed to be a non-political, technical program of livestock development. Instead, the expansion of bureaucratic state power unfolded behind the backs of the participants as a result of the conceptual apparatus of the discourse of development. Power was exercised, but it took the form of "unintended outcomes" which were "incorporated into anonymous constellations of control" containing, nonetheless, "a kind of political intelligibility." The exercise of state power, in Foucault's terms, was an instrument effect of the discourse, which on the surface was apolitical. In Ferguson's words, the "unintended yet instrumental elements in a resultant constellation" produced "the expansion of a particular kind of state power while simultaneously exerting a powerful depoliticising effect."[24] This expansion of state power through the apparently contradictory process of depoliticisation represents the essence of the antipolitics machine. In this manner, development discourse serves to depoliticise and disempower local communities to the benefit of the state.

[22] Frederick Cooper and Randall Packard, *International Development and the Social Sciences: Essays on the History and Politics of Knowledge* (Berkeley: University of California Press, 1997): 2–3.

[23] Arturo Escobar, "Power and Visibility: the Invention and Management of Development in the Third World." *Cultural Anthropology* 3, No. 4 (1988): 430, 435.

[24] James Ferguson, *The Anti-politics Machine: 'Development,' Depoliticization and Bureaucratic Power in Lesotho* (Cambridge: Cambridge University Press, 1990), xv, 18–21.

Ferguson locates the origins of the antipolitics machine in the late colonial period, when a new idea of development emerged after 1945 that sought to transform tribes into nations capable of competing on the modern world stage. Cooper and Packard agree, arguing that "development" emerged alongside the new system of post-war states created by decolonisation and symbolised by the United Nations. However, Cooper traces the roots of this shift further back, to the late 1930s when a wave of labour resistance swept across the colonial world. Rather than deal with these protests as a labour problem, colonial officials responded with new programs of economic and social development and the new idea of development was born.[25] In the process, experts concerned with development shifted from the passive to the active voice. Before the 1940s, colonial officials and anthropologists were content to describe evolutionary processes in colonies; afterwards, they wanted to modernise colonial societies. "Development," writes Ferguson, had become "applied."[26]

Ferguson's argument reflects a common assumption about the origins of the modern idea of development, but it is seriously misleading when applied to British West Africa. In the case of Northern Ghana, colonial development had become "applied" well before 1945, or even 1930, in terms very similar to Ferguson's description of post-war discourse. The colonial vision of developing tribes into nation-states stretches back at least to 1918, which is significant because its emergence provided the backbone for indirect rule. In fact, the origins of this discourse can be traced even further back in time, to the European scramble for Africa during the late nineteenth century. During the scramble, British colonial officials developed a discourse which justified colonial interventions on the assumption that slave raiders had disrupted the evolution of some West African societies. Colonial officials thus spoke of reviving the natural evolution of African states. By 1918, this notion had expanded to include the development of native states into a modern nation. The policy of indirect rule, therefore, was based on a discourse of development which Ferguson mistakenly identifies with the period after World War Two. If we stretch Ferguson's ideas back to the period from

[25] Frederick Cooper, *Decolonization and African Society: The Labor Question in French and British Africa* (Cambridge: Cambridge University Press, 1996).

[26] James Ferguson, "Anthropology and Its Evil Twin: 'Development' in the Constitution of a Discipline," in Cooper and Packard, 159–161.

1895 to 1918, it is thus possible to link up his argument with Mamdani's notion of decentralised despotism. Colonial discourse seemingly constructed a knowledge-power regime which underwrote British hegemony in the rural areas of the Gold Coast.

But did the discourse itself instrumentally produce the expansion of bureaucratic colonial power? Hawkins' recent study of colonial writing in north-western Ghana suggests that this was the case. In an intriguing book, Hawkins argues that writing was "an indispensable instrument of colonialism" which reflected a "capitalist culture with imperial pretensions eager to assert its dominance over large numbers of cultures in northern Ghana that did not possess a similar medium of communication." The colonial project was successful, replacing "the logic of the ancestors worn into the land with words written on paper." The ancestors represented noumenal authority, in which power resided beyond individual consciousness in the realm of collective ritual. The world on paper subverted noumenal power by imposing western, capitalist culture onto the African population. This process forced Africans to live under "the jurisdiction of writing" rather than their ancestral earth shrines, which robbed them of their autonomy by imposing "mimetic tyranny" from which the people have yet to escape.[27]

Hawkins rightly argues that colonial officials consciously sought to appropriate and dominate African societies. However, as the author himself observes, the book is not concerned with colonial policy and thus "its contribution to our understanding of colonial intentions is limited".[28] In contrast, I am concerned precisely with colonial intentions and policy, which were tied intimately to the idea and practice of development in Northern Ghana. Indeed, if we are to understand the history of development, it is critically important to examine the relationship between ideas, policies and practices. Furthermore, these aspects of colonial rule were interrelated in a context under which the colonial state had rather less power than the idea of mimetic tyranny implies. As Hawkins himself acknowledges, colonialism succeeded more on paper than in practice.[29] In the official mind, the

---

[27] Sean Hawkins, *Writing and Colonialism in Northern Ghana: The Encounter Bewteen the LoDagaa and the "World on Paper"* (Toronto: University of Toronto Press, 2002), xiii, 10–11, 23, 325–328.

[28] Ibid., xiii.

[29] Ibid., 24.

lack of colonial power manifested itself in a process of uncontrolled development, which undermined African social cohesion and produced the corruption of an organic process of socio-economic change. By the 1920s, one of the main goals of colonial policy in the Northern Territories was to set development back onto its natural, organic path. This goal embroiled colonial officials and traditional authorities in debates over development, individualism and community. Most colonial officials emphasised community against individualism, or, in other words, community against the development of civil society. This was a major preoccupation of the colonial administration, and we cannot understand it fully by considering only the intersection of colonialism and writing.

Carola Lentz delves more deeply into colonial policies and their outcomes in her work on north-western Ghana. Drawing on extensive fieldwork and archival material, Lentz's work demonstrates the relative weakness of the British project of turning "tribes" into "nations."[30] In north-western Ghana this project dated to the early twentieth century, when British officers divided the region into tribal territories, appointed the first chiefs and created a ruling hierarchy based on assumptions about tradition and evolution. The chiefs appeared to be invented, since colonial officers found few obvious political leaders among the apparently stateless areas of the Middle Volta Basin. British officers considered these areas especially "primitive" because they had not yet evolved chiefs or states. However, this was not entirely true, because strongmen and social inequality had developed in the precolonial period.[31] Largely unaware of this fact, colonial officers set out to push the natural evolutionary process along by developing chiefs and consolidating tribal native states. In the colonial imagination, authentic development required a tribal foundation.

As Lentz argues, however, colonial policies did not simply impose a tribal straitjacket on a victimised population. Instead, they set the stage for complex struggles over ethnicity and power during which African actors actively appropriated and subverted colonial notions of tribe and evolution to their own ends. Chiefs, labour migrants

[30] Carola Lentz, *Ethnicity and the Making of History in Northern Ghana*, manuscript, forthcoming as *Ethnicity and the Making of History in Northern Ghana* (Edinburgh: Edinburgh University Press, 2006), 18.
[31] Ibid.

and the educated elite "mobilis(ed) ethnicity politically" as they struggled for power within the colonial system.[32] These struggles were deeply historical, embedded in precolonial power structures which had given rise to complex and shifting social relations based on patriclan affiliation, ritual fields of power and the authority of local strongmen. During the colonial period, various actors mobilised ethnicity either to preserve older inequalities or to challenge the strongmen of the past. As a result, colonial tribal categories were not as rigid as they appeared, but rather became "subject to continuous debate and negotiation."[33] In other words, local actors persistently refused to follow the colonial ideal of African community.

Allman and Parker echo Lentz's argument in their fascinating history of the Tongnaab god of the Talensi in northern Ghana. The study focuses on the development of Tongnaab shrines in the Tong Hills during the nineteenth and twentieth centuries. This period witnessed the expansion of pilgrim traffic to the shrines from as far away as Asante. In the early twentieth century, Tongnaab also became the centre of resistance to British rule, and colonial officers attacked the Hills and closed one of the main shrines. However, pilgrims continued to visit another shrine, and the growing pilgrimage networks eventually were captured by a lineage of the indigenous inhabitants of the Tong Hills. The main figure was a British-appointed chief, who used the shrine's popularity for personal economic gain. This development undermined the British ideal of African community, but there was little colonial officials could do to stem the flow of pilgrims to the Tong Hills. As Allman and Parker observe, the story of Tongnaab "challenges the analytical distinction between tradition and modernity" and points to the need to place African religion in its historical perspective. Viewed historically, Tongnaab emerges as a vibrant god which "held its own in the increasingly competitive ritual marketplace of colonial West Africa." Far from being mere victims of colonialism, African actors subverted colonial intentions by "author(ing) . . . their own scripts for colonial rule."[34] Once again, local actors subverted the colonial project of preserving African community.

[32] Ibid., 3.

[33] Ibid., 12.

[34] Jean Allman and Jonathan Parker, *Tongnaab: The History of a West African God* (Bloomington: Indiana University Press, 2005), 5, 73–4.

On a broader level, Sara Berry has shown that the colonial discourse of African tradition was not particularly successful in shoring up British power in British West Africa. Berry argues that indirect rule, which she perceptively labels "hegemony on a shoestring," did not succeed in imposing English versions of African customary law on African societies in the British colonies. Instead, it promoted instability in rural Africa by triggering ongoing debates about "tradition" and "shap(ing) struggles over authority and access to resources." The British might have tried to separate urban citizens from rural subjects, as Mamdani argues, but this attempt was not entirely successful. Decentralised despotism was more effective on paper than in reality. According to Berry, British power was limited by four main factors: lack of financial resources, because the Exchequer provided little funding; contradictions in the colonial project, because economic development promoted African prosperity, which threatened the colonial state's access to cheap labour; dynamics of African societies, because indirect rule rested on the assumption of static, closed African "tribes"; and conflicting claims of tradition, because competing African claims undercut the colonial project of identifying customary law. Limits on colonial power meant that hegemony on a shoestring shaped the terrain of local struggles over economic activity and resource mobilisation, but it "didn't block the commercialisation of agriculture and resource mobilisation in Africa."[35]

Beyond the question of state power, an exclusive focus on discourse in Ferguson's terms also ignores the material roots of development interventions, which in the case of Northern Ghana included a concern for order and emerged as a reaction to previous periods of development. On this issue, we should be careful not to apply Ferguson's particular formulation unquestioningly to African colonial development, especially considering his assumptions about its intentions. In order to demonstrate the unintended instrument effects of the conceptual apparatus of development, Ferguson must first outline the intentions of the developers, which in a familiar fashion he identifies as economic growth and/or the elimination of poverty. The fact that the Lesotho project failed to achieve these goals opens the door to Ferguson's analysis of its unintended instrument effects. This is convincing in the case of Lesotho between 1975 and 1984, but it

[35] Sara Berry, *No Condition is Permanent: the Social Dynamics of Agrarian Change in sub-Saharan Africa* (Madison: University of Wisconsin Press, 1993), 24–30.

breaks down when we turn our gaze to the Northern Territories of the Gold Coast, where colonial development was driven by a powerful third intention: the amelioration of the negative effects of capitalist development. Before indirect rule, British colonial officials tried to facilitate capitalist production by developing private property and African landlordism.[36] It was in reaction to the negative effects of this project, especially the perceived breakdown of African social cohesion, that colonial development policy turned towards preserving African community through indirect rule. Indirect rule therefore was not just about discourse or the conscious imposition of mimetic tyranny. But it was also more than just hegemony on a shoestring, because its material roots, as a reaction to previous periods of development, ran deeper than mere political expediency. They also reflected, in Cowen and Shenton's terms, a deeply rooted agrarian doctrine of development.

Following Cowen and Shenton, "doctrine of development" refers to the intention to develop expressed in state policy, where the state acts as trustee over a less-developed people. Throughout the history of British colonialism, this intention came in reaction to the negative effects of the development of capitalism, which unfolded as an immanent process outside the control of the colonial state. In the Gold Coast, the negative side of capitalist development was labelled corruption and it manifested itself in the breakdown of African community.[37] This breakdown occurred as the aggressive British development policies of the late nineteenth century opened the door to the growth of a land market, which spiralled out of the control of the colonial state and threatened the orderly development of the colony. In this case, colonial development doctrine thus stood opposed to perceived corruption produced by the immanent process of capitalist development. Indirect rule, in other words, represented a reaction to past processes and policies believed to have produced corruptions of development. After the failed push for private property and African landlordism, colonial development policy rested on an agrarian doctrine

---

[36] M.P. Cowen and R.W. Shenton, *Doctrines of Development* (London: Routledge, 1996). Anne Phillips, *The Enigma of Colonialism: British Policy in West Africa* (London: James Currey, 1989). R.W. Shenton, *The Development of Capitalism in Northern Nigeria* (Toronto: University of Toronto Press, 1986).

[37] M.P. Cowen and R.W. Shenton, "The Invention of Development," in *Power of Development*, ed. Jonathan Crush, 28 (London: Routledge, 1995). Cowen and Shenton, *Doctrines of Development*, viii, 56.

of development based on preserving African community while extracting resources and labour for colonial accumulation.[38]

In the Northern Territories, British administrators attributed the breakdown of community to "premature" westernisation. In the official mind, economic growth between 1899 and the 1940s undermined African community by triggering the development of labourers, accumulating chiefs and the educated elite. This process pressed against the British ideal, ascendant after the Northern Nigerian Lands Committee of 1908 and the West African Lands Committee of 1912–17, of preserving community in the face of economic, political and social change. This ideal threatened to crumble in the wake of the Depression as a series of working class strikes (on the mines and railways) and peasant "strikes" (produce hold-ups) shot through the West Indies and British Africa. As Cooper notes, Britain and France labelled these processes "detribalisation" and responded by invoking development as a means to ameliorate economic and social conditions in the colonies.[39] In other words, Britain turned to development doctrine to mitigate what was considered the corruption produced by past periods of development. For British colonial officials, the converse of the breakdown of community was the rise of "premature individualism." As Gibbon observes in his critique of Mamdani, the substantive threat behind African individualism was the potential recombination of individuals into new classes based on the division of labour under capitalism.[40] Although this process did not proceed very far in the Northern Territories, colonial officers constantly worried about its possibility. In other words, the potential breakdown of African community threatened to produce the rise of civil society, whose members many colonial officers considered dangerous to the colonial project.[41]

---

[38] Cowen and Shenton, *Doctrines of Development*, 57,433–6.

[39] Cooper, *Decolonization and African Society*, 72.

[40] Peter Gibbon, "Civil society and political change, with special reference to 'developmentalist' states," paper presented to the Nordic Conference on "Social Movements in the Third World," University of Lund, 1993, 29. Gibbon's comments are directed at Mahmood Mamdani, "State and Civil Society in Contemporary Africa: Reconceptualizing the Birth of State Nationalism and the Defeat of Popular Movements." *Africa Development* 15, Nos. 3–4 (1990): 47–70.

[41] Hutchful, 63; Reinhart Kössler and Henning Melber, *The Concept of Civil Society and the Process of Nation-Building in African States, NEPRU WORKING PAPER 44* (Windhoek, The Namibian Economic Policy Research Unit, 1994), 2. Mamdani, *Citizen and Subject*, 13–16.

This study, then, draws on the arguments of Mamdani and Ferguson, as well as the informative historical material in Hawkins' study of north-western Ghana. Hawkins in particular provides valuable material on the imposition of British ideas about chieftaincy. However, he takes an explicitly cultural perspective, assessing the colonial attempt "to subjugate and regulate an oral culture and force within the conceptual framework of a literate society."[42] In contrast, I am more concerned with intellectual and political history, revolving around the intentions and application of colonial development policy. In this sense, the book is rooted more strongly in the ideas of Berry, Lentz, Allman and Parker, and Cowen and Shenton. Taken together, these scholars provide an excellent framework for explaining the history of development in Northern Ghana. In particular, Berry, Lentz, and Allman and Parker demonstrate convincingly that colonial officials were not able simply to impose the straitjacket of "tribe" onto a victimised African population. Instead, colonialism set the stage for struggles over power and resources, in which African actors drew on precolonial as well as colonial precedents. This process blurred the distinction between tradition and modernity so dear to most colonial administrators. As such, African actors subverted colonial intentions for their development.

Focusing on these intentions, my analysis complements the excellent recent work on Northern Ghana by providing an alternative analytical framework, drawing on Cowen and Shenton's study of development doctrine. Covering a broader geographical area than Lentz, Hawkins and Allman and Parker, the book investigates the colonial state's attempt to support community against the growth of civil society between 1899 and 1957. The precise nature of this project fluctuated in reaction to previous periods of development. The core vision, however, remained consistent after 1912, firmly rooted in the agrarian doctrine of development and dedicated to preserving African community while mobilising resources for the colonial economy. This focus contributes to the historiography in a number of ways. First, the book fills a gap in the literature on Northern Ghana by fully assessing colonial intentions and development policy. In this sense, this book links the others together through the lens of colonial development doctrine. In my opinion, this approach provides an important framework for understanding the historical events

[42] Hawkins, *Writing and Colonialism in Northern Ghana*, 32.

analysed with such skill in recent studies of Northern Ghana. As such, it contributes to the literature on development studies as well as African history.

Geographical Focus

The book investigates the history of development doctrine at the levels of the Colonial Office, the colonial government in Accra and the northern administration in Tamale. Evidence is drawn from several regions of the Northern Territories, particularly the areas around Lawra, Tumu and Zuarungu. During the colonial period, these areas either formed Districts in and of themselves or existed as parts of larger Districts. All of them contained communities whom the British labelled "primitive" and whom many present writers refer to as "stateless." These labels reflected a significant misreading of local power relations by colonial officials. "Chiefs" might not have existed in the British sense, but strongmen had developed in many settlements by the mid-nineteenth century. These men often worked their way into the first chieftaincies of the colonial era.[43] The result was a hierarchy of chiefs, arranged according to ethnic boundaries that exist to this day. In today's terminology, the major ethnic groups included in this study are the Dagara (Lawra), the Sissala (Tumu and parts of Lawra), and the Talensi (Zuarungu). From the perspective of colonial development, Lawra-Tumu and Zuarungu were connected on several levels. First, both areas experienced the creation of chiefs where none had existed before, at least in the British sense. Second, the colonial state constructed both areas as victims of slave raiders in the nineteenth century. Many colonial officers believed that these raids triggered the depopulation of some areas and the overpopulation of others. Development thus involved resettling people from overcrowded areas into depopulated regions. Finally, the colonial state used models of resettlement, created in Lawra-Tumu and Zuarungu, to move settlers into the site of the Gonja groundnut project, which was located on an uninhabited tract of land in the middle belt of the Northern Territories.

[43] Carola Lentz provides a detailed account of this process in her work on Namdom. See for example Lentz, *Ethnicity and the Making of History in Northern Ghana*, 54, 128–9.

Contents

Beginning with a brief overview of the European scramble for the West African hinterland, Chapter Two discusses the shift in development doctrine from the aggressive stance of Joseph Chamberlain—supported by the early Gold Coast administration—to the preservationist stance of the West African Lands Committee. By providing infrastructure to attract expatriate capital, Chamberlain sought to trigger an agrarian transformation and a revolution in mineral production in West Africa. Chamberlain's program included the policy of developing a class of African landlords and supporting the development of agrarian capitalism on West African soil. By 1906, however, Chamberlain's vision was being challenged by the rise of a powerful British humanitarian lobby led by Mary Kingsley and Edmund Dene Morel. Kingsley and Morel belonged to the liberal camp allied to British merchant capital, and led a campaign against the exploitative nature of Chamberlain's West African development programme.[44] The Liberal lobby drew inspiration from the anti-landlord ideas of American utopian socialist Henry George, who argued for eliminating the landlord class through single tax equal to their ground rents. This idea worked its way through Morel into the Northern Nigerian Lands Committee (NNLC) of 1908 and the West African Lands Committee (WALC) of 1912–17. Arguing against the development of land markets and landlordism, these two committees advocated African production on African terms, that is, through peasant producers working communal land. Land nationalisation and direct taxation figured prominently in the recommendations of both committees.[45] In the Northern Territories, the transition from developing the estates to developing community mirrored the rise of the liberal reaction to Chamberlain. Chapter Two closes with the observation that by 1919 the Gold Coast government had accepted the peasant road for the Northern Territories, although it fell short of the NNLC/WALC prescription for land nationalisation. Chapter Three discusses the arrival of the full WALC framework between 1919 and 1927 during the Governorship of Sir F.G. Guggisberg,

[44] Anne Phillips, *The Enigma Of Colonialism: British Policy In West Africa* (London: James Currey, 1989), 66.

[45] Shenton, *Development of Capitalism*, 46–7. Phillips, 76.

who drafted a land nationalisation Ordinance before he left the Gold Coast.

But more than this, the chapter assesses the ideas of one of Guggisberg's subordinates, A.C. Duncan-Johnstone, who implemented Guggisberg's vision in the north-west. Duncan-Johnstone's idea of development drew on the work of Charles Temple in Northern Nigeria and, through Temple, the anthropology of Sir Henry Maine. Out of these influences Duncan-Johnstone implemented a system of native tribunals, which some later colonial officers criticised for producing chiefly despotism. In reaction, the northern administration worked to implement a full system of indirect rule, supported by the reports of the first professional anthropologist to visit the Northern Territories, R.S. Rattray. The chapter concludes by analysing Rattray's reports, along with the studies of several administrative officers. These studies have been analysed very effectively for the Lawra District by Carola Lentz, whose work on Nandom has contributed significantly to our knowledge of the north-western Northern Territories.[46] We shall expand this story to consider the implications of colonial anthropology for development in the Northern Territories more generally. Chapter Four surveys the implementation of indirect rule between 1932 and 1936, which marked the arrival of the West African policy to the Northern Territories. As Anne Phillips notes, during this era the Northern Territories became the only region outside Northern Nigeria to experience the full implementation of the idea of the NNLC and WALC.

The second half of the book focuses on development policies in the Northern Territories between 1935 and 1957. Chapter Five analyses the British "discovery" of food insecurity in the north-east and the remedy of mixed farming, especially the work of agriculturalist Charles Lynn and anthropologist Meyer Fortes. The chapter also

[46] See especially Carola Lentz, "Stateless Societies or Chiefdoms: A Debate Among Dagara Intellectuals," in *Ghana's North: Research on Culture, Religion, and Politics of Societies in Transition* (Kroger, Franz and Meier, Barbara, Frankfurt am Main: Peter Lang, 2003), "Colonial Constructions and African Initiatives: The History of Ethnicity in Northwestern Ghana," *Ethnos* 65, No. 1 (2000): 107–136. "Colonial Ethnography and Political Reform: the Works of A.C. Duncan-Johnstone, R.S. Rattray, J. Eyre-Smith and J. Guiness on Northern Ghana." *Ghana Studies* 2 (1999): 119–69. "A Dagara Rebellion Against Dagomba Rule? Contested Stories of Origin in North-Western Ghana." *Journal of African History* 35 (1994): 457–92; "Histories and Political Conflict: A Case Study of Chieftaincy in Nandom, Northwestern Ghana." *Paideuma* 39 (1993).

includes another key aspect of development doctrine in the north: the eradication of disease. This issue is discussed through the work of entomologist K.R.S. Morris, who sought to eradicate tsetse flies and trypanosomiasis from the Lawra-Tumu District. All of these initiatives were framed within the doctrine of indirect rule. As time progressed, however, colonial officers began to criticise indirect rule as an inadequate framework for development. Chapter Six discusses this debate, in which the critics argued that working through chiefs would not achieve the economic growth necessary for development and social welfare. Nor would indirect rule preserve African community, as evidenced by the development of a pilgrimage trade, in which the guardians of earth shrines accumulated individual wealth by providing services to pilgrims from Ashanti and the Colony. The inadequacy of indirect rule led to more forceful state intervention into development in the Northern Territories. One of the casualties of this shift was indirect rule itself, which was gradually replaced by local government as a preferred administrative framework for development. Also, during this period the colonial state rejected mixed farming by individual peasants as capable of producing the newly required levels of subsistence and export crops. Chapter Seven discusses these changes to colonial political and agricultural policy between 1945 and 1948. After 1948, the development themes examined in Chapters Five through Eight (mixed farming, tsetse eradication, resettlement and the mechanisation of agriculture) converged in the largest single agricultural project in the history of the Gold Coast before 1950: the Damongo Groundnut scheme. Chapter Eight discusses the process through which the scheme was presented to the Colonial Office, its rejection by the Colonial Development Corporation, and its ultimate transformation into an internally funded foodstuff production project. The chapter ends with a discussion of the simultaneous emergence of community development in the Northern Territories, its relation to the Gonja scheme, and its close link to the development doctrine of the colonial state. Chapter Nine presents the book's major conclusions.

CHAPTER TWO

FROM DEVELOPING THE ESTATES TO PRESERVING THE PEASANTRY: DEVELOPMENT IN THE NORTHERN TERRITORIES, 1895–1919

Introduction

Britain annexed the Northern Territories as a Protectorate of the Gold Coast in late 1901, driven by Joseph Chamberlain's 1895 decree that the British had a duty to develop their colonial estates. Chamberlain's development program was very aggressive, seeking to open the Gold Coast to British capital in order to extract raw materials and develop markets for British manufactured goods. Chamberlain set out to achieve this goal by nationalising African lands, building state-sponsored infrastructure, destroying what he considered to be "unprogressive" African political and social systems, imposing direct taxation, and encouraging the development of landlordism and agrarian capitalism on African soil. Officials in the Gold Coast complied with Chamberlain's development program as they campaigned to bring the Northern Territories under British control. The main figure in the early period was Chief Commissioner Lt. Colonel H.P. Northcott, who produced a plan to develop the region along Chamberlainite lines after securing it against European and African competitors. However, this vision for West Africa did not last long, for between 1906 and 1912, Chamberlain's program was eclipsed by a Liberal reaction to the exploitation of the British West African colonies. During this period the colonial doctrine of West African development shifted from encouraging the development of agrarian capitalism to blocking its growth in favour of preserving peasant production and African community.

In Britain the transition was led by the liberal Third Party of Mary Kingsley, E.D. Morel and John Holt, allies of merchant capital in the search for global opportunities for trade. The Third Party strove to preserve African peasant production and use trade as a means of "civilising" the African population. Through Morel's influence, they drew on the ideas of the American utopian socialist Henry

George, especially his belief in land nationalisation as a tool for the state to appropriate ground rents in the interests of community development. This idea took root in West Africa during the deliberations of the Northern Nigerian Lands Committee (NNLC) in 1908 and the West African Lands Committee (WALC) between 1912 and 1916. From this date onwards, the British West African policy sought to achieve two development goals simultaneously: extracting African resources and labour, and preserving African community. At the root of this project stood the African peasant, whose production was to be hitched to the global economy without destroying the social bonds of traditional village communities.

The Gold Coast moved towards this vision in the Northern Territories between 1901 and 1919. Northcott's successors abandoned the main planks of Chamberlain's program, including direct taxation and plantation agriculture driven by expatriate capital. Instead, the administration built a system of chiefdoms and established the chiefs as labour contractors for public works and migrant labour. Under this plan, the north would not be developed economically beyond its role as supplier of labour for the Colony and Ashanti. Local communities would remain intact and subsistence would be based on peasant production. By the time of Governor Hugh Clifford (1912–1919), the policy of preserving the peasantry was firmly in place in the Northern Territories. In the far north, some colonial officers argued that the peasants should be placed under chiefs who would be subsumed under the neighbouring states of Wa and Mamprusi. This plan reflected the belief that Wa and Mamprusi had controlled the "decentralised" communities to the north before the slave raids of the nineteenth century.

At the level of discourse, this policy reflected an important colonial trope of interrupted evolution. The natural evolution of traditional African societies had been disrupted by African slave raiders. Fortunately, the evolution of the tribes of the Northern Territories could be set back on track because the region had not been corrupted by westernisation. More important than its reflection of colonial discourse, however, the shift towards the peasantry also marked a transition in development doctrine, from Chamberlain's constructivist policies towards the Georgeist program of the NNLC and the WALC. Though Clifford rejected land nationalisation, he supported the WALC's objective to preserve the African peasantry, and thus African community, in the Northern Territories. This vision was based on the assumption that discrete tribes existed and that evolution required the appointment of chiefs over their ethnic communities. As Lentz, Hawkins, and Allman and Parker have shown, this assumption was misleading because territorially defined "tribes" did not exist in the Lawra, Tumu and Zuarungu areas, nor were the people simply subject to the authority of the surrounding states. As such, colonial development doctrine was problematic from the beginning.

Joseph Chamberlain, the Undeveloped Estates and the Scramble for Greater Asante

In 1895, Secretary of State for the Colonies Joseph Chamberlain proclaimed that Britain had a duty to develop its colonies. "Great Britain," he declared,

> the little centre of a vaster Empire that the world has ever seen, owns great possessions in every part of the globe, and many of these possessions are still almost unexplored, entirely underdeveloped. What would a great landlord do in a similar case with a great estate? If he had the money he would expend some of it at any rate in improving the property, in making communications, in making outlets for the products of his land.[1]

This vision of the "underdeveloped estates of the realm"[2] signalled Chamberlain's intention to rescue Britain from the downturn of the 1870–80s by developing the British Empire. This was an aggressive program to revolutionise the organisation of land and labour in the colonial world through a partnership between the state and expatriate capital. Britain would attract private capital by developing communications infrastructure, granting private concessions and securing a stable labour supply by taxing the indigenous population.[3]

By the time of Chamberlain's appointment to the Colonial Office, the Gold Coast administration already had tried to implement legislation resembling his vision of development. Responding to a rush of concession-seeking, in 1889 Governor Brandford Griffith declared

---

[1] Quoted in Dennis Judd, *Radical Joe: A Life of Joseph Chamberlain* (London: Hamish Hamilton, 1977), 190.

[2] Ibid.

[3] M.P. Cowen and R.W. Shenton, *Doctrines of Development* (London: Routledge, 1996), 254–5, 274–5. Anne Phillips, *The Enigma of Colonialism: British Policy in West Africa* (London: James Currey, 1989), 65.

the entire Colony Crown Land in order to exert government control over expatriate capital. In 1894, Griffith drafted a Crown Lands Bill empowering the government to appropriate all unoccupied ("waste") land for the purposes of development. Griffith's successor W.E. Maxwell withdrew the Bill in the face of opposition from the chiefs, the coastal elite and European merchant firms. However, Maxwell drafted a new lands bill in 1897 which proposed to create "public" as opposed to "state" lands over which the Crown could exert control but not outright ownership.[4] Maxwell hoped that the 1897 Lands Bill would secure Griffith's goal of state control over concessions and alienation without portraying the colonial state as the illegitimate landlord of African lands. As a secondary effect, Maxwell hoped that the Bill would encourage the growth of a land market and the emergence of private property.[5] These goals fit nicely with Chamberlain's vision of developing the West African estates.

The real prize, however, was Asante and its northern hinterland.[6] Chamberlain's project sought to open "Greater Asante" to expatriate capital by wresting control of the region away from competing interests, which included not only France and Germany, but also the Juula revolutionary Samory Touré, the Zabarima warrior Babatu and Asante itself. From the perspective of development in the Northern Territories, the campaigns of the Zabarima, Samory's Sofa warriors and Asante were particularly important. These three states formed but one chapter in a long history of indigenous state-building in West Africa, based on control at various times over the trades in gold, slaves and kola nuts between the forest, savannah and desert. At the time of the European scramble, several powerful African states had emerged, which included the Zabarima and Samorians, using European weaponry and military techniques to reform or build empires across the West African savannah. As we shall see, the leaders of these states, especially Samory and Babatu, greatly influenced British ideas about development in the Northern Territories.

---

[4] R.B. Bening, "Colonial Development Policy In Northern Ghana, 1898–1950," *Bulletin of the Ghana Geographical Association* 17 (1975), 69–70. Phillips, 63–4.

[5] Olemufu Omosini, "The Gold Coast Land Question: Some Issues Raised on West Africa's Economic Development," *International Journal of African Historical Studies* 5, No. 3 (1972): 455–462.

[6] John Hargreaves, *West Africa Partitioned, Volume 1: The Loaded Pause* (London: MacMillan Press, 1974), 215.

Chamberlain's immediate goal was to secure the "Hinterland of the Gold Coast Colony," an area stretching into the savannah that had been incorporated into the Asante polity in the eighteenth century. The region contained two distinct types of societies: the "decentralised" peoples of the Middle Volta Basin, and the surrounding states of Mossi to the north and Gonja, Dagomba and Mamprusi to the south. The precolonial history of the decentralised societies is difficult to capture in the absence of local written accounts. However, some scholars have pieced together the most probable accounts from local oral histories and later colonial sources. Writing about the north-west, for example, Lentz and Hawkins conclude that the area was settled initially by dispersed and peaceful migrations of patriclan sectors in search of agricultural land. As a result, power was diffused among households/patriclans (*yir*) and earth shrines (*tengaan*).[7] Neither realm of power was connected very tightly to territorial boundaries. As Lentz observes, patriclans could be very large and they often cut across linguistic, cultural and ethnic lines. Earth shrines were arranged into "parishes", but *tengaan* represented "fields of ritual power" and their territorial boundaries could be negotiated and renegotiated, resulting in fluid shrine hierarchies.[8] A similar pattern appears to have been true for the Talensi of the north-east, where the people probably were isolated from neighbouring societies before the eighteenth century. As in the north-west, power operated at the household level and within the ritual communities of the earth shrines. In this area, however, there was a distinction between the indigenous clans (Talis), who provided the earth priests (*tengdaana*), and immigrants from Mamprugu to the south (Namoos), who provided secular leaders (headmen and local chiefs). Chiefship, however, was not the defining institution of authority. Instead, the people were bound together more fundamentally by the power of the earth shrines, within which were housed local variants of the Tongnaab god, whom Allman and Parker call the "readily accessible refraction of the withdrawn High God, Naawun". Tongnaab's "ritual field of power"

[7] Carola Lentz, *Ethnicity and the Making of History in Northern Ghana*, manuscript, forthcoming as *Ethnicity and the Making of History in Northern Ghana* (Edinburgh: Edinburgh University Press, 2006), 23, 431. Sean Hawkins, *Writing and Colonialism in Northern Ghana: The Encounter Between the LoDagaa and the "World on Paper"* (Toronto: University of Toronto Press, 2002), 114.

[8] Lentz, *Ethnicity and the Making of History in Northern Ghana*, 25–6, 30–1.

blurred ethnic distinctions and bound the people together as one community.[9] As in the north-east, therefore, there is little evidence in the north-west of discrete ethnic communities with clear territorial boundaries, at least before the nineteenth century. As such, the settlements of the Middle Volta Basin stood in contrast to the neighbouring areas, where centralised, territorially defined states had emerged among the Mossi to the north, and the Mamprusi, Dagomba and Gonja to the south.

This entire area had been brought into the Asante polity between 1700 and 1750 when Asante expanded northwards to capture the trade in slaves and gold to the coast and kola nuts to the Sokoto Caliphate (see Map 1). Between 1732 and the 1780s, Asante's leaders negotiated tributary relations with Gonja, Dagomba and Mamprusi, who provided a regular tribute in slaves to Kumasi in return for military protection.[10] Most of the slaves came from the Middle Volta Basin, which served as an important supply area to the Americas during the eighteenth century. However, slave-gathering expeditions continued after abolition into the nineteenth century. In 1867, for example, Dagomba invaded the hinterland after the Asantehene asked the Dagomba paramount chief, Ya Na Abdallah, to revive the slave tribute that had fallen into abeyance when Asante was diverted by the British advance in the south. Joining the Dagomba were a group of Zabarima horsemen from the Sokoto Caliphate, who had allied with Dagomba around 1860. During the expedition of 1867, the Zabarima broke away from Dagomba and launched a thirty-year campaign of their own on the fringes of the Asante hinterland.[11]

At the time of the Zabarima expansion the British and French were attempting to move northwards along the eastern side of Greater Asante. The Asantehene effectively blocked the European expansion until the British sacked Kumasi in 1874 and gained access to the caravan routes to the Sokoto Caliphate. In 1876, the British Special Commissioner V.S. Goldsworthy and the French trader M.J. Bonnet reached Salaga and Yendi and a significant European trade developed between Dagomba, Eastern Gonja and Accra along the Volta

[9] Jean Allman and Jonathan Parker, *Tongnaab: The History of a West African God* (Bloomington: Indiana University Press, 2005), 29, 44, 53–4.

[10] Ibid., 30.

[11] J.J. Holden, "The Zabarima Conquest of North-West Ghana." *Transactions of the Historical Society of Ghana* 8 (1965): 60–64.

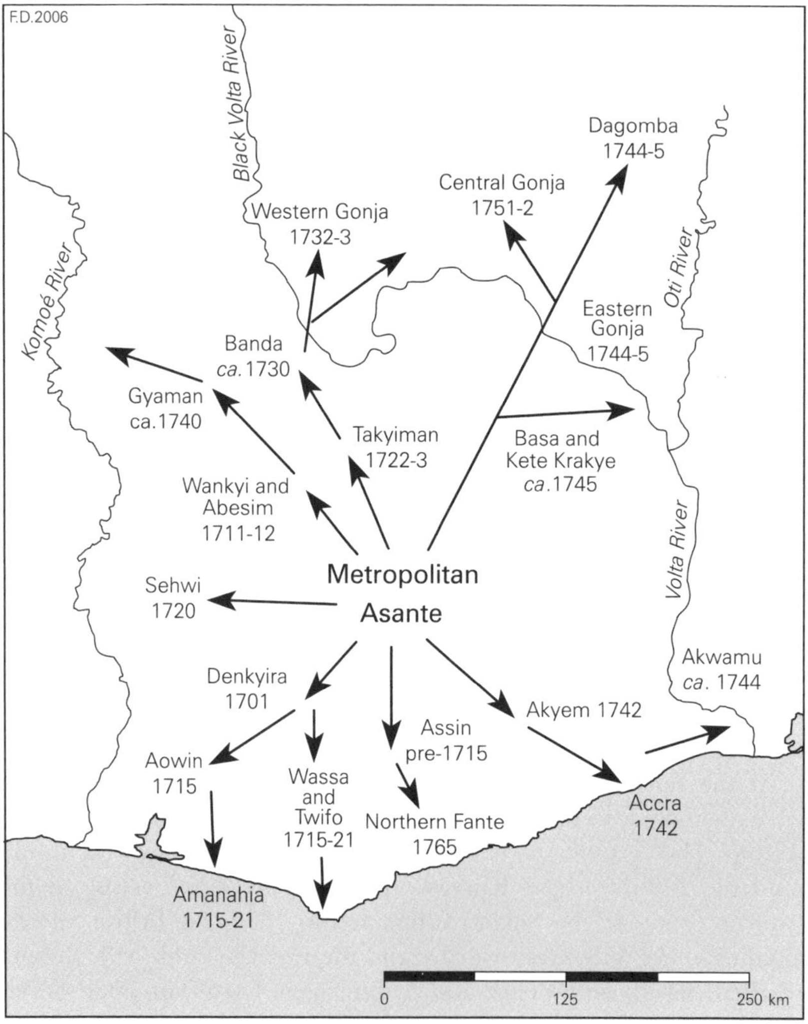

Map 1: Asante Expansion in the Eighteenth Century
Source: Ivor Wilks, *Asante in the Nineteenth Century: The Structure and Evolution of a Political Order*. London: Cambridge University Press, 1975.

River outside the control of the Asante.[12] In 1884 the Germans solidified their position by declaring a Protectorate over Togoland. The Berlin Conference of 1884/5 further intensified European activity to the north of Asante and over the next three years German and French officials visited major settlements in Dagomba, Gonja and Mamprusi and began to secure treaties of friendship and trade with local leaders. This flurry of activity prompted Britain to negotiate a neutral zone with Germany in 1887, which included Dagomba and parts of Eastern Gonja (Salaga, Yapei and Daboya).[13] The next year, the French official Louis Binger travelled further into the savanna. As part of his mission, Binger recorded and mapped the "tribes" of the Middle Volta Basin, based on information from second-hand sources, including Muslim informants from Wa. Constructing his ethnic map, Binger identified the Gourounsi as one of the largest groups, whom local sources claimed had been forced into the area by raids by the surrounding states of Gonja, Dagomba, Mamprusi. To the west of Gourounsi lived the Lobi, Dagarti and Dagabakha. On a later journey, Binger identified the Talensi, whom he identified ethnically with the Mamprusi.[14]

By the time of Binger's journey, the Zabarima had united under a strong and effective leader, Mahama dan Issa (Babatu), who sacked and occupied Wa in 1887/8. Meanwhile, by 1897 the French also had moved into the region from their base in Senegal, pushing into the Upper and Middle Niger as far as Ouagadougou.[15] Concerned about these developments, the British sent Fante official George Ekem Ferguson to secure treaties against the advances of the other powers. Ferguson's main goal was to secure sole trading rights for the British along a large corridor in the Northern Territories.[16] Drawing on Binger's account, Ferguson assumed that the decentralised peoples of the Middle Volta Basin had come under the control of the

[12] Paul Andre Ladouceur, *Chiefs and Politicians: the Politics of Regionalism in Northern Ghana* (London: Longman, 1979), 39. R.B. Bening, "The Definition of the International Boundaries of Northern Ghana, 1888–1904." *Transactions of the Historical Society of Ghana* 14, No. 2 (December 1973), 229.

[13] Ladouceur, 39. Bening, "Definition," 229.

[14] Hawkins, *Writing and Colonialism in Northern Ghana*, 45–7; Lentz, *Ethnicity and the Making of History in Northern Ghana*, 126–7; Allman and Parker, 55.

[15] Ivor Wilks, *Wa and the Wala: Islam and Polity in Northwestern Ghana* (Cambridge: Cambridge University Press, 1989), 7.

[16] Brenda Chalfin, *Shea Butter Republic: State Power, Global Markets, and the Making of an Indigenous Commodity* (New York: Routledge, 2004), 94–5.

surrounding states.[17] On two missions in 1892 and 1894, Ferguson signed treaties with the rulers of the major states, including Gonja, Dagomba, Wa and Mamprusi and Mossi. The French and Germans, however, continued to contest these territories. In 1894, British forces occupied Salaga and Yendi on the pretence that the Germans had attacked and burned the settlements. In 1895 France signed a treaty with the Wa Na and the following year the Germans threatened Britain's control over Dagomba by defeating a Dagomba force near Yendi.[18] The following year, however, the situation in Wa was complicated by the arrival of yet another force, the army of the Juula revolutionary Samory Touré.

Samory's revolution began in the 1830s in present-day Guinea and by the 1870s had produced a sophisticated state rivaling French interests in West Africa. In 1895, driven inland by the French, Samory's forces entered Bonduku on the fringes of the Asante empire. From Bonduku, Samory captured Kong, a close ally of the French, and from Kong he sent his son to rule over the Gonja kingdom. In 1896, Samory attacked Wa and installed his lieutenant Ali Wangara to rule over the Wala as part of the Samorian state. Worried about a possible Samorian-Asante-French alliance—although in reality this was never a threat—Britain stepped up its campaign against the Asante, and in 1896 Chamberlain ordered the invasion of Kumasi and the arrest of Asante's paramount chief, Asantehene Agyeman Prempe I. The attack was successful and it allowed British forces to occupy Gambaga in 1896, which provided a base to move northwards to attack Samory's army in Wa and bring the Wala back into the British sphere. British forces captured Wa in 1897, the French retreated from the area, and the Wala polity became part of the "Hinterland of the Northern Territories of the Gold Coast Colony." The annexation of Wa was formalised with a second treaty with the Wa Na, this time for trade and protection, which recognised him as the "King of Dagarti."[19]

Shortly after the capture of Wa, the "Asante Hinterland" was renamed "The Northern Territories of the Gold Coast" and put

---

[17] Hawkins, *Writing and Colonialism in Northern Ghana*, 47.

[18] Phyllis Ferguson and Ivor Wilks, "Chiefs, Constitutions and the British in Northern Ghana," in *West African Chiefs*, ed. M. Crowder and O. Ikeme, 330 (New York: Africana Publishing Corporation, 1970). Bening, "Definition," 247.

[19] Wilks, *Asante in the Nineteenth Century: the Structure and Evolution of a Political Order* (London: Cambridge University Press, 1975), 302–4.

under the charge of Commissioner and Commandant Lt.-Col. H.P. Northcott (see Map 2). By this time the French had occupied Ouagadougou, the Germans controlled Sansanne Mango and Britain had secured Wa, Bouna and Gambaga. All three powers continued to make new treaties to secure their territories more concretely. Britain finally secured the Northern Territories in 1898/9 through separate agreements with the French and the Germans. Through the Anglo-French Convention (1898) Britain received Wa and Mamprusi, while the Anglo-German Agreement of 1899 divided Dagomba and Gonja between Britain and the Germans.[20] The Colonial Office instructed Northcott to secure the boundaries of the Northern Territories and recommend a plan for its development.

The Development Program of H.P. Northcott, 1897–1901

Northcott's immediate task was to continue to sign treaties of friendship and protection with the northern chiefs, a policy which he personally favoured very strongly. Presenting his vision to the Colonial Office in the summer of 1898, Northcott wrote that

> the agency employed will be that of the native chiefs, and their power will, during good behaviour, be uniformly supported, except in their relationship with neighbouring chiefs and of offences of a capital nature, which will be reserved for decision by a member of the Administration.[21]

The Colonial Office approved Northcott's policy, believing that rule through the chiefs was more important in the Northern Territories than among the more "advanced" societies of the Colony. They also instructed him to adhere as closely as possible to "racial boundaries," which colonial officials believed corresponded to defined territories, in appointing the chiefs and consolidating their power. Northcott's ideal, therefore, was to find and recognise chiefs who controlled large territories and who would agree to co-operate with the colonial administration.[22] He achieved this goal through persuasion and force, negotiating agreements if possible but threatening to bring in the military when necessary.

---

[20] Bening, "The Definition of the International Boundaries," 239. Ladouceur, 40.
[21] Bening, "Foundations," 118.
[22] Ibid., 118–19.

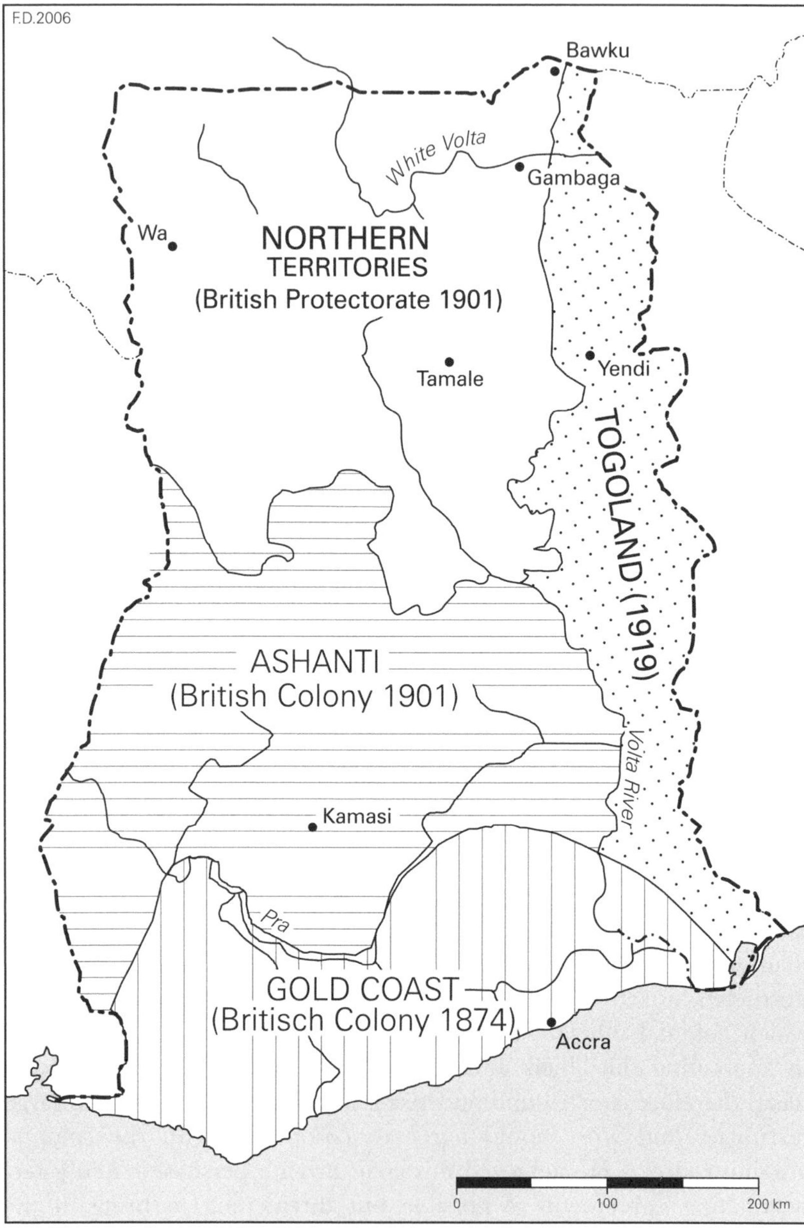

Map 2: Colonial Ghana as of 1919
From Brenda Chalfin, *Shea Butter Republic: State Power, Global Markets and the Making of an Indigenous Commodity*, New York: Routledge, 2004.

It was at this time that we see the emergence of what would become a familiar colonial discourse about African development. Northcott believed that several big kingdoms had existed before the military campaigns of Samory and Babatu, including Gonja, Dagomba, Mamprusi and Wa, and that their development had been interrupted by the slave raids of the "freebooters." Based on this belief, Northcott's main goal was to revive the development of these African states by amalgamating the northern chiefs based on the boundaries of the former kingdoms. His plan focused mainly on Mamprusi and Wa, where the slave raiders seemed to have caused the most damage. In the north-east he believed that the most powerful state was the Mamprusi Dynasty, formed when a migrant named Tosoga conquered the hinterland and developed an empire based in Gambaga. From this centre a series of immigrants settled among the stateless societies to the north of Gambaga and formed ruling lineages accountable to the Mamprusi paramount chief.[23] The stateless peoples north of Gambaga including the Talensi, whom British officials by this time included under the tribal name "Frafra" and who would become very important in the story of British colonialism in the Northern Territories.[24] Meanwhile, in the northwest the state of Wa extended similar control over a "tribe" that the British initially called Dagaba or Dagarti. According to Northcott, Mamprusi and Wa ruled over the stateless peoples to the north until the raids of Samory and Babatu destroyed the fledgling kingdoms between 1879 and 1897. In addition to severing political ties, the slave raids also cut off the evolution of the stateless peoples into centralised states and rendered them suspicious and hostile to foreigners. During Northcott's expedition, Britain, France and Germany defeated the slave raiders and negotiated boundaries of European jurisdiction in the areas formerly controlled by Mamprusi and Wa.[25] In appointing the chiefs, Northcott believed that he could maintain these traditional boundaries and construct a hierarchy of chiefs subject to the authority of the paramount chiefs of Wa and Mamprusi (the Wa Na and Nayiri, respectively).

---

[23] H.P. Northcott, *Report On the Northern Territories of the Gold Coast* (London: HMSO, 1899), 12–13.

[24] "Frafra" referred to the Talensi, Nabdam, Gurensi and Nankanni. See Carola Lentz, "Colonial Constructions and African Initiatives: The History of Ethnicity in Northwestern Ghana," *Ethnos* 65, No. 1 (2000): 125.

[25] Bening, "Definition", 229–61.

The construction of paramountcies, which formed the core of Northcott's program, was closely connected to domestic slavery and tribute. Northcott recommended the quiet retention of domestic slavery which, he argued, "must be regarded as a harmless form of labour contract, so deeply rooted in the social economy of the native that it is most undesirable to modify it" except under gradual self-emancipation facilitated by gradual education and economic growth. In fact, according to Northcott chiefly coerced labour operated on the same principle as taxation in "civilised communities," that is, a form of debt payment by free citizens to their governments in return for peace and good government.[26] More important, however, was the commutation of tribute into direct taxes. Writing in 1899, Northcott stated that

> The essence of easy rule over the natives of West Africa is the existence of some convincing proof of paramountcy. This is displayed by the native rulers in various forms, but the only one of these that does not conflict with public opinion as known in Great Britain is the exaction of tribute.[27]

By "tribute" Northcott meant direct taxation, and he pushed for its implementation once the paramountices had been placed on a strong footing.

Beyond its role in legitimating chiefs' power, direct taxation also would deliver a steady and stable labour supply for public works to support Northcott's economic plan to capture and develop the caravan trade to the West African interior.[28] Britain would benefit by supplying agricultural surpluses to the traders, taxing the caravans and inserting British goods into the trading networks. Trade would focus on Gambaga (see Map 3), which Northcott believed could be developed as an "entrepot for the supply of European goods to the whole bend of the Niger." This project would require the policing of trade routes, the development of transportation infrastructure (preferably up the Volta River), the introduction of currency and the support of major market centres.[29]

---

[26] Northcott, *Report on the Northern Territories*, 33.

[27] Northcott, "Further Correspondence on the Northern Territories of the Gold Coast," CO879/58: Africa (West), Great Britain, Public Record Office (PRO), 183.

[28] On the caravan trade, see Paul Lovejoy, *Caravans of Kola* (Zaria, Ahmadu Bello University Press, 1980).

[29] Northcott, *Report on the Northern Territories*, 46–8, "Further Correspondence," 25/6, 180, 270/1.

In Northcott's opinion the project of reviving the northern chieftaincies posed a major challenge because slave raiding had rendered the stateless peoples predisposed to violence against foreign intruders. Northcott's plan to re-establish the embryonic chiefs of the pre-slave raiding days thus began with military "pacification," under which a form of violence similar to the slave raiders was invoked by the British in the name of development. Northcott began the campaign in 1897/8 with a particular focus on the Talensi in the north-east, presumed to be under Mamprusi, and the Dagara in the north-west, presumed to be under Wa. Between 1907 and 1918, Northcott's successors believed that they had successfully pacified the Northern Territories and revived the political structures which existed before Samory and Babatu appeared in the Northern Territories (see Map 3). It is to these campaigns that we will no turn.

The Politics of "Pacification" and the Development of the Chiefs, 1894–1918

Talensi

After setting the boundaries in 1898/9 it took almost fifteen years for the colonial administration to bring the Talensi under their control. From their base at Gambaga, the Mamprusi capital, the administration sent a series of military expeditions against the Talensi, whom the British included under the tribal label "Frafra," in response to complaints from immigrant Hausa traders. In 1899, Captain Giffard secured treaties with most of the settlements and established a British post at Bolgatanga. Resistance persisted, however, from the settlement of Tongo at the base of the Tong Hills, which served as the gateway to an important sacred shrine. In 1899, Captain Donald Stewart attacked the area and captured the chief of Tongo (the *Tongrana*), whom Stewart believed was the key to conquering the Talensi. "The author of all this trouble," he wrote, "is the Chief of Tong (Tongo) who is also the chief fetish priest of all the Frafra. He is the man who gave the orders to have us driven out of the country and established a boycott whereby Mr. Fenton (at the British station at Bolgatanga) could get not food for his men and therefore had to withdraw from Tanga." Having captured the Tongo chief and eliminated the power of the Tong Hills shrine, Stewart believed

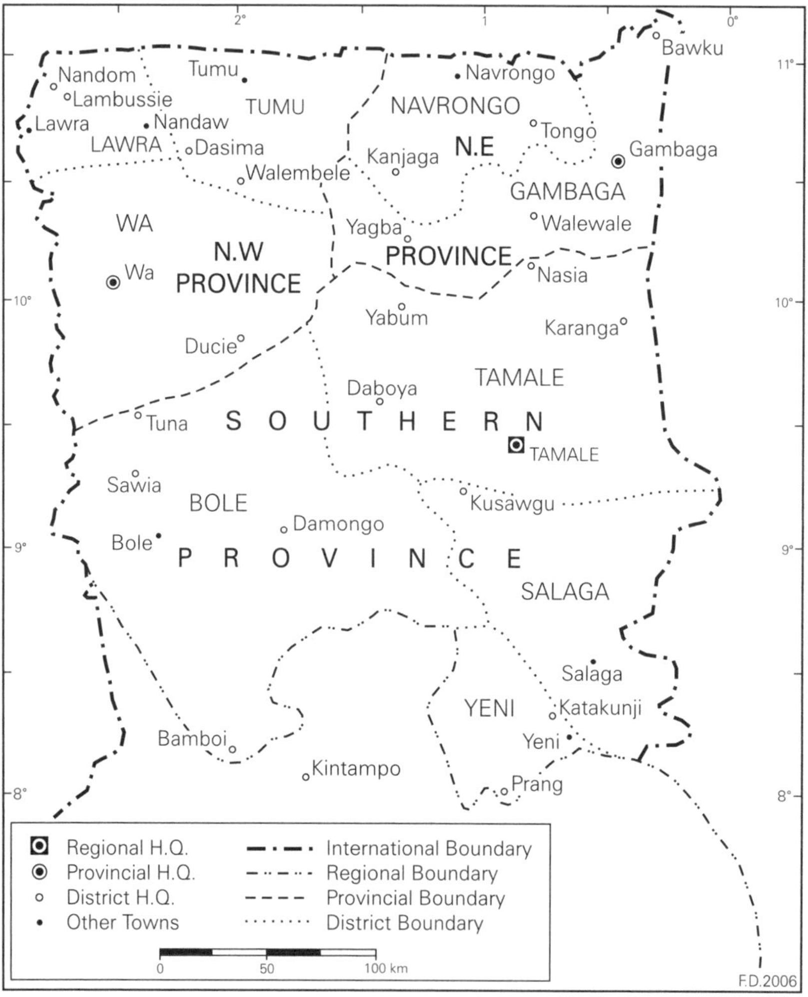

Map 3: Northern Territories of the Gold Coast, Provinces and Districts, 1907
Source: Carola Lentz

that the Frafra could be "thoroughly beaten in every direction" and British rule secured on a permanent basis.[30] Most of the Talensi chiefs indeed did submit to British rule during Stewart's campaign, but he was mistaken about the *Tongrana*'s control over the Tong Hills shrine. Stewart mistook the Tongrana for a *tengdaana*, but in fact he was a Namoo, not a Tali, and he had no connection to the earth shrine. Despite his arrest and the destruction of Tongo, the Talis of the Tong Hills continued to resist between 1900 and 1905.[31]

Faced with declining imperial funding for the Northern Territories, after 1905 the administration extended their administrative control over the north-east to capture taxes from the caravan trade. Between 1905 and 1908 the administration built stations along the main trade route in Navrongo (others were constructed along caravan routes at Bawku and Tumu). In 1907, when the northern military administration gave way to civilian rule, Navrongo District Commissioner Captain O'Kineally became the first British officer to visit Tenzugu in the Tong Hills, the gateway to the Tongnaab shrines. O'Kineally's visit was peaceful, and he urged the administration to suspend further punitive expeditions in the hopes that the people would "come in" peacefully.[32]

At this time the northern administration was led by A.E.G. Watherston, who intended to resurrect the Mamprusi Dynasty's supposed paramountcy over the Talensi.[33] Watherston's project of political amalgamation would provide a framework for socialising the African population into the market by nurturing the expansion of their wants and expectations along Western lines. To this end Watherston moved the administrative capital southwards from Gambaga to Tamale with the intention of developing markets and exposing northerners to "progressive" southern ideas.[34] In order to minimise the pain of this transition, Watherston attempted to divide the northern population

---

[30] M. Anafu, "The Impact of Colonial Rule On Talensi Political Institutions, 1898–1967," *Transactions of the Historical Society of Ghana* 14, No. 1 (June 1973): 18–19; Allman and Parker, 58–9.

[31] Jack Goody, "The Political Systems of the Talensi and Their Neighbours, 1888–1915," *Cambridge Anthropology* 14, No. 2 (1990): 10. Anafu, 19–20.

[32] Allman and Parker, 60–1.

[33] In 1908, Watherston reproduce Northcott's argument verbatim, without crediting Northcott, in a speech to the Royal African Society. See A.E.G. Watherston, "The Northern Territories of the Gold Coast," *Journal of the Royal African Society* 7, No. 28 (July, 1908), 350 and Northcott, *Report on the Northern Territories*, 13.

[34] Watherston, 355–70.

"into their original divisions, so as to come under the paramount chiefs they were in the habit of obeying before Samory and Babatu overran the country."[35] However, Watherston left his post before his plans could be fulfilled, and in any case his successor, Cecil Armitage, faced renewed resistance in the Nabdam village of Nangodi in 1910. Armitage sent a punitive expedition into the area, which destroyed crops and compounds in no less than six villages.[36]

After this expedition the colonial administration opened a District Office in Zuarungu, less than five miles from the Tong Hills. The Talensi resisted the increased colonial presence, which included the demand for forced labour for road work at a time of food shortages and cattle disease. Responding to Talensi resistance, the colonial government sent in a force to occupy the Tong Hills and break the last bastion of resistance to the colonial occupation. British forces attacked Tenzugu ferociously, at the end of the dry season when people were short of water and during an important harvest festival (*Gologo*), when they were not permitted to fight. Five elders were arrested, Tenzugu and the sacred grove were destroyed, and the people were banned from living in the Tong Hills. In the summer of 1912, Armitage reported that the "Fra-Fra" were co-operating with British authorities and that they were "the most tractable and amiable people imaginable." Three years later, however, Armitage discovered that pilgrims had been visiting the Tenzugu shrine against British orders and he ordered it destroyed once again. The fact that Talensi volunteers helped to set it on fire convinced Armitage that he had finally broken the power of the shrine. However, Armitage failed to realise that the volunteers were Namoos, without a ritual connection to the Tongnaab, and that the shrine in question was the Bonaab shrine, one of many Tongnaab shrines in the area. Another important shrine, Yanii, remained untouched.[37] Convinced that he had destroyed *the* Tong Hills shine, Armitage wrote that "the breaking of the Tong Hills 'Fetish' power, which was a cloak, under cover of which a band of unscrupulous raiders carried on their work, gives us an excellent opportunity to revive the authority of the chiefs."[38]

---

[35] Ibid., 357.
[36] Allman and Parker, 63.
[37] Ibid., 63–7, 79–81.
[38] Goody, 17.

While he "pacified" the Talensi area between 1910 and 1915, Armitage also set out to re-create the Mamprusi Dynasty by constructing a hierarchy of chiefs under the paramount chief of Mamprusi (the *Nayiri*). In his own words, Armitage wanted to amalgamate the small chieftaincies into larger districts under the control of a few "really big chiefs." Under the scheme Armitage intended to make Mamprusi the hub of the district administration of the northeast, in which the Nayiri would become paramount not only over the "Frafra," but also the Gurunsi, Builsa, and Kusasi. The result was the creation of the "Kingdom of Mampurugu," consisting of five subdivisions: Mampurugu, Frafra, Kusasi, Gurunsi and Builsa. Armitage installed the *Nayiri* as the chief of Mampurugu and the paramount ruler of the Northeast District; he also asked his district staff to find suitable Head Chiefs for the other four subdivisions as representatives accountable to the *Nayiri*. Single head chiefs were chosen to head up Gurunsi, Builsa and Kusasi. Among the Talensi, however, Captain S.D. Nash chose to deputise four separate chiefs to serve under the *Nayiri*, representing the settlements of Bongo, Nangodi, Sekoti and Tongo. In the first three, local Talensi chiefs were placed directly under the authority of the *Nayiri* in Mampurugu. In Tongo, however, Nash refused to recognise the Tongrana as head chief directly under the *Nayiri*. Instead, he recruited the chief of Kurugu (the *Kunab*), from a Mamprusi village across the Talensi border, moved him to Zuarungu and proclaimed him head chief of the Talensi, with the Tongrana relegated to the third rung below the *Nayiri*. Nash justified this move on the basis of some rather shadowy information that the Kunab had ruled over the Talensi before the slave raiding days. Governor J.J. Thorburn presided over the creation of the new "Mamprusi kingdom" in 1912, at which time the head chiefs proclaimed their allegiance to the *Nayiri* and agreed to pay an annual tribute to the Mamprusi paramount chief. The end result therefore was the division of Frafra into the sub-divisions of Bongo, Nangodi, Sekoti and Kurugu.[39]

In constructing his scheme Armitage claimed that he had revived traditional Mamprusi hegemony over the northeast, an accomplishment whose legitimacy appeared to be confirmed by his staff's investigations of oral tradition. According to local informants, oral traditions

[39] Anafu, 19–23. Illiasu, 6–11.

said that Mamprusi immigrants had settled in Taleland[40] in the distant past, which meant that Talensi were divided into two distinct groups: the indigenous Talis and the immigrant Namoos. The Namoos were descended from a Mamprusi chief named Mosuor who had fled to Taleland after losing a succession struggle in Mampurugu. In Taleland, Mosuor founded the village of Tongo and negotiated an agreement with the Talis permitting his descendents to remain on the land, who eventually spread out to establish Namoo colonies in Yamriga, Sie and Biuk. When Mosuor died, his son traveled to Mampurugu to be formally invested by the *Nayiri* as the new chief of Tongo. This set the precedent of Mamprusi authority over Namoo chieftaincy. After a succession dispute over the fourth Tongo chieftaincy, the *Nayiri* sent a representative to Kurugu—a Mamprusi settlement just across the White Volta River from Taleland—to keep an eye on the Talensi and act as the elector of the chief of Tongo.[41] This oral tradition was filtered through the British imagination to construct a story of Mamprusi hegemony over the Talensi in the era before the slave raids of Samory and Babatu, and it was on this basis that Armitage created the hierarchy of Talensi chiefs under the control of the Mamprusi. Not only did the oral traditions appear to justify placing Bongo, Nangodi and Sekoti under the *Nayiri*; they also seemed to rationalise inserting the chief of Kurugu between the *Nayiri* and the chief of Tongo.

Beneath the head chiefs, Armitage deputised a series of village chiefs and headmen subject to the authority of the four divisional chiefs. This process was relatively less problematic in the Namoo settlements, whose clan heads were called "chief" (*naab*), than it was among the Talis who had no tradition of chieftaincy. In the latter case, Provincial Commissioner Captain S.D. Nash found no chiefs as such, but in 1911 he discovered a group of hereditary lineage heads who, he argued, had served as the chiefs' elders in the precolonial period. Nash recorded the names of the family heads but because of their old age and perceived incapacity he refused to recognise them as chiefs. Instead, he deputised some of their "helpers"—often the elders' sons and brothers—to recruit labour for public

[40] "Taleland" refers to the land of the Talensi.

[41] Keith Hart, "The Economic Basis of Talensi Social History in the Early Twentieth Century." in *Research in Economic Anthropology, Volume One*, ed. George Dalton, 192 (Greenwich: IAI Press, 1978). Anafu, 28.

works. In reality these men were a diverse lot. Some of them had simply agreed to collaborate and were made chiefs, some were elders or former slaves or outcasts, and some had been minor *tengdaanas*. For the most part, they had little indigenous authority, hence their only power came from the British, and their offices were often bought and sold. These men usurped the power of the elders and religious leaders and became the recognised chiefs of the Talis. They were given the title *kambonaaba*, a term derived from the Mamprusi/Dagomba military office of *Kambonse* (gunmen captain) and an appropriate title for British-appointed "sergeant-major chiefs" who had no hereditary claim to rule and whose main function was to recruit forced labour for public works. The *kambonaabas* were supported by the colonial state and they quickly solidified their position as local rulers against the claims of the lineage heads and *tengdaanas*.[42]

The most important example of the usurpation of traditional authority by *kambonaabas* occurred among the exiled people of Tenzugu, among whom Nash appointed a *kambonaaba* named Tengol in 1911. Tengol replaced two former authority figures, the *kpatarnaaba* (head of the Kpatar section of Tenzugu) and the *tengdaana* of the Bonaab shrine. These two men had been important political leaders of Tenzugu before they were jailed by the British after the attacks on the Tong Hills in 1911 and 1915. For his part, Tengol used his position to accumulate wealth through labour recruiting. More importantly, he also cultivated a growing clandestine pilgrim trade to the Yanii Tongnaab shrine, which continued to operate beyond the knowledge of the British into the 1920s.[43]

As Allman and Parker brilliantly demonstrate, British officials were unaware that their intervention had destroyed the authority of only one Tongnaab shrine, and one specific Tali clan, while opening the door to the machinations of Tengol and the "ritual collaborators" of another shrine, Yanii.[44] Armitage believed differently. With the *kambonaabas* in place, he claimed that he had recreated the native state of Mamprusi, with a hierarchy of chiefs and headmen stretching down from the *Nayiri* through the divisional chiefs to the *kambonaabas* at the village level. As we shall see later, this false belief

[42] Anafu, 26. Illiasu, 6–11. Allman and Parker, 84–5.

[43] Allman and Parker, 76. Meyer Fortes, *The Dynamics of Clanship Among the Talensi, Being the First Part of an Analysis of the Social Structure of a Trans-Volta Tribe* (London: Oxford University Press, 1969 (originally published, 1945), 110–14.

[44] Allman and Parker, 100–101.

would produce complicated struggles for power during the development of indirect rule in the 1930s.

The North-west

The colonial project in the north-west was similar in its attempt to "reconstruct" the authority of a traditional state believed to have been destroyed by the slave raiders. As noted above, this project sought to resurrect the power of the Wa Na over the Dagarti and Lobi to the north. This notion was problematic from the outset because "Dagarti" and "Lobi" did not reflect distinct ethnic groups, much less "tribes." Instead, the area to the north of Wa contained settlements whose inhabitants defined themselves differently in different ritual settings. In the 1950s anthropologist Jack Goody invented the term "LoDagaa" and "LoWiili" to describe this constellation of villages, not as a tribal label but rather as directional categories resembling the Western categories "Easterners" and "Westerners."[45] Lentz very perceptively points out the flaws in Goody's classification and his tendency to fall back into essentialised tribal categories.[46] She prefers the term "Dagara," which is more useful because it refers to the constellation of communities in what became the Lawra District in the early twentieth century (see Map 4). Early on, British officials subsumed two "tribes" within this category, which formed part of a confusing variety of shifting tribal labels over time (see Figure 1). The earliest designations included "Lobi", "Dagarti" and "Isala", formulated between 1903 and 1905, and drawn from earlier sources such as Binger.[47] Some British officers, such as Northcott, believed that the Lobi and Dagarti had been subjects of the Wa polity before the slave raids of the nineteeth century. The labels themselves referred to perceived levels of "civilisation" rather than any meaningful social or political structures, with the Lobi being the least advanced.[48] As such the Lobi became the main target of British pacification.

The pacification campaign grew out of the search for wealth. Britain's interest in the north-west emerged after G.E. Ferguson

[45] Goody, *The Social Organisation of the LoWiili, Second Edition* (London: Oxford University Press, 1967), iii.

[46] Lentz, "Colonial Constructions and African Initiatives," 118–20.

[47] Lentz, "Contested Identities: the History of Ethnicity in Northern Ghana," 140.

[48] Hawkins, *Writing and Colonialism in Northern Ghana*, 43. Lentz, "Colonial Constructions and African Initiatives," 113–14.

reported that Wa was an important gateway to a lucrative trading and gold-producing region along the Black Volta river.[49] Ferguson believed that the Wa Na was the paramount ruler over a sizeable portion of the north-west, and the British treaties recognised him as the king of the Dagarti. In 1897, Lieutenant F.B. Henderson reinforced this belief when he signed a Treaty of Friendship and Protection with the Wa Na, stating that his authority stretched from the Black Volta to Dasima in the north-east and Kulmasa in the south. The true picture, however, was rather more ambiguous. Not all colonial officials shared the view that the north-west had once been under Wa's paramountcy, and Northcott himself soon discovered that only one "Dagarti" settlement recognised the paramount authority of Wa.[50] Accepting the Dagarti as an independent tribe, Northcott signed a treaty with the chief of Kaleo as "King of Dagarti," offering him gifts of money, sheep, salt and cloth in return for allegiance to the British forces.[51] Similar treaties were signed with "sub-chiefs" in Issa, Busi, Wogu, Nadawli and Dorimon. These chiefs, however, complained that they had only united under Kaleo to fend off Samory and Babatu, and thus they were treated as independent chiefs for the time being. As a final step, the colonial administration divided the "Country of Dagarti" into the Wa Sub-District and the Dagarti Sub-District, and placed them along with the Gurunshi and Bole Sub-Districts into the Black Volta District with its headquarters at Wa.[52]

The British administration extended its authority northwards from Wa through the threat of force. Captain Berthon took over the Black Volta District in 1901, and for two years he suppressed resistance through piecemeal expeditions. With Northcott's permission, Berthon mounted a larger expedition in 1903, traveling from Wa to Tumu and back again, and passing through many of settlements along the way. Moving north from Kaleo between 1903 and 1905, Berthon's men conducted pacification campaigns and recognised chiefs in and around the settlements of Lawra, Nandom, Jirapa, Lambussie and

[49] Brenda Chalfin, *Shea Butter Republic: State Power, Global Markets and the Making of an Indigenous Commodity* (New York: Routledge, 2004), 89; Bening, "Definition," 232–4.
[50] Wilks, *Wa and the Wala*, 9–10,142.
[51] Northcott, *Report on the Northern Territories*, 16.
[52] Wilks, *Wa and the Wala*, 9–10,144. Lentz, "Histories and Political Conflict: A Case Study of Chieftaincy in Nandom, Northwestern Ghana," *Paideuma* 39 (1993): 183. Martin Staniland, *The Lions of Dagbon: Political Change in Northern Ghana* (Cambridge, Cambridge University Press, 1975), 42.

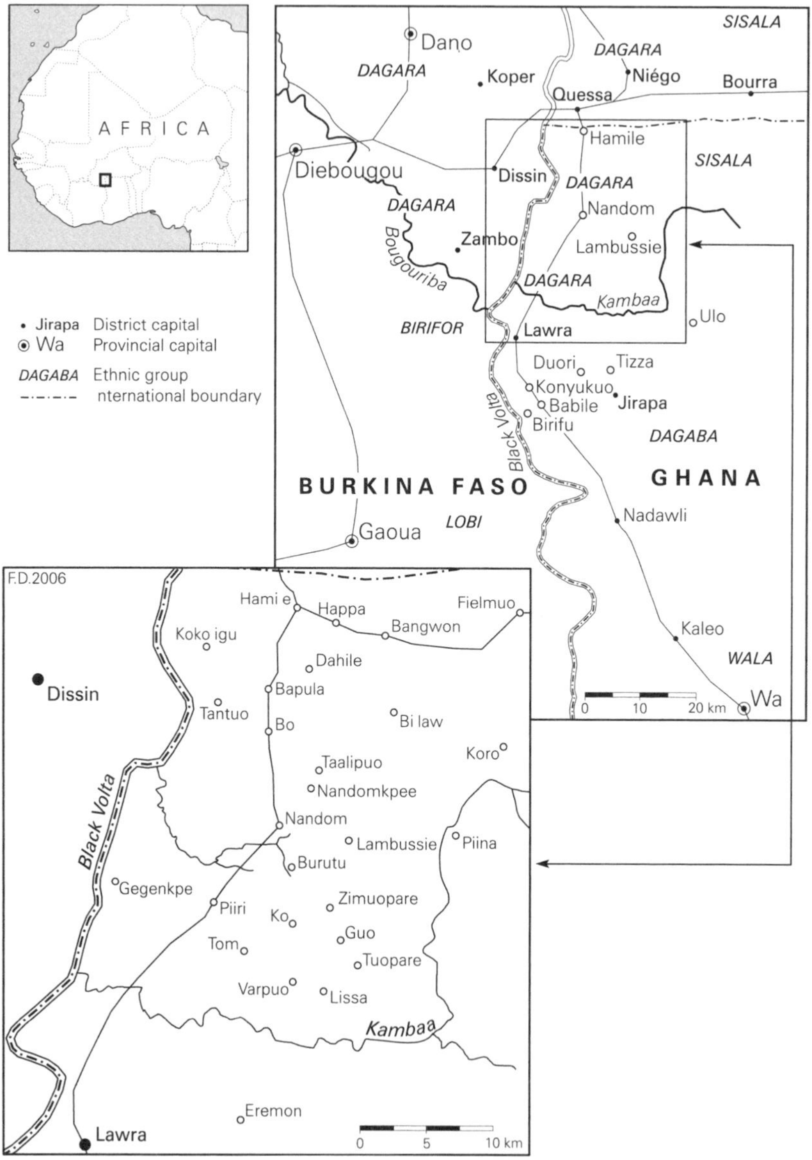

Map 4: North-Western Ghana: Ethnic Groups
Source: Carola Lentz

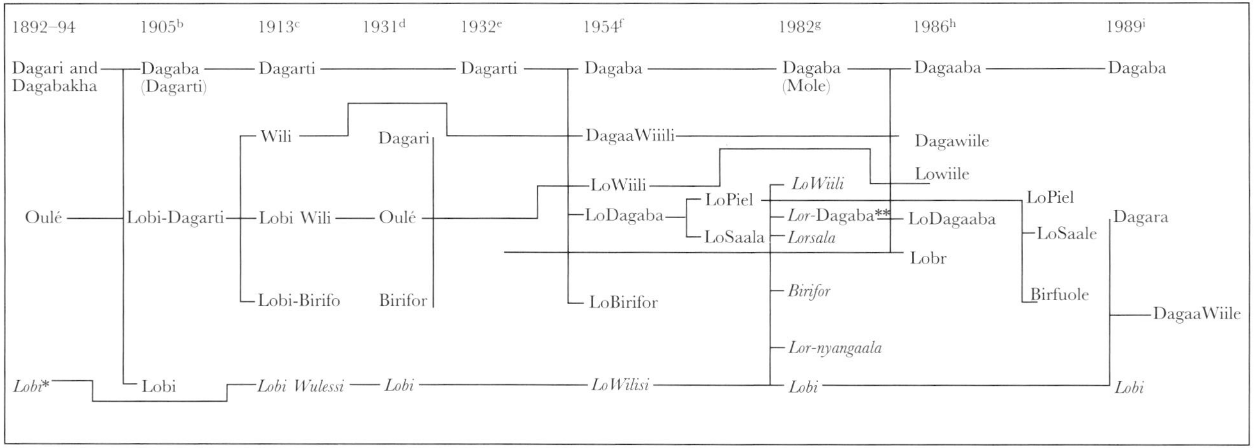

Sources:
a Binger 1982; George Ekem Ferguson (1894) in Arhin 1974.
b NAG ADN 56/1/50, Reports on Tours of Inspection North West Province, March-May 1905.
c NAG ADM 61/5/1, Lawra District Record Book, 6 (11 October 1913).
d Labouret 1931.
e Rattray 1932.
f Goodry 1954.
g Tuurey 1982.
h Archbishop Peter Dery (1984) cited in Angsotinge 1986.
i Der 1989.
* Italics indicate that these were deemed to be people linguistically and culturally separate from the LoDagaa.
** Allegedly a linguistic and cultural hybrid of the *Lobi* and Dagaba.

Figure 1: Colonial "Tribal" Names in the North-West
Source: Sean Hawkins, *Writing and Colonialism in Northern Ghana: The Encounter Between the LoDagaa and the "World on Paper."* Toronto: University of Toronto Press, 2002.

Tumu. Ostensibly a peaceful mission, Berthon nonetheless took a force of one hundred troops and attacked whenever the people would not cooperate with the British contingent. The attacks laid the ground for Berthon's successor Moutray Read to continue the pacification program after 1905, securing the cooperation additional villages whose memories of Berthon's attacks led them to concede the rule of the British administration. Resistance continued, however, and throughout 1906 Read regularly used the threat of punishment to force the people of the north-west to obey the chiefs that had been created by the colonial administration.[53]

With the onset of civilian rule in 1907 the administration renamed the Black Volta District the "North-Western Province," which included only the three Districts of Wa, Lawra and Tumu. Each District was to have a head chief, with the Wa Na acting as the paramount ruler over all three, but the people of Lawra and Tumu neither accepted the overlordship of the Wa Na nor agreed on head chiefs for their Districts. As a result, thirty-eight small, independent "native states" were established in the three Districts between 1906 and 1907. By 1913 these had been reduced to thirty-six: ten in the Lawra District, twelve in Tumu and fourteen in Wa.[54] In 1914, Armitage attempted once again to amalgamate the native states under Wa, declaring the Wa Na paramount over the three Districts. He also placed the Tumu District under the paramountcy of the chief of Tumu. Most settlements, however, still would not accept the authority of the paramount rulers, and the divisions continued to act independently.[55]

In both the Talensi area and the north-west, the difficulty experienced by successive Chief Commissioners in amalgamating the chieftaincies of the Northern Territories reflected the divergence between the colonial discourse of African "tribe" and reality on the ground. British officials from Northcott to Armitage believed in an evolutionary scheme whereby "primitive" societies evolved from family units into tribal chiefdoms and finally to centralised states.[56] They believed that several states had evolved in the Northern Territories and then had extended their rule over a series of defined tribes.

---

[53] Lentz, "Histories and Political Conflict," 181–6. Bening, "Foundations," 118. Lentz, *Ethnicity and the Making of History in Northern Ghana*, 59–62.

[54] Bening, Foundations, 120. Lentz, *Ethnicity and the Making of History in Northern Ghana*, 84.

[55] Bening, "Foundations," 120.

[56] Lentz, "Colonial Constructions and African Initiatives," 113.

Having quelled the disruptions of the slave raiders, the colonial administration could set the natural evolution of the Northern Territories back on its proper path by resurrecting the authority of the traditional states over the surrounding tribes. In reality, however, the authority of kingdoms such as Wa and Mamprusi over their territories was never as absolute as the Europeans believed, and the "subject" peoples rarely identified themselves as belonging to specific "tribes." Mamprusi, for instance, had exerted control over the appointment of local rulers among the Talensi, but it was restricted to Namoo settlements and it did not provide any sort of executive or administrative powers over other local affairs. In the northwest the case for Wa hegemony may have been stronger, but the people of the north-west did not identify themselves as a single ethnic group, much less an ethnic group under the rule of the Wala.

Furthermore, we do not know for certain whether precolonial societies in the Black Volta area were centralized or "stateless," although a vigorous debate has taken place over this question since the 1970s.[57] As we shall discover, most colonial officials after 1930 believed that chiefs had not existed prior to British rule. Many later scholars have accepted this view, including Goody and Hawkins.[58] In opposition, Ghanaian scholars such as Benedict Der argue that the Dagara were organised into centralised chieftaincies in the eighteenth and nineteenth centuries. Lentz persuasively refutes both arguments by stating that, first, the precolonial history of the north-west was too complex to make generalisations, and, second, that precolonial political structures fell somewhere between centralisation and "acephalousness." Drawing on oral histories and colonial documents, Lentz argues that "strongmen" developed in the north-west, as successful farmers whose power was deepened during the slave raids of the nineteenth century. In some cases, these men provided protection from the slave raiders; in others, they joined their ranks and became warriors themselves.[59] The same appears to have been true among the Talensi.

[57] Lentz provides several good overviews of the debates, but see especially Carola Lentz, "Stateless Societies or Chiefdoms: A Debate Among Dagara Intellectuals," in Franz Kroger and Barbara Meier (eds.), *Ghana's North: Research on Culture, Religion, and Politics of Societies in Transition* (Frankfurt am Main: Peter Lang, 2003).

[58] See Goody, *Social Organisation of the LoWiili* and Hawkins, "Disguising Chiefs and God As History: Questions on the Acephalousness of LoDagaa Politics and Religion." *Africa* 66, No. 2 (1996), and Hawkins, *Writing and Colonialism*, Chapter 1.

[59] Lentz, *Ethnicity and the Making of History in Northern Ghana*, 68–77.

In the early 1890s, Ferguson noted that "big men" had developed, gathering captives and followers to build forces for looting caravans plying the route between Ouagadougu and Salaga.[60]

The notion of precolonial strongmen is important because it attempts to sort out the actual identities of the chiefs appointed by the British between 1903 and 1907. Many early chiefs were drawn from the ranks of the strongmen, although in some cases they had been messengers of the *tengaansobs*. These men were not chiefs in the British sense, nor were they simply the heads of lineages in a kin-ordered society. Thus, Lentz concludes, "the Volta area in the nineteenth century was characterised neither by a strict hierarchy with permanent chiefdoms, nor by egalitarianism and a total lack of leadership."[61] What we can say for certain is that British officials changed the political landscape by seeking out local strongmen and appointing them chiefs. In this sense the chiefs were "invented," but not entirely so, since their power was rooted in the precolonial period.

These complications did not dissuade the colonial authorities from retaining Northcott's idea of "tribe." Indeed, the administration continued to search for natural tribal boundaries as a basis for the district administration in the Northern Territories. As we shall see below, colonial officials did not, however, retain Northcott's vision for direct taxation and the development of agriculture and trade to the West African interior.

Land, Labour and Development in the Northern Territories, 1901–1919

As the pacification campaigns unfolded, the colonial administration cast around for revenue-generating opportunities in the Northern Territories. The military activities had been costly and had imposed a significant drain on the British Treasury through a series of Imperial Grants-in-Aid between 1898 and 1908.[62] This cost created pressure for economic development, and for a few decades the colonial administration tried to develop marketable surpluses in the Protectorate. In March, 1908, for instance, a travelling investigator from the

---

[60] Allman and Parker, 56.

[61] Lentz, "Stateless Societies or Chiefdoms: A Debate Among Dagara Intellectuals," 137.

[62] Ladouceur, 45.

Imperial Institute visited and praised the north's suitability for cotton, hibiscus, rubber, shea butter and tobacco. This finding provoked the state to place an Agricultural Inspector in Tamale, who investigated but failed to develop the production of tobacco and shea butter. Investigations into cotton similarly produced no results, despite the continual re-voting of public funds for research work performed by the British Cotton Growing Association.[63] In the area of trade, stores and shops developed by Watherston in Tamale failed to cover their costs. In 1910, the lack of economic development in the north promoted Chief Commissioner Arthur Festing to declare that "one must be possessed of great optimism to be able to throw out hopes of much export trade from the Northern Territories, at any rate for some years to come. The great bar to such trade is, of course, the existing lack of transport facilities."[64] Governor Thorburn laid the situation bare in 1912. "Until the Colony and Ashanti have been thoroughly opened up and developed," he wrote, "the Northern Territories must be content to wait their turn, and any extensive program designed to render the area more accessible must be suffered to stand over for a long time to come."[65]

In the absence of agricultural surpluses, the colonial administration attempted to raise revenues through direct taxation and levies on the existing caravan trade. Northcott initiated these taxes in the hopes of making the Protectorate self-supporting. He believed that the people would accept a standardised, regular tax in place of the unpredictable exactions of the slave raiders in the precolonial period. The revenue would be small at first, £875 per annum, but it would increase steadily over time. As it turned out, however, the tax was inefficient and expensive to collect and it provoked chiefs to extort money for their personal use. For example, in the north-west it appears that only the settlements to have paid the colonial maintenance tax were those which had previously paid tribute to Babatu.[66]

---

[63] *Northern Territories Annual Report for 1910*, Accra: Government Printer, 1911, 365–66. K.O. Dike-Nworah, "The West African Operations of the British Cotton Growing Association, 1904–1914," *African Historical Studies* 4, No. 2 (1971): 315–331. Marion Johnson, "Cotton Imperialism in West Africa," *African Affairs* 73, No. 291 (April, 1974): 178–187.

[64] *Northern Territories Annual Report, 1910* (London: HMSO, 1911), 6.

[65] David Kimble, *A Political History of Ghana: The Rise of Gold Coast Nationalism, 1850–1928* (London: Oxford University Press, 1965), 534.

[66] Lentz, *Ethnicity and the Making of History in Northern Ghana* forthcoming, 57.

More successful were the caravan tolls levied on the transit trade between the savannah and the coast, consisting mainly of cattle moving southwards into Ashanti and kola nuts moving northwards to the Western Sudan. The tax was set between 6d and 2/-, depending on the item, and it provided most of the revenue for the Northern Territories between 1900 and 1908.[67]

The Abandonment of Direct Taxation and the Rise of Chiefly "Communal" Labour

Northcott's ideals did not hold up long after his departure in 1901. After Northcott left the Gold Coast, Governor Sir Mathew Nathan decided against the direct tax and persuaded Joseph Chamberlain and Northcott's successor A.H. Morris that it should be dropped. Although Chamberlain supported the principle of direct taxation, he agreed that it might not be appropriate for the Northern Territories. He thus informed Governor Nathan that the Colonial Office would drop the tax in return for forcing the he chiefs to call up compulsory labour for public works. Morris accepted Chamberlain's alternative and declared himself "head chief" with the power to force the northern chiefs to obtain forced labour for public works and the fledgling mining industry in the Gold Coast Colony. As a result, the tax was only levied in 1900 and 1901 before it was abolished due to local opposition. In its place, Chief Commissioner Irvine instituted forced labour through the chiefs of twenty-four days per year for every adult male, which lasted until the introduction of a poll tax of 1936. This policy shift initiated the era of the "sergeant-major chiefs" in the Northern Territories.[68] Morris' successor Chief Commissioner Irvine also supported this policy, stating his preference for forced labour over direct taxation among the Dagarti, Frafra, Gurunshi and Lobi-Dagarti "since little has been done to open up the country."[69] Despite a revival of the debate by the Colonial Office between

[67] Ladouceur, 44–5. Ferguson and Wilks, 333–4.

[68] Ferguson and Wilks, 334; Anthony P. Hayden, *Sir Matthew Nathan: British Colonial Governor and Civil Servant* (St. Lucia: University of Queensland Press, 1976), 70–72. Anne Phillips, 26. Stephen Constantine, *The Making of Colonial Development Policy, 1914–1940* (London: Frank Cass and Company, 1984), 11. Lentz, *Ethnicity and the Making of History in Northern Ghana*, 57.

[69] Goody, "Political Systems," 14.

1909 and 1911,[70] the Gold Coast maintained the forced labour system until the administration reintroduced direct taxation in the 1930s. Until this time, the chiefs remained in their role as labour contractors for the colonial administration. Most of the "communal" labour was used for public works projects such as road-building and porterage, but the chiefs also recruited many northerners for the Gold Coast Constabulary and for a brief period also recruited workers for the mines in the south.[71]

Land and Development, 1904–1912

While the chiefs were providing migrant labour for the southern mines, concession-seekers became active in the Northern Territories itself. Worried about a flood of requests, Governor Nathan drafted a Mineral Rights Ordinance (MRO) vesting control over the north's mineral-bearing land in the state. The MRO was triggered by a request in 1901 from an expatriate firm, the Wa Syndicate, for a concession near Wasipe, west of Wa. The Ordinance permitted the government to appropriate mineral-bearing land, and it required concession-seekers to complete a cumbersome, multistage application process with fees paid to the colonial state at every stage. These strict requirements reflected Nathan's fear that the Syndicate's activities would trigger a wave of illegitimate companies, as had occurred in the Gold Coast and South Africa after the Asante and Boer Wars. At the same time, however, the Gold Coast government also needed mining taxes—especially in the absence of direct taxation—to pay for the railways constructed during Chamberlain's campaign to pacify and control Asante.[72]

Although it fell short of land nationalisation the MRO set a precedent for the colonial administration to appropriate land in the Northern Territories, with the stated intention of protecting local communities from foreign capital. The Ordinance succeeded in limiting the concession-seekers, but as B.G. Der indicates it also "partly dispossessed the Northern Territories peoples of their lands" and placed them

---

[70] See for example Sgd T.H. Dugan, Acting District Commissioner, Lorha, 14 December 1909, ADM56/1/87, National Archives of Ghana, Accra (NAGA). Frafra District Commissioner, N.D., ADM56/1/87, NAGA. Sgd. H.C. Wheeler, Navaho District Commissioner, 14 November 1909, ADM56/1/87, NAGA.

[71] Ladouceur, 48.

[72] Hayden, 85–6, 130–3.

under the control of the state.[73] The administration had tried a similar strategy in the south but it had been abandoned in the face of resistance from the coastal elites and the chiefs. The most that the Governor achieved in the Colony and Ashanti was a Concessions Ordinance in 1900, which gave the administration some control over concessions but upheld the chiefs rather than the government as the trustees over community lands. This measure came after the defeat of the Lands Bills of 1894 and 1897, when the elites and chiefs effectively argued that most land in the south was occupied and under the traditional jurisdiction of the chiefs.[74]

By contrast, Governor Nathan justified outright appropriation in the north on the grounds that much of the land was "totally uninhabited, and that there are no native rights to deal with." The Dagarti, he continued, were a tribe "not using money and having no kings or central power of government. The mining rights in this country would not interfere with their lands and villages but would be a benefit to them if worked by a Company." Nathan accepted Morris' view that large tracts of the area were uninhabited "or sparsely populated" and that "the Gold Coast system of concessions would be quite inapplicable to such tracts."[75] Based on this assumption the MRO gave the state the right to grant concessions, bypassing the chiefs completely. The precedent for land nationalisation had been set in the Northern Territories.

The Transition to the Peasant Road, 1907–1919

Between 1904 and 1923 the colonial state extended the intent of the legislation by using the MRO to appropriate land at will for the purposes of development. After 1911, however, the intent of the state's trusteeship began to change, from the regulation of concessions to environmental protection and, ultimately, the protection of African community. This change in emphasis reflected the colonial state's reaction to the negative side of the development of the cocoa industry between 1900 and 1911. By 1911, the Gold Coast had emerged

[73] Ibid., 132.
[74] Omosini, 465–468.
[75] B.G. Der, "Colonial Land Policies in the Northern Territories of the Gold Coast, 1900–1975," *Universitas, New Series*, 4, No. 2 (1975): 130–1.

as the world's largest single producer of cocoa.[76] The cocoa industry emerged outside the control of the colonial state and, while contributing significantly to the colonial economy, its growth also threatened to bring severe environmental damage to the Colony and Ashanti. The peasant-based system of cocoa production lent support to liberal advocates of community, such as E.D. Morel, who fought against Chamberlain's program of smashing the African peasantry to make way for large, European owned plantations. Responding to these trends, the colonial administration gradually evolved a doctrine of development designed to encourage peasant production while protecting African community and guarding against environmental deterioration.

In environmental terms, the rapid growth of cocoa production drew a negative response from colonial officials in the form of an attempt to control the apparent destruction of the forests. Cocoa had been introduced into the Gold Coast by Basel Missionaries and, most famously, by the local trader Tettie Quashie, who introduced the crop to Akuapem farmers faced with declining prices for oil palms. Thus encouraged, the farmers began to experiment with the crop in the 1880s. Around 1896 a number of Akuapem farmers moved across the Densu river into the neighbouring state of Akyem Abuakwa. The Akuapem migrants were followed by other groups of farmers, including settlers from Krobo and Ga areas to the east and south of Akyem Abuakwa. By 1911, when the Gold Coast was one of the world's leading producers of cocoa, most of the crop was grown in Akyem Abuakwa by migrant farmer who had bought land outright from local chiefs. According to Polly Hill, the Akuapem farmers resembled capitalists more than peasants inasmuch as they migrated to Akyem Abuakwa to buy land from chiefs for cash crop production.[77] Labour in Akyem Abuakwa had also become partially commodified between 1896 and 1919 and by the end of World War One many Akuapem farmers were using wage labour on their farms. In neighbouring south Asante, capitalist relations in cocoa production

[76] On the growth of cocoa production, see Polly Hill's pioneering study, *The Gold Coast Cocoa Farmer: A Preliminary Survey* (London: Oxford University Press, 1956). See also Hill, *The Migrant Cocoa Farmers of Southern Ghana: A Study in Rural Capitalism* (Cambridge: Cambridge University Press, 1963). For a more recent analysis, see Gwendolyn Mikell, *Cocoa and Chaos in Ghana* (New York: Paragon House, 1989).

[77] Polly Hill, "The Migrant Farmers of Southern Ghana," *Africa* 31, No. 3 (1961): 109–112.

also appear to have developed after 1916.[78] These relations were not purely capitalist, for much cocoa was produced by family labour or by tenant farmers under sharecropping arrangements. However, a circular migrant labour regime had developed by this time, where migrant workers from the Northern Territories and French colonies worked for wages on a contract basis during the cocoa season, then returned to their homes and families during the off-season.[79] The development of markets in land and labour underwrote a massive expansion of the cocoa industry as well as the related extension of foodstuff production into new areas of the Akan forests. In the eyes of many colonial officials, these processes carried serious environmental implications.

Forestry, H.C. Belfield and the West African Lands Committee, 1907–1916

As cocoa production outstripped mining the colonial state passed a Forestry Bill designed to conserve the colony's forests. The forestry question had been on the table since a Native Jurisdiction Ordinance of 1883 empowered chiefs to make by-laws for forest conservation. After the chiefs failed to make any such by-laws, the state enacted a Timber Protection Ordinance in 1907 and introduced a full-scale Forestry Bill into the Legislative Assembly in 1910.[80] Dissatisfied with the Bill, the colonial state amended the legislation and re-introduced a new Forestry Bill in 1911. The second Bill was amended in the face of criticism from the ARPS and the African members of the Legislative Council. Though the amended version passed in 1911, its enactment provoked heated protest from the APRS because it gave the state the right to grant leaseholds to "strangers," including foreign capitalists, in cases of poor conservation by the original owners.

The ARPS argued that this provision, while stopping short of wholesale land appropriation, would produce the same result: the expropriation of indigenous lands for the benefit of expatriate capital. After the Bill's enactment the ARPS sent J.E. Casely-Hayford to London to protest the state's intention to retain leasehold powers. While the delegation pursued its lobbying in London, the Colonial

[78] Gareth Austin, "The Emergence of Capitalist Relations in South Asante Cocoa Farming, c. 1916–33," *Journal of African History* 28 (1987): 263–4.
[79] Austin, 273–4.
[80] Kimble, 365.

Office sent forestry expert H.C. Belfield to the Gold Coast to study the issue in detail. Though Belfield conceded some points to the ARPS, his report of 1912 supported the spirit of the 1911 Ordinance, and, indeed, the plans of Griffith and Maxwell to appropriate indigenous lands in the interests of agrarian development. The Colonial Office, however, decided to shelve Belfield's report as it turned to the deliberations of the newly created West African Lands Committee (WALC).[81]

Created out of the Northern Nigerian Lands Committee (NNLC) of 1908/9, the WALC's membership included prominent figures such as E.D. Morel and British Liberal MP Josiah Wedgewood.[82] During the Nigerian negotiations, Northern Nigerian Resident Charles Temple worked with Governor Percy Girouard and Richard Palmer, Resident of Katsina and Temple ally, to undermine Frederick Lugard's plan to develop Northern Nigeria's Emirs into a landlord class.[83] In 1908 Temple, Girouard and Palmer orchestrated the deliberations of the NNLC, whose members advocated protecting against landlordism by implementing a taxation structure similar to Henry George's single-tax. An American utopian socialist, George cast landlords as parasites and developed a neo-Ricardian theory equating ground rents with an "unearned increment," siphoned off by the landlords to the detriment of the labouring communities. If this increment were appropriated by the state as a single tax, George argued, the proceeds could be used for community development instead of lining the pockets of a parasitic landlord class.[84] As Anne Phillips has noted, the NNLC membership considered Africa an approximation of "the ideal world of Henry George" and its recommendations sought to preserve this world by nationalising Northern Nigeria and levying direct taxes roughly equivalent to ground rents.[85] As a strategy to keep Northern Nigeria safe from Lugard's vision of landlordism, Temple and Girouard proposed to nationalise the region and appropriate ground rents in order to satisfy "the common wants of the inhabitants" rather than

---

[81] Ibid., 362. Phillips, 74–5.

[82] Phillips, 75. R.W. Shenton, *The Development of Capitalism in Northern Nigeria* (Toronto: University of Toronto Press, 1986), 41, 46–7.

[83] Shenton, 26–30.

[84] Cowen and Shenton, 259. See also Phillips, 67–68 and Shenton, 29–30.

[85] Phillips, 68. Shenton, 29.

lining the pockets of a landlord class.[86] A clearer argument for George's single tax could not have been made.

The Nigerian colonial state fulfilled the NNLC's vision in 1910 by implementing a *Northern Nigerian Lands Proclamation* and a direct tax in the form of a Hausa institution, the *biet-al-mal*, implemented by Palmer in the Katsina Emirate in 1910/11 and controlled by a native police force, the *dogari*. The land proclamation and direct tax intended to block the growth of private property and landlordism by rendering land inalienable (through nationalisation) and redistributing rents through the colonial state as trustee for the African population. In 1912 the ideas of the NNLC worked their way into the newly formed West African Lands Committee, whose single-tax bias was reflected by the inclusion of Morel and Wedgewood in its membership. Although World War One prevented the publication of the WALC's findings, the committee's draft report of 1916 solidified the British West African policy along the lines of the NNLC. Through their recommendations, the NNLC and WALC turned the British towards preventing the commercialisation of land and attempting to develop and preserve Henry George's ideal world in West Africa.[87] This plan found support in the Gold Coast. In 1913, for example, the *Gold Coast Leader* supported the WALC's argument against private property on the grounds that the chiefs would barter their ancestral lands away to foreigners. "Are we going to suffer ourselves," stated the *Leader*, "to be reduced to the miserable status of the proletarian for exploitation purposes by foreign settlers to enrich themselves and make us a landless people in the land of our birth?"[88] The Northern Territories provided an ideal venue for this project of preventing proletarianisation and landlessness, since individual land tenure had not yet developed.

Sir Hugh Clifford and the Northern Territories, 1912–1919

Due to its political implications, however, the full Georgeist program of the WALC received little support from the West African colonial governors.[89] In the Gold Coast, Sir Hugh Clifford—the Governor

---

[86] "Land Tenure and Political Evolution in West Africa," *American Review of Reviews*, 47 (January–June, 1913): 617, no author, 618.
[87] Shenton, 41–5. Phillips, 67–8, 74–5.
[88] Quoted in "Land Tenure and Political Evolution in West Africa," 617.
[89] Phillips, 77–8.

during the WALC period—flatly rejected the policy of land nationalisation as political suicide. Clifford's stance was not surprising considering the long history of indigenous resistance to the Crown appropriation of land in the Gold Coast. Clifford agreed, however, with both the WALC and the *Gold Coast Leader* that African communities required protection against the negative side of westernisation.[90] In Clifford's formulation, the coastal elite represented the worst of the evils of the west; he believed that the Gold Coast professionals had absorbed the worst of civilisation through early contacts with exploitative and ruthless European traders.[91]

Though Clifford stopped short of land nationalisation, he believed that British trusteeship could save the Northern Territories from the disintegration brought by westernisation in the south. Such trusteeship, Clifford believed, could take the Gold Coast across "seven or eight centuries" in a "single bound" while protecting the people from the "speedy degenerations which the rapid changes effected in their environment and conditions of life are only too likely to occasion."[92] The north provided a particularly clean slate for this project, because the region's lack of development had saved it from the southern experience. Clifford thus turned the non-development of the north into a positive achievement. Although the Northern Territories had not been visibly developed, Clifford wrote in 1913, the British had brought "peace," "security" and "liberty" to the region and thus saved the people from the tyranny of slave raiding and the "horrors of frequent inter-tribal conflicts."[93] In other words, the Pax Britannica had set the stage for development along African lines, which for Clifford meant peasant-based systems of rural production.[94] To guard against the "degeneration" of the peasantry, Clifford proposed to keep "tribal systems" intact and simultaneously modernise them as "efficient instruments of government," all the while guarding against

---

[90] H.A. Gailey, *Clifford: Imperial Proconsul* (London: Rex Collings, 1982), 76.

[91] Sir Hugh Clifford, "The Gold Coast," *Blackwoods Magazine*, MCCXXVII, No. 203 (January 1918): 56–7,65. "The Gold Coast and its Dependencies," *United Empire*, August 1915: 646.

[92] Sir Hugh Clifford, "Recent Developments on the Gold Coast," *Journal of the Royal African Society* 18, No. 72 (July, 1919): 244.

[93] Clifford's speech to the Legislative Council, 13 October 1913, quoted in G.E. Metcalfe, *Great Britain and Ghana: Documents of Ghana History, 1807–1957* (London: Thomas Nelson and Sons, Ltd., 1964), 546–7.

[94] Clifford, "Recent Developments," 244, 245.

challenges from the educated elite.[95] In contrast to Watherston, trusteeship for Clifford meant battling southern influences instead of encouraging their spread to the Northern Territories.[96] Led by this vision, Clifford committed the Gold Coast to the peasant road, described by Anne Phillips as the basis of the British West African policy. In assuming this stance Clifford took up the spirit of the project of liberal preservationism advocated by E.D. Morel and Josiah Wedgewood. Clifford did not, however, accept the Georgeist project of land nationalisation. In fact, between 1914 and 1917, Clifford strongly opposed suggestions from the Colonial Office to vest lands and minerals in the colonial state.[97] As we shall discover in Chapter Three, land nationalisation would have to wait until the tenure of Clifford's successor, Sir F.G. Guggisberg, between 1919 and 1927.

Conclusion

In British West Africa, the period between 1899 and 1919 witnessed a shift in development doctrine from Chamberlain's program of constructivist, capitalist trusteeship, towards the Georgeist project of protecting peasant producers from the perceived evils of private property and landlordism. This shift worked itself out in the Northern Territories, albeit haltingly, through political policies that created Native States ruled by chiefs, and economic policies intended to provide the colonial state with control over land and labour. These policies rested on a particular reading of the history of the Northern Territories, according to which the evolution of native states under the influence of the Mamprusi Dynasty and the Wa polity was interrupted by the slave raiding activities of Samory and Babatu. Rooted in oral testimony, this story had some elements of truth in that Samory and Babatu both campaigned in certain parts of the Northern Territories. However, in drawing on European ideas of evolution and "primitive society," the colonial narrative misinterpreted the extent and nature of the influence of Mamprusi and Wa, as well as the rela-

[95] Ibid., 246, 251–2. Sir Hugh Clifford, "Some Facts Concerning the Gold Coast," *Journal of the Royal African Society* 14, No. 53 (October, 1914): 20–1. Clifford, "The Gold Coast," 55.

[96] Clifford, "Recent Developments," 243–252.

[97] Phillips, 77–8, 113.

tive impact of Samory, Babatu and the British themselves in disrupting local communities after the 1880s. As Lentz has shown for the Dagara, and Allman and Parker for the Talensi, while not simply "inventing" chiefs, British officers nonetheless transformed the basis of social and political power in their appointment of chiefs and the construction of chiefly hierarchies. As Lentz writes, the British "redefined the personal networks of the strongmen, their kin and client relationships, as territorial spheres of authority."[98] This project was related to the colonial discourse of development, based on a European trope of an evolutionary ladder, which constructed the Northern Territories as a region in need of European trusteeship.

We must not, however, allow the analysis of discourse to distract us from the material and philosophical roots of the transition to the agrarian doctrine of development. At the level of the Colonial Office, the policy shift grew out of the liberal reaction to the destructive side of Chamberlain's development philosophy. As such, the attempt to resurrect tradition in the Northern Territories mirrored the rising influence of E.D. Morel, Percy Girouard and other Georgeists on development doctrine in West Africa. The WALC's recommendations reflected a concern with the negative side of capitalist development. In a similar manner, the concern with preserving tradition in the Northern Territories increasingly sought to counter the perceived evils produced by the uncontrolled development of mining and cocoa production. These evils included, most significantly, the emergence of private property in land and the destruction of the colony's forests. Acting individually, without the guidance of British trustees, African peasants threatened to trigger the development of agrarian capitalism and thus produce the negative consequences of capitalism which Morel and his allies fought against. Efforts to use state control to "protect" the African population from capitalist development, however, provoked heated resistance from the professional elite of the coastal towns. Colonial officials considered the rise of this elite as part of the problem of uncontrolled development in the south. According to this line of thinking, economic change in the south had produced corruption rather than development.

After 1900 the colonial state's development policy in the Northern Territories increasingly came to represent a reaction to the perceived

[98] Lentz, *Ethnicity and the Making of History in Northern Ghana*, 79.

corruption of development in the south. Governor Nathan's MRO, for instance, blocked the penetration of mining capital and provided the state with legislation for controlling the appropriation and distribution of land. Later colonial officials, most notably Armitage and Clifford, argued more explicitly against permitting the colony's educated population to undermine the authentic, peasant-based development of the Northern Territories. For the Georgeists the solution to these problems lay in land nationalisation, permitting the state to block the development of private property in land. Before 1919 colonial governors would not go this far out of the fear of the political backlash against the appropriation land by the state. As we shall see in Chapter Three, Clifford's successor Sir F.G. Guggisberg took this step near the end of his governorship in the 1920s, and the Northern Territories would become the only region outside Northern Nigeria to adapt Henry George's ideas to colonial West Africa. This program grew out of Northcott's project of reviving the traditional states of the Northern Territories in response to a previous period of development. Between 1919 and 1927, one prominent northern official portrayed this program as leading the African population up the "steep slope of civilisation." We shall now turn to the colonial state's attempt to implement this idea in the Northern Territories.

CHAPTER THREE

CORRUPTIONS OF DEVELOPMENT AND THE "STEEP SLOPE OF CIVILISATION," 1919–1933

Introduction

If Governor Clifford committed the Gold Coast to the peasant road, it was left to his successor Sir Frederick Gordon Guggisberg to lay the foundation for the full WALC program in the Northern Territories. Guggisberg accomplished this task through the Land and Native Rights Ordinance (LNRO) of 1927, which vested the Protectorate's land in the hands of the state. As Anne Phillips observes, with this measure the Northern Territories would join Northern Nigeria in adopting the WALC's recommendations on land tenure.[1] But Guggisberg's LNRO was part of a larger development program that rested on two additional pillars: amalgamating "tribes" into larger units under paramount chiefs, and restricting education to the minimum required to support the amalgamated native states. These policies were to lay the foundation for indirect rule and development without "denationalisation," where the social cohesion of traditional African communities would be preserved during a process of modernisation and state building. Since chiefs would have to be the agents of this process, and since their authority depended on communal land tenure, it was imperative for Guggisberg to implement nationalisation as a hedge against the development of private property.

Guggisberg's implementation of his development vision was complex and contradictory, beginning with a Ten-Year Development Plan in 1919 and culminating in the LNRO of 1927. The Ten-Year Plan concentrated on the cocoa and mining industries rather than the potential exports of the north, since Guggisberg needed immediate surpluses to fund his program of education and development. Since these industries relied on workers from the Northern Territories, Guggisberg also had to accept the reality of labour migration; in

[1] Anne Phillips, *The Enigma of Colonialism: British Policy in West Africa* (London: James Curry, 1989), 114, 117.

fact he encouraged it for a brief period during the 1920s. But labour migration and the growth of trade contributed to commodification in the north through remittances and, in some areas, through the commercialisation of religious shrines. Migrant workers, chiefs and earth priests became accumulators, and accumulation pressed against the idealised vision of African community. As Berry, Lentz and Allman and Parker argue, colonial rule was not all-powerful but rather established a framework for local struggles over authority and resources. These processes intensified until northern officials began to call for reforms to strengthen indirect rule and, in a throwback to Northcott's development plan, to impose direct taxation. In this sense, Guggisberg's attempt to create development without denationalisation laid the foundation for indirect rule as a reaction to the uncontrolled consequences of export-led development in the Colony and Ashanti. In doing so, Guggisberg set the stage for his successors to attempt to create the "ideal world of Henry George" in the Northern Territories.[2]

Guggisberg and Development, 1919–1927

In 1919 Guggisberg introduced the first ten-year development plan in British colonial Africa. As Chalfin notes, the plan marked a shift in development policy towards programmatic, large-scale export-oriented development, supported by the improvement of infrastructure in the north and south.[3] Beyond the mere expansion of exports, however, Guggisberg also planned to use the surpluses to develop social services and education. Economic growth was a means to this end. "For progress we must have education," he wrote in 1921, "for Education of the right kind we must have a bigger revenue. To get a bigger revenue we must have a bigger trade, and to get a bigger trade we must have more agriculture and far better systems of transport than at present exist."[4] In the short-term the plan targeted cocoa production and mining, by far the Colony's two biggest sectors, to

[2] Ibid., 68.

[3] Brenda Chalfin, *Shea Butter Republic: State Power, Global Markets and the Making of an Indigenous Commodity* (New York: Routledge, 2004), 106.

[4] 1920/1 Legislative Council Debates, quoted in *The Political Economy of Colonialism in Ghana: A Collection of Documents and Statistics, 1900–1960*, ed. Geoffrey Kay, 11 (Cambridge: Cambridge University Press, 1972).

which end Guggisberg pledged to improve the roads and railways to the cocoa and mining areas and to construct a new deep-water harbour at Takoradi. In the long-run, however, the Governor foresaw the diversification of the Gold Coast's exports and he set his sights on developing the Northern Territories. "The whole future of the Gold Coast," wrote Guggisberg in 1920,

> is bound up with the development of the ground-nut and shea butter industries in the Northern Territories . . . I have seen millions of acres of country where ground-nuts are indigenous and can grow in prodigious quantities without the constant labour of clearing the forest and bunch of the Colony and Ashanti . . . As for the shea-nut, we should be in an unrivalled position. I have seen thousands of acres rotting on the ground . . . a loss easily avertible by the cultivation of surrounding belts of ground-nuts.[5]

To this end Guggisberg planned to build a Kumasi-Tamale railroad, which he believed would produce "trains heavily loaded with groundnuts, shea-butter, corn and cattle steaming South across the Volta."[6] The north thus figured very prominently in Guggisberg's ten-year plan.

Guggisberg considered himself an "Engineer" constructing a "Highway of Progress along which the races of the Gold Coast may advance, by gentle gradients over the Ridges of Difficulty and by easy curves around the Swamps of Doubt and Superstition to those far off Cities of Promise—the Cities of Final Development, Wealth and Happiness."[7] The end goal of development would be a modern nation-state equal to the "European nations with which they must inevitably contend in the world's struggle for existence."[8] Guggisberg emphasised that this process should not "denationalise" the African leaders, but rather "graft skilfully on to their national characteristics the best attributes of modern civilisation." "For without preserving his national characteristics," Guggisberg continued, "and his sympathy

---

[5] *Report on the Northern Territories of the Gold Coast, 1920* (London: HMSO, 1921), 6.

[6] Piet Konings, *The State and Rural Class Formation in Ghana: A Comparative Analysis* (London, KPI Limited, 1986), 164. For an excellent analysis of colonial investigations into shea production during Guggisberg's tenure, see Chalfin, *Shea Butter Republic*, 103–22.

[7] F. Agbodeka, "Sir Gordon Guggisberg's Contribution to the Development of the Gold Coast," *Transactions of the Historical Society of Ghana* 13, No. 1 (June, 1972): 53. R.E. Wraith, *Guggisberg* (London: Oxford University Press, 1967), 100.

[8] Sir F.G. Guggisberg, *The Gold Coast: A Review of the Events of 1920–1926 and the Prospects of 1927* (Accra: Government Printer, 1927), 86.

and touch with the great illiterate masses of his own people, no man can ever become a leader in progress, whatever other sort of leader he may become."[9] For Guggisberg, therefore, development hinged on creating a class of leaders capable of modernising tribal societies and amalgamating them into a nation-state while simultaneously "preserving and sublimating the sanctions on which the whole of their lives have been based." Guggisberg's "Cities of Final Development" thus referred to tribally-based native states stitched together into a modern Gold Coast nation, whose development would not undermine the social cohesion of the north's African communities.[10]

This program was framed in reaction to the perceived corruption of the development process in the Colony and Ashanti, where Guggisberg believed that economic change had been too rapid and had disrupted the social and moral progress of the people. Mine workers symbolised the corruption of authentic development. "The inhabitants in mining villages," wrote Guggisberg in 1926, "form a cosmopolitan crowd of hired labourers, whose moral development compares very unfavourably with that of the rest of the country. It may safely be assumed that they are, generally speaking, the scallywags of West Africa."[11] Education was not helping matters, because the school system in the Colony and Ashanti merely produced a class of "semi-educated" school leavers who refused to do manual labour and vocally resisted the colonial state.

From Guggisberg's perspective little could be done to reverse this situation in the south because it had gone too far. Accordingly, he neither challenged the development of private property nor chose to impose land nationalisation or other NNLC/WALC policies.[12] However, the Northern Territories provided Guggisberg with a clean slate for his experiment in development without denationalisation. As in

[9] Ibid., 202.

[10] Sir F.G. Guggisberg and A.G. Fraser, *The Future of the Negro: Some Chapters in the Development of a Race* (London: Student Christian Movement, 1929), 65.

[11] Guggisberg's comments on Ormsby-Gore's report, 1926, quoted in *Colonialism and Underdevelopment in Ghana*, Rhoda Howard, 202 (London: Croom Helm, 1978).

[12] The main proponent of private property in the south was Lt-Colonel R.H. Rowe, Gold Coast Surveyor from 1920–27 and later Commissioner of Lands in Nigeria. Phillips, 120–7. See also Bjorn Edsman, *Lawyers in Gold Coast Politics c. 1900–1945: From Mensah Sarbah to J.B. Danquah* (Stockholm: Almqvist & Wiksell International, 1979), 83. David Kimble, *A Political History of Ghana: The Rise of Gold Coast Nationalism, 1850–1928* (Oxford: Clarendon Press, 1963), 440. Wraith, 179. Agbodeka, 53. F.M. Bourret, *Ghana: The Road to Independence, 1919–1957* (Stanford: Stanford University Press, 1960), 51.

the past, the vision hinged on appointing paramount chiefs and amalgamating their territories into larger, economically viable native states. In Guggisberg's opinion this had not happened in the past, in fact there had been a tendency "for the bigger states to break up to the detriment of development and trade." Based on this observation, Guggisberg proclaimed that his policy was

> to maintain any paramount chiefs that exist and gradually absorb under these any small communities scattered about. What we should aim is that some day the Dagombas, Gonjas and Mamprusis should become strong native states. Each will have its own little Public Works Department, and carry on its own business with the Political Officer as a resident and advisor. Each state will be more of less self-contained.[13]

To achieve this vision, Guggisberg set out to amalgamate the chieftaincies, roll back the education system and nationalise the land of the Northern Territories.

Amalgamation of Chieftaincies

Guggisberg initiated the amalgamation project by asking his District Commissioners to combine the existing native states of the Northern Territories into larger administrative units. In Lawra-Tumu, District Commissioner A.C. Duncan-Johnstone used legal reforms to establish a formal hierarchy of chieftaincies centred around Native Tribunals in Lawra, Nandom, Jirapa, Lambussie and Tumu.[14] In Mamprusi, the District Commissioner combined the three districts of Zuarungu, Navrongo and Bawku into "North Mamprusi," a single administrative unit subject to the authority of the paramount chief of Mamprusi.[15] These reforms sparked an important debate over whether British-imposed chiefs or land priests represented the best trustees of their traditional communities. Because this debate affected the development of Native Administration in the 1930s, the process of amalgamation in the 1920s must be discussed in some detail.

---

[13] Quoted in R.B. Bening, "Foundations of the Modern Native States of Northern Ghana," *Universitas* 5, No. 1 (November, 1975): 121.

[14] Carola Lentz, "Histories and Political Conflict: A Case Study of Chieftaincy in Nandom, Northwestern Ghana," *Paideuma* 39 (1993): 188.

[15] Bening, "Foundations," 121.

The North-west

In Lawra-Tumu, Duncan-Johnstone attempted to sort out the area's tribal divisions through interviews with the chiefs of Lawra and Jirapa. Duncan-Johnstone also conducted a census in 1921, with an eye towards reducing the number of ethnic groups and consolidating the native states of the District.[16] The process resulted in the retention of the ten Paramount Chiefs created between 1905 and 1907, based on four tribal categories—Lobi, Dagarti, Sissala and Grunshi—arranged into a hierarchy with the chief of Lawra as the President of a new chiefs' council and the chiefs of Nandom, Jirapa and Lambussie as ex-officio members.[17] Beneath the paramountcies Duncan-Johnstone assembled a system of twenty-one divisions, answerable to the Paramount chiefs and ruling over a series of subordinate chiefs, local chiefs and headmen.[18] Emphasising the law, Duncan-Johnstone also created a Divisional court presided over by the Paramount Chiefs as the highest in a hierarchy of courts reaching down to the level of the village. Native Tribunals were headed by chiefs, with few if any powers given to elders who would have had significant authority in the precolonial period.[19] To improve communication, Duncan-Johnstone adopted the Northern Nigerian system of Hausa native police, the *dogari*, and converted it into a system of chiefs' messengers responsible for relaying messages between the tribunals.[20] A school was built in Lawra in 1917 to provide Hausa-language instruction to the *dogari*. Two years later, the administration built an official government school with classes in English.[21]

Drawing on a familiar discourse, Duncan-Johnstone believed that his reforms had resurrected the natural evolution of the north-western societies that had been disrupted by the slave raids of the nine-

---

[16] Carola Lentz, *Ethnicity and the Making of History in Northern Ghana*, manuscript, forthcoming as *Ethnicity and the Making of History in Northern Ghana* (Edinburgh: Edinburgh University Press, 2006), 136, 146–9.

[17] A.C. Duncan-Johnstone, Intelligence Report, June, 1921, NRG61/5/11, Lawra-Tumu District Record Book, National Archives of Ghana, Accra (NAGA), 210.

[18] Duncan-Johnstone, 210,263. Michael Dasent, 24 June 1924, ADM56/1/309, NAGA, 1.

[19] Lentz, *Ethnicity and the Making of History in Northern Ghana*, 98.

[20] Duncan-Johnstone, 210, 230–1. See also James Merriman Lance, *Seeking the Political Kingdom: British Colonial Impositions and African Manipulations in the Northern Territories of the Gold Coast Colony* (Ph.D. dissertation, Stanford University, 1995), 168.

[21] Sean Hawkins, *Writing and Colonialism in Northern Ghana: The Encounter Bewteen the LoDagaa and the "World on Paper"* (Toronto: University of Toronto Press, 2002), 123.

teenth century and then corrupted by the British-imposed chiefs. Without conducting village-level investigations among the people, Duncan-Johnstone reiterated a familiar colonial refrain about pre-colonial communities in the north-west.[22] Before the slave raids of the nineteenth century, he believed, there had been no chiefs among the Lobi, Dagarti and Sissala, only "heads of each compound, known as the Tengdaanas or owners of the land."[23] This lack of unity rendered the people defenceless against Samory and Babatu, so that when British forces reached the northwest in 1903 the people were "weak and disintegrated." Early British policies failed to unify the chieftaincies and by 1918 rivalries between the chiefs had undermined their natural bonds of community. Seeking to regenerate those bonds, Duncan-Johnstone implemented reforms designed to teach the chiefs "to rule themselves and to manage intelligently their own affairs."[24] Law formed the basis of the reforms and the conduit for realigning evolution after it had been thrown off of its proper path by the slave raids of the nineteenth century.

Although precolonial "chiefs" as such probably did not exist in the north-west, Lentz has shown that strongmen had developed in many communities before the colonial period.[25] Duncan-Johnstone missed this fact, surely because his ideas drew as much on anthropological theory as reality on the ground. In particular, his philosophy of development through legal reforms drew heavily on the work of Charles Temple in Northern Nigeria and reflected the influence of Victorian anthropology and Henry George's philosophy of anti-landlordism. In Nigeria, Temple had worked with Governor Percy Girouard and Kastina Resident Richard Palmer to undermine Frederick Lugard's plan to develop Northern Nigeria's Emirs into a landlord class.[26] This debate eventually produced the Northern Nigerian Lands Committee and it gave Temple the opportunity to express his desire to lead the African up the "steep slope of civilisation without reducing him to a state of collapse on the journey."[27] Temple borrowed

[22] Lentz, *Ethnicity and the Making of History in Northern Ghana*, 99; Hawkins, *Writing and Colonialism*, 117.

[23] Duncan-Johnstone, 9.

[24] Ibid., 210, 234, 267–270.

[25] Lentz, *Ethnicity and the Making of History in Northern Ghana*, 68–77.

[26] Robert W. Shenton, *The Development of Capitalism in Northern Nigeria* (Toronto: University of Toronto Press, 1986), 28–30.

[27] Duncan-Johnstone, 209.

this image from Walter Bagehot's 1873 *Physics and Politics*, which in turn drew from Sir Henry Maine's *Ancient Law*, one of the founding texts of Victorian anthropology.[28] The "steep slope of civilisation" referred to Maine's theory of the evolutionary change from kinship organisation to local contiguity, or "status" to "contract," through the mechanism of the development of law.[29] This European discourse provided a handy image to justify British trusteeship over African development, under which colonial officials would manage the Africans' journey up the evolutionary ladder so that it unfolded along African lines. This idea was crucially important for Temple. "By implanting in his mind a contempt for his own institutions," he wrote in 1918, "by persuading him or compelling him to adopt our modes of life, we divorce him from his own natural entourage, and he becomes alienated."[30]

In the Victorian vision of primitive society, the "natural entourage" of the African included "fellowship, the society of equals, pride of race, (and) patriotism."[31] When Duncan-Johnstone spoke of "pride of race" and set out to reform the customary law of the Northern Territories, he called up the ghosts of Maine and Bagehot to invoke the important European discourse of the steep slope of civilisation as a guiding idea behind his reforms.[32] Duncan-Johnstone invoked this model as a direct response to the corruption of the evolutionary process caused by the growth of labour migrancy and the chiefs' abuse of authority under direct rule. In other words, Duncan-Johnstone framed his intention to develop the Northern Territories in response to immanent forces which he considered corruptions of the transition from status to contract. In 1921, convinced that his plan had worked, he wrote that "it is certain that were we now to vacate the Country an invader would no longer find a weak and disintegrated people, but would probably encounter a formidable resistance from the united Lobi country led by chiefs who have learnt the value of cooperation and unity."[33]

---

[28] Walter Bagehot, *Physics and Politics, or, Thoughts on the Application of the Principles of 'Natural Selection' and 'Inheritance' to Political Society* (New York: D. Appleton and Company, 1873), 23.

[29] Adam Kuper, *The Invention of Primitive Society: Transformations of an Illusion* (London: Routledge, 1988), 27–8.

[30] Duncan-Johnstone, 209.

[31] Ibid., 209.

[32] Lance, 169.

[33] Duncan-Johnstone, 287. Duncan-Johnstone also worked on native courts in the

The North-east

In the North-East colonial officers were not nearly as active as Duncan-Johnstone in reforming the chieftaincies established before 1919. There was some tinkering over boundaries, as in Armitage's decision in 1920 to set the White Volta River as the boundary between the Navrongo and Zuaraungu Districts.[34] However, there were no reforms on the scale of Duncan-Johnstone's and the basic structures laid down in 1912 remained in place during Guggisberg's governorship. The Talensi, for instance, remained part of the Kurugu Division despite the fact that the Kunab's authority was tenuous at best and that some colonial officials felt that the Division should be disbanded. Less than a year into the Kunab's reign, District Commissioner Warden complained the new chief lacked the character necessary to gain the respect of the Talensi.[35] Captain Nash echoed this complaint at the end of 1913, stating that the Kunab's power was so weak that he had to approach Nash for help in forcing the sub-chiefs to deliver foodstuffs and call up labourers to build his house. By this time Nash already had decided not to enforce the Mamprusi paramountcy over Taleland, arguing that the Kurugu Division was a "mere paper scheme" and that the Talensi did not accept the Kunab as their head chief. Rather than reorganise the Division, however, Chief Commissioner Armitage decided in early 1914 to retain the Kunab in the hope that he would eventually develop into a respected paramount chief. Subsequently, Armitage took no steps to reform the system before his retirement in 1920.[36]

Beyond this veneer of stability, however, important changes took place which fed into local power struggles in the north-east. The biggest change occurred in the Tong Hills in 1925, when the colonial administration officially recognised Tongnaab and permitted pilgrims to visit the shrines without fear of punishment. This momentous event occurred after the chief of Yinduri, a Namoo settlement at the base of the Tong Hills, informed the colonial administration that the

south. See Victoria B. Tashijan, 'The diaries of A.C. Duncan-Johnstone: a preliminary analysis of British involvement in the "native courts" of colonial Asante', *Ghana Studies* 1 (1998): 135–50.

[34] Austin-Cathrie to District Commissioner, North Mamprusi, 13 January 1926, ADM56/1/336, NAGA.

[35] A.A. Illiasu, "The Establishment of British Administration in Mampurugu, 1898–1937," *Transactions of the Historical Society of Ghana*, 16, No. (1975): 16.

[36] Ibid., 17.

shrine had been operating clandestinely for six years. The accusation prompted an enquiry by Provincial Commissioner Cutfield, during which the British discovered the Yanii shrine for the first time in the rocks above Tenzugu. Cutfield's informants, who did not include any of the clients of the destroyed Bonaab shrine, told him that the Bonaab and Yanii shrines were different. They referred to the Yanii shrine as the "good" Tongnaab shrine, and the Bonaab shrine as independent and evil. In this manner, one Tali lineage, Bukiok, convinced the British that their shrine, Yanii, was *the* Tongnaab shrine, to the exclusion of another lineage, Kpatar, and their Tongnaab shrine Bonaab. As guardians of the Yanii shrine, Tengol and his followers thus used the reopening of the Tong Hills to further their interests against the Kpatar lineage and the *kpatarnaab*.[37] As we shall discover, these struggles would intensify over the years, reinforcing the arguments of Berry, Lentz and Allman and Parker, that colonial rule established a framework for local struggles over power and authority.

Guggisberg and Education

Unaware of the local struggles unfolding underneath colonial institutions, the administration continued its plan to develop the native states of the Northern Territories. Education formed an important part of this process. For the "big native states" to be put on a proper footing, Guggisberg believed that the north's education system had to be reformed to guard against "premature westernisation." Educational progress had to be slow and sure, inculcating a sense of duty to the chiefs and tribes as much as the British administration, since rapid change would undermine the basis of the entire project. "History shows," Guggisberg stated in 1921, "that too quick an advance at any period in the development of a race means delay in the end."[38] In Guggisberg's opinion the advance had been too quick indeed in the coastal towns and mining areas, where alienated, westernised elites and morally degenerate wage labourers had been corrupted by

[37] Jean Allman and Jonathan Parker, *Tongnaab: The History of a West African God* (Bloomington: Indiana University Press, 2005), 98–101.
[38] Gold Coast, Legislative Council Debates, 1920/1, quoted in Kay, 8.

the "disintegrating waves of western civilisation."[39] This experience had to be avoided at all costs in the Northern Territories. "It is obvious," wrote Guggisberg in 1925, "that to do anything at the present moment that would extend or perpetuate this (Southern) system in the Northern Territories would be extremely inadvisable. In the Northern Territories we have virgin ground on which to work as far as education is concerned, guided by the lessons brought to us by the failures in the Colony and Ashanti."[40]

With this concern in mind Guggisberg sent the Deputy Director of Education, R.F. Honter, to visit the north in 1924 to forge a new educational policy for the Protectorate. Honter reported that the government schools' focus on literary education produced "semi-literate" graduates unwilling to perform manual labour and prone to resist colonial rule. He recommended converting all government schools except Tamale into junior trade schools, which would provide basic skills up to Standard III but focus on practical training in areas such as masonry and farming. This training would equip the graduates to return to their villages and become "useful citizens" of the Northern Territories. A very small number of students would be sent to the Tamale school, which would be the only institution in the Protectorate offering degrees up to Standard VII. Guggisberg agreed with this approach and endorsed Honter's views on a visit to Wa in 1925. Warning against repeating the mistakes of the Colony and Ashanti, he instructed the school to reduce its maximum training from Standard VII to Standard III. The Colonial Office backed Guggisberg's plan and gave him permission to sever the administration of education in the north from the rest of the colony to ensure its separate development. With the green light from the Secretary of State, Guggisberg appointed Rev. A.H. Candler as the Director of Education in the Northern Territories, directly responsible to the Governor rather than the Department of Education. Soon after his appointment, Candler decided to roll back all schools except Tamale to Standard III. He also tried to promote "tribal" loyalties by instructing student in loyalty to their chiefs, housing them according to tribes, and, in 1928, making Dagbani rather than English the *lingua franca* in the government

[39] Guggisberg, *The Gold Coast*, 23.

[40] Bening, "The Development of Education in Northern Ghana, 1908–1957," *Ghana Social Science Journal* 1. No. 2 (November 1971): 25.

schools.[41] Students also were required to wear local smocks rather than western clothing, a fact which S.W.D.K. Gandah remembered none too fondly in his recent memoir.[42]

Guggisberg, Land Nationalisation and the LNRO, 1923–1927

Guggisberg's final policy for developing the Northern Territories was land nationalisation through the Land and Native Rights Ordinance of 1927. The drift towards nationalisation began in 1923 with an amendment to the Mineral Rights Ordinance, which vested all government-occupied land and buildings in the colonial state and empowered the Governor to appropriate land at will for public works.[43] Initially, Chief Commissioner Arthur J. Philbrick simply wanted to obtain Deeds of Gift from chiefs who had transferred land to the state, but Guggisberg rejected Philbrick's request on the grounds that "the chiefs have no clear idea of private property in land, and it is very undesirable to encourage them in the idea that they have the power to make such grants."[44] In 1926, Acting Governor J.C. Maxwell argued that broader control of land by the state would be needed to protect the people from exploitation by "alien" land speculators (Europeans and southerners) once a proposed railway reached the Northern Territories. To this end, Maxwell passed the *Land Transactions (Restriction on Operation) Ordinance*, which guaranteed indigenous rights of occupancy but prohibited alienation. Upon his return in 1927 Guggisberg extended Maxwell's reforms by drafting the Land and Native Rights Ordinance (LNRO), which was implemented shortly after he left the Gold Coast in the spring of 1927. Based on Northern Nigeria's land proclamation of 1910, the LNRO recognised indige-

[41] Dagbani was chosen on the (inaccurate) assumption that all northern languages were related as part of the Mole-Dagbani language group. R.B. Bening, *A History of Education in Northern Ghana, 1907–1976* (Accra: Ghana Universities Press, 1990), 59–61.

[42] Lentz, *Ethnicity and the Making of History in Northern Ghana*, 215–16.

[43] Under the amended ordinance the government could appropriate land simply by posting a sign that read "Taken for the Government." R.B. Bening, "Land Policy and Administration in Northern Ghana, 1898–1976," *Transactions of the Historical Society of Ghana* 16, No. 2 (1995): 236–7.

[44] Guggisberg, quoted in B.G. Der, "Colonial Land Policies in the Northern Territories in the Gold Coast, 1900–1975." *Universitas (New Series)*, 4, No. 2 (1975): 134.

nous occupancy rights, prevented land sales and asserted "complete control over any acquisition of land by non-natives."[45] Under the Ordinance the entire Protectorate was declared "public land," subject to the control of the Governor and "held for the use and common benefit, direct or indirect, of the natives."[46] The Governor asserted the right to validate land titles, set rents and permit or disallow mortgaging. All of the rents collected in rural areas would be deposited directly into the central Treasury, and urban rents would be split between the Treasury and the chiefs.[47] At the local level, all occupants remained subject to the customary laws enforced by chiefs as trustees of their communities. In this manner, the Ordinance officially vested the land in the people through their chiefs, but the colonial administration reserved the right to appropriate land at will for the purposes of development.

Resistance and the Transition to Indirect Rule, 1927–8

Guggisberg's policies of amalgamation, education and land nationalisation were meant to shore up the power of the chiefs as trustees of their communities. It turned out, however, that problems of chiefly authority accelerated during Guggisberg's governorship to the point where the northern administration raised calls for reforms in the late 1920s. The result was a complex series of negotiations over chiefs' authority and territorial jurisdiction, which reinforces the argument that indirect rule established a terrain of struggle rather than simply imposing British notions of tribe on African communities. There were at least three categories of conflicts in the Northern Territories during the 1920s: lower chiefs against higher chiefs, commoners against chiefs, and subjects from one "tribe" against chiefs of another. The first category occurred frequently in the Lawra District, where problems quickly arose between the chiefs in the new hierarchy.

---

[45] Gold Coast Colonial Secretary (Sir James Maxwell) to Colonial Office, 13 March 1926, Document #5 in "Proposed Reforms in respect of the Land Legislation of the Gold Coast, Primarily in order to Promote Security of Title," Enclosure 2 in Gold Coast Conference of 10 February 1930, CO96/693/17, Great Britain, Public Record Office (PRO), 52, 56.

[46] Bening, "Land Policy," 239.

[47] Phillips, 114.

In one case, for example, Duncan-Johnstone had placed the chief of a small border settlement, Babile, under the chief of a slightly larger one, Birifu, who in turn was placed under the paramount chief at Lawra. In 1919, the Babile chief, who happened to be the brother of the chief of Lawra, refused to submit to the authority of Birifu. The British administration responded swiftly, accusing the Babile chief of recalcitrance, corruption and extortion, and removing him from office.[48] This move resolved the issue temporarily, but in 1927 District Commissioner Eyre-Smith suspended the medallion of chief Gandah of Birifu for "repeated attempts to make himself independent of Lawra."[49]

An illustration of the second class of conflict occurred in Tumu, where paramount chief Kantom faced charges of corruption and extortion. Kantom was a classic example of the British-imposed chiefs criticised so harshly by Duncan-Johnstone, having been installed in 1918 primarily because of his knowledge of the English language.[50] By the early 1920s Kantom had become very wealthy and faced numerous allegations of graft, and in 1921 the Chief Commissioner himself agreed that he was not a legitimate chief. While the British investigated Kantom, the Muslim section of Wallembelli accused him of extorting labour from the village. The Liman claimed that many of Wallembelli's settlers were illegitimate because they were Wala rather than Sissala.[51] Duncan-Johnstone accused the Wallembelli Muslims of inciting resistance against Kantom.[52] When the Liman allied with one of the headmen Duncan-Johnstone had them arrested and sent into political detention in Lawra. Upon their release, the two men gathered their followers and established a new settlement south of the Kulpawn River, subject to the paramountcy of a sympathetic chief.[53] In this and other cases the administration supported Kantom rather than the resistors, at one point refusing to remove

[48] Lawra-Tumu District Record Book, 1927–1938, ADM61/5/11, NAGA, 6,10.

[49] Lawra-Tumu District Record Book, 1927–1938, ADM61/5/11, NAGA, 10. Eyre-Smith, 3/2/27, 27/8/27, ADM56/1/290, NAGA.

[50] Provincial Commissioner, North-West Province to Chief Commissioner, 3 June 1918, 18 July 1918, ADM56/1/309, NAGA.

[51] S.D. Nash to Acting Provincial Commissioner, 24 November 1920, ADM56/1/309, NAGA.

[52] Duncan Johnstone to Provincial Commissioner, 10 March 1921, ADM56/1/309, NAGA.

[53] Nash to Acting District Commissioner, Tumu, 6 April 1921, ADM56/1/309, NAGA.

him from office on the grounds that it was better to have a "strong crook" than a "weak honest man" in the Tumu paramountcy.[54] Despite several subsequent challenges to his authority, Kantom held onto power during the 1920s.[55]

Turning to the north-east we find an important example of the third category of resistance, involving ethnicity and administrative boundaries. In one case, Armitage's new boundary between Navrongo and Zuarungu provoked resistance from the affected settlements. The boundary left the village of Gardima, primarily Dagomba in ethnicity, straddling the two districts, and the Chief Commissioner decided to place them under the authority of the chief of Sandema (the Sandemanab) in the Navrongo District. The Dagombas of Gardima resisted, ignoring the Sandemab's requests for communal labour and refusing to allow him to appoint a successor to the Gardima chief when he died in 1923. At a meeting in 1926 with Navrongo District Commissioner Austin-Cathrie, the locally elected Gardimanab stated that he would rather "return to his own country than serve Sandema." Arguing that the Sandemanab had no traditional jurisdiction over the Dagombas, Austin-Cathrie allowed them to move to a new settlement in the Zuarungu District.[56] After they agreed to submit to the authority of Passankwia, in the Zuarungu District, the Gardima Dagombas moved across the border in early 1926.[57] To fill the gap, Austin-Cathrie moved a new group of settlers from a nearby village, whom he described as "generally hungry," into Gardima and ordered them to accept the authority of the Sandemanab.[58]

These examples illustrate the problems with Guggisberg's attempt to amalgamate the northern chieftaincies, most of which stemmed from the fact that the chiefs' hierarchies were arbitrary and tended to create rifts between settlements. Paramount chiefs used their new offices to accumulate wealth and in so doing provoked resistance from their subjects. Ethnic conflicts emerged over chiefly authority

[54] P.F. Whittal to Walker-Leigh, 11 March 1931, ADM56/1/301, NAGA.

[55] See E.S. Eyre-Smith to Freeman, 11 November 1921. Walker-Leigh to Freeman, 2 November 1921. Freeman to Walker-Leigh, 24 November 1921. Freeman to Walker-Leigh, 12 December 1921, ADM56/1/301, NAGA.

[56] Austin-Cathrie to District Commissioner, North Mamprusi, 13 January 1926, ADM56/1/336, NAGA.

[57] "Zongo" referred to a section of a village or town set aside for "strangers," usually traders.

[58] Austin-Cathrie to District Commissioner, North Mamprusi, 13 January 1926, ADM56/1/336, NAGA.

and land rights and the administration tried in vain to determine who rightly belonged where. In the end, questions over the chiefs' jurisdiction were settled by negotiation and compromise rather than the hegemonic construction of colonial-defined customary law.

Calls for Reform, 1924–8

Persistent problems with chiefs' authority prompted calls for reform in the 1920s. In the north-west, for example, Duncan-Johnstone's successor Michael Dasent recommended amalgamating the ten divisions into three ethnically based states ruled by the paramount chiefs of the Lobi-Dagarti, "Grunshi" and Sissala.[59] Explaining his suggestion, Dasent informed the Chief Commissioner of his belief that "the idea for the future" was

> (some) sort of Native States with their own Administration, Treasury (Taxes will have to come), Police, etc., under the supervision of a Commissioner such as the big Emirates of Nigeria, therefore what I mean to suggest is that the fewer Administrations there are, the greater number of people of the same race which can be brought under one chief, the more speedy and easier of attainment will be (the) ultimate object, presumably that of the natives administering under supervision, their own country.[60]

Dasent believed that his three categories reflected the true racial division in the north-west. He had no doubt that the "Issala" and "Grunshi" were single tribes, and he argued that the "Dagarti" were actually "of Lobi stock". In Dasent's opinion, amalgamation under these three tribal categories was a pressing matter because individual divisional loyalties were growing very quickly and threatened to undermine the project of amalgamation.[61]

In 1928, Dasent's successor Eyre-Smith proposed a more radical plan for reform, arguing as Dasent did that Duncan-Johnstone's reforms had not paid enough attention to tribal boundaries. As a case in point he cited a conflict between the settlements of Ulu and Karni. In 1928, the family sections of the Ulu had their chief removed

---

[59] M. Dasent, 6 August 1924, ADM56/1/309, NAGA.

[60] Ibid.

[61] Michael Dasent, 1924, quoted in Lentz, *Ethnicity and the Making of History in Northern Ghana*, 175.

and imprisoned for extorting fines from conscripted labourers.[62] The administration installed the chief of Karni, a sub-chief under Ulu, in his place. The elevation of the Karni chief prompted the village to assert its independence from Ulu and a struggle for authority and dominance broke out between the two settlements. Eyre-Smith blamed the troubles on two factors: the fact that neither of the chiefs appeared to come from royal families, and the failure to build local political structures from the ground up. To redress the problem, Eyre-Smith pledged to restructure the villages "in the groups to which the land belongs."[63]

Eyre-Smith's actions reflected an underlying criticism of Duncan-Johnstone's reforms: that by installing the wrong people as chiefs they had encouraged despotism and corruption. On the surface, despotism was not hard to prove, especially after Eyre-Smith discovered several large chiefs' farms worked by forced labour. For example, Chief Kayani of Tugu, who had been appointed a sub-chief of Jirapa in 1918, developed a farm of twelve hundred acres on the backs of his subjects, even though it undermined their own food production. By 1928 half of the population of one of Kanayi's villages had fled and many others complained regularly to the District Administration. Eyre-Smith attempted to punish Kayani, but hid not believe that the chief of Jirapa would have treated the people any better, for they had been mistreated by his sons before Kayani's appointment. In Eyre-Smith's opinion this problem was generalised across the north-west, and its roots could be found in the system of chiefs and native tribunals developed by Duncan-Johnstone between 1917 and 1921.[64]

The trouble with Duncan-Johnstone's system was that it imposed chiefs rather than land priests as territorial rulers. This move was premature, because the people had not progressed to the stage where political leadership was attached to religion. Expressed in Maine's terms, Duncan-Johnstone imposed relations of contract prematurely upon a people governed by ties of status, substituting despotic rulers for an organic form of African democracy. Eyre-Smith believed that

[62] G.F. Mackay, Acting District Commissioner, Lawra-Tumu, 12 September 1928, ADM56/1/290, NAGA.

[63] Eyre-Smith, 9 May 1929, ADM56/1/290, NAGA.

[64] Eyre-Smith to Commissioner, Northern Province, 3/9/27, 2–6. See also Sean Hawkins, *Writing and Colonialism*, 111–12.

the authentic leaders were the land priests, In this argument he was supported by colonial anthropologist R.S. Rattray who had "discovered" their significance in the late 1920s. When the British toured the north to appoint chiefs, the land priests thrust forward commoners because they were suspicious of outsiders after the slave raids of the nineteenth century. Lacking legitimacy, the new chiefs ignored the land priests and evolved into "something which every one, African and European alike, who understands anything about the real Africa, knows to be an anomaly, and under ordinary circumstances an impossibility, i.e., the local despotic ruler." Duncan-Johnstone's system reproduced the hierarchy of "petty unconstitutional European-made Chiefs," when he should have searched out and appointed the land priests as the political leaders.[65]

Were Eyre-Smith and Rattray correct in believing that they had found a more authentic group of chiefs than Duncan-Johnstone? Hawkins applauds them for recognising "ethnographic facts" instead of "historical fiction."[66] As Lentz argues, however, this clearly was not the case because precolonial communities were not defined by territorially bounded *tengani* areas, but rather by complex and shifting socio-political networks based on kin and patriclan affinities. These networks, including *tengani* fields of ritual power, were not tied to territorial boundaries, nor did they reflect simple descent from a common ancestor.[67] Rattray himself had evidence for clan membership based on in-migration and co-residence, but he ignored it in favour of the idea of descent-based clans and tribes.[68] This idea drew on anthropological theory, Victorian ideas about "primitive society" and British, Irish and Scottish analogies. In Eyre-Smith's opinion, for instance, early British history was the story of invading bands of foreigners who had established themselves as feudal landlords by

---

[65] Rattray, *Report by the Anthropology Commissioner*, Accra: Government Printer, 1930, 10, CO98/50, PRO. For an excellent overview of Rattray's and Eyre-Smith's ideas on this point, see Carola Lentz, "Colonial Ethnography and Political Reform: the Works of A.C. Duncan-Johnstone, R.S. Rattray, J. Eyre-Smith and J. Guiness on Northern Ghana," *Ghana Studies* 2(1999): 119–69, and Lentz, *Ethnicity and the Making of History in Northern Ghana*, 150–2.

[66] Sean Hawkins, "Disguising Chiefs and God as History: Questions on the Acephalousness of LoDagaa Politics and Religion," *Africa* 66, No. 2 (1996): 209.

[67] Carola Lentz, "Contested Identities: the History of Ethnicity in Northern Ghana," in *Ethnicity in Ghana: the Limits of Invention*, ed. Carola Lentz and Paul Nugent, 152 (Houndmills: Macmillan Press, 2000).

[68] Lentz, *Ethnicity and the Making of History in Northern Ghana*, 153–4.

expropriating indigenous peasants. This process corrupted the peasants' historical development because the invaders failed to build their rule upon the social systems of the indigenous peoples. In the primitive societies of medieval England, Scotland and Ireland, argued Eyre-Smith, religion encapsulated law and morality and courts were "entirely ecclesiastical in nature."[69] The "ecclesiastical" court leaders, whose offices combined law, religion and politics, ruled over parishes defined by religion, implying that they were organised according to status. The development of feudalism corrupted this organic social order and produced "much discontent in Europe," presumably because the invaders disrupted the natural growth of the kinship-based parishes.[70] The natural evolutionary transition from ecclesiastical to secular rule was truncated by the corrupting influence of outside forces.

In the Northern Territories, Eyre-Smith and Rattray perceived signs of a similar breakdown of "primitive" society at the hands of a group of foreign invaders, the British themselves. According to Rattray the people of Lawra provided the best example of the "old order," equivalent to "primitive Ireland" or Maine's conception of status: matrilineal, governed by religious laws and organised along bloodlines.[71] As in medieval England, courts were ecclesiastical, politics were religious and social groups were organised into parishes (*tengani*) controlled by land priests (*tengansobes*) who were appointed on the basis of genealogy. The convergence of religion, law and kinship meant that social sanctions emanating from the *tengansobes* flowed directly from blood ties. Under this system male family heads settled intrafamily matters while wider concerns fell to the authority of the *tengansobe* of the appropriate *tengani*, "advised by the heads of kindred groups."[72] According to Eyre-Smith the *tengani* areas, whose boundaries defined communities on the basis of descent from a common ancestor, represented "the most primitive form of community." Social sanctions binding individuals to their communities were rooted

---

[69] St. J. Eyre-Smith, *A Brief Review of the History and Social Organisation of the Peoples of the Northern Territories of the Gold Coast* (Gold Coast: Government Printer, 1932), 35–6.

[70] Ibid., 17, 22, 23, 27, 42.

[71] R.S. Rattray, *Tribes of the Ashanti Hinterland, Volume Two* (Oxford: The Clarendon Press, 1969, originally published, 1932), 426.

[72] St. J. Eyre-Smith, "Response to John Guiness," 2 March 1933, NRG8/2/14, National Archives of Ghana, Tamale (NAGT).

in organic ties of kinship and contained a series of natural checks and balances. Within this system the *tengansobes* represented the true leaders of the stateless peoples of the Northern Territories.[73]

In the absence of foreign contact, the *tengansobes* would have evolved into chiefs and the people would have developed, organically, into patrilineal societies with territorial as opposed to religious boundaries. Eyre-Smith characterised this process as a "natural cell-like growth" from the "childhood" of family compounds to the "maturity" of a state-based polity.[74] The transition began with the expansion of families into villages, which eventually became amalgamated into *tengani* areas (earth shrine parishes). This process (a movement from status to contract) had occurred in Asante and it would have unfolded in Lawra-Tumu because, Rattray argued, the *tengansobes* were "the exact prototype of the Ashanti chief."[75]

However, the natural process of evolution had been interrupted by "external influences" that were "gnawing at the foundations of the structure upon which the lives of the people are based." The growth of migrant labour was part of the problem, since it produced a "vast body of natives who are no longer bound by the religious sanctions of their family or tribe, and who are evolving from the superstitions and beliefs which governed their lives in the past." But the administration worsened the situation by ignoring *tengani* boundaries in appointing chiefs after 1903. In Eyre-Smith's words, "the land organisation in some instances bears no relation to the political authority we have imposed." This process freed chiefs from the checks on abusive behaviour emanating from the *tengansobes*, since subjects now served different *tengansobes* than their chiefs. Severed from traditional sanctions, the chiefs became despotic feudal landlords. Europe had discarded this form of rule, and Eyre-Smith believed that the Northern Territories should not permit it to take root on African soil.[76]

In Eyre-Smith's opinion, the rapid and inappropriate reforms had not allowed the people of Lawra-Tumu to evolve individual ethics, much less a sense of obligation to the State. This made it imperative, at such a "critical transition stage," for the British quickly to

---

[73] Eyre-Smith, *Brief Review*, 27.
[74] Ibid., 23.
[75] R.S. Rattray, *Tribes of the Ashanti Hinterland, Volume 1*, xix.
[76] Eyre-Smith, *Brief Review*, 40–5.

devise "a direct means of maintaining the moral and economic responsibility of the individual to the family, and thus indirectly to the State."[77] The solution was to realign "land organisation" with "political authority" by redrawing political boundaries according to *tengani* areas and reasserting the authority of the *tengansobes* over their rightful "parishes." Eyre-Smith believed this would be possible because the *tengani* areas and *tengansobes* had remained intact as of the 1920s. Despite the "transition" of the north and the penetration of "western ideas and institutions," he argued, "the fundamental basis of the social organisation and religion, namely the family system and the land organisation, though modified, remain."[78] Rattray believed that this strategy would result in "what many of the old-time Chiefs had themselves evolved, i.e. a combination of what was in existence when their first ancestors came here, and what they borrowed from elsewhere and built upon that underlying structure."[79] Eyre-Smith agreed, advocating the establishment "on an economic basis" of "the democratic form of government and land organisation which were in existence on our advent."[80]

Once the boundaries were redrawn, the administration would limit the power of existing chiefs to their earth shrine boundaries, then allow the chieftaincies to lapse on the deaths of chiefs and appoint land priests in their place. Political boundaries thus would reflect kinship ties and *tengani* parishes. Unlike the unconstitutional chiefs, the *tengansobes* would not be corrupt—indeed, *could* not be corrupt—because their authority would be rooted in kinship through blood and soil. For Eyre-Smith, everything flowed from this fact. With true leaders in place, the experience of Ireland and Scotland would be avoided and the people of Lawra-Tumu would evolve naturally from "primitive" communalism to a modern system ruled by a "well-ordered State run for the greatest good of the greatest number."[81]

Eyre-Smith did not object to Duncan-Johnstone's system of tribunals itself. On the contrary, he fully supported native tribunals and direct taxation as long as the "native states" were based on *tengani* areas and the *tengansobes* became chiefs (or at least controlled

[77] Ibid., 42.
[78] Ibid., 37.
[79] Rattray, *The Tribes of the Ashanti Hinterland*, xx.
[80] Eyre-Smith, *Brief Review*, 45.
[81] Ibid., 43.

their appointment). Indeed, Eyre-Smith considered western institutions indispensible for the transition to modern statehood and he argued that political and economic decentralization and direct taxation would make individuals "directly responsible to the State as individualism and individual property evolved." Their implantation would allow the chiefs to develop into capable, self-governing administrators assisted by family elders acting as state councillors. Such a system would reinstate the *tengansobes'* proper powers as "fathers" of their people and thus preserve the family character of traditional society. Landlordism and feudalism would give way to a patchwork of co-operative agrarian producers who would amalgamate eventually into a regional federation and ultimately join the Gold Coast nation. "In the N.T.s," concluded Eyre-Smith, there existed "the material for the establishment of a model State, economic forces properly directed serving to unite together the sections of the kingdoms, making the whole into one vast Co-operative State having in course of time a representative or representatives of its divisions on the Legislative Council of the Colony."[82] In this way Eyre-Smith's vision mirrored Duncan-Johnstone's except that the *tengansobes* rather than the British-made chiefs would be the agents of modernisation. As Lentz had documented very effectively, Eyre-Smith thus believed that political modernisation had to be based on the age-old, traditional institution of the earth-shrine.[83]

But to what extent were the land priests untouched by "westernisation?" Rattray's experience in the north-east raises questions about whether the colonial state could ever shield traditional authorities in the Northern Territories from outside influences. In 1928, Rattray trekked up to the Tong Hills to visit an important Tongnaab shrine, the Yanii *bo'ar*, accompanied by his mission-educated Nankani translator Victor Aboya.[84] Upon arriving at the shrine Rattray was surprised to be sharing the cave with numerous "well-dressed" African businessmen and women who "had motored hundreds of miles from Kumasi, Kwahu and Mampon" to participate in the ritual. The crowd also included several of Rattray's "friends of old days" from

[82] Ibid., *Brief Review*, 43–45.

[83] Carola Lentz, "Colonial Constructions and African Initiatives: the History of Ethnicity in Northwestern Ghana," *Ethnos* 65, No. 1 (2000): 116.

[84] The full story of Rattray's visit to the shrine, including Aboya's subsequent contribution to *Tribes of the Ashanti Hinterland*, is told in admirable detail in Allman and Parker, 107–15.

Asante. These friends were educated southerners who had travelled from Accra to Kumasi to the sacred Talensi cave. Writing up his field notes for publication, Rattray described the festival as "the most interesting and extraordinary of many curious rites which it has been my privilege to attend in the course of many years of anthropological fieldwork." Most extraordinary was the level of commercialisation of the supposedly "traditional" festival. Many of the requests to the shrine's priest revolved around financial matters, as in the case of one pilgrim from Mampon, near Kumasi:

> I was at my town of Mampon (Ashanti), and I heard about grandfather (Rattray: *nana*, here a term of respect), so I came to lean on him that he might give me health, which I once had. I keep a store and I have two motor-cars. From that store I derive no profit whatever. As for my two motor-cars, when I ply them for hire and people enter them, I only incur debts and there is no profit in them. Because of that, and because I have heard of grandfather, I have come to ask him if he will show me the way to make profit.

The Mampon pilgrim completed his request by asking for children from his wives and good health for his relatives and promised to return with payment if his wishes were fulfilled.[85]

Rattray's discovery demonstrated the extent to which economic change had affected the Northern Territories. As the colonial state turned away from developing the north, migrant labourers began to drift southwards in response to wage labour opportunities in the new cocoa belt in northwest Asante. The guardians of the Tongnaab shrines used the migrant workers to "advertise" their shrines by spreading information about their powers to southern professionals. This was especially true of the Yanii shrine, which operated under the radar of the British for a decade after the Bonaab shrine was outlawed in 1915. When the colonial administration recognised Tongnaab officially in 1925, the Yanii shrine was well placed to emerge as paramount over the others.[86] As we shall discover later, the increased pilgrim traffic to the Yanii shrine enabled its guardian—a *kambonaaba*-turned-religious-leader named Tengol—to accumulate wealth on an impressive scale.

In the name of preserving tradition against the forces of economic change, observers like Rattray portrayed "land priest accumulation"

---

[85] Rattray, *Tribes of the Ashanti Hinterland, Volume Two*, 361–5.
[86] Allman and Parker, 80, 100.

as the corruption of authentic development. Sent north at the request of Provincial Commissioner A.W. Cardinall, Rattray's specific task was to investigate the customs of the northern peoples in preparation for indirect rule. On a personal level, Rattray moved north out of a missionary-like zeal to find, in McCaskie's words, "the key to an essentially synchronic and immutable perfection—a first cause."[87] The commercialisation of the Tong Hills shrine demonstrated the difficulty of such a task. Indeed for Rattray it simply filtered into the belief that British rule had corrupted traditional society in the Northern Territories, and that the northern tribes had to be put back on the natural track of their evolution.

New Calls for Indirect Rule and Direct Taxation

The need to revive authentic development by strengthening the chiefs prompted Guggisberg's successor Governor Thomas to push aggressively for indirect rule. Blaming Northern Territories Chief Commissioner Walker-Leigh for the lack of progress, Thomas declared that "definite lines should be laid down without delay on which Administrative officers can work; so that when the time is ripe, a system of indirect rule can be introduced and the natives themselves given a share of the government in the country." In 1928, Thomas also revived the issue of direct taxation, saying that "we missed our chance in the Colony, we missed it in Ashanti." Thomas went on to say that "one thing is certain. No administration can be of any use if it has no power, and power connotes financial control . . . a system of taxation will be necessary."[88] This possibility had been raised a year earlier, in similar terms, when Northern Provincial Commissioner A.J. Cutfield convened a political conference to discuss strengthening the northern chieftaincies.[89] "The Chiefs must be upheld," wrote Cutfield, "we rule through the Chiefs, they are held responsible for various duties and must keep up state." "It must be borne in mind," he continued, "that with the march of civilisation the power of the chiefs will decrease and the supply of labour be less unless matters

[87] T.C. McCaskie, "R.S. Rattray and the Construction of Asante History: An Appraisal," *History in Africa* 10 (1983): 189–190.

[88] Phyllis Ferguson and Ivor Wilks, "Chiefs, Constitutions and the British in Northern Ghana," in *West African Chiefs*, ed. M. Crowder and O. Ikeme, 334–5 (New York: Africana Publishing Corporation, 1970).

[89] Eyre-Smith, 23/8/27, NRG8/2/14, NAGT.

be put on an orthodox legal basis." In Cutfield's opinion the forces of progress, which colonial officials had not controlled, had undermined traditional chiefly authority. The administration thus had to capture "the march of civilisation" in order to guide the process of modernisation without further threatening the authority of the chiefs. Cutfield believed that this project necessitated granting the chiefs formal legal powers by making them salaried employees of the government. In the absence of public funding, putting the chiefs on salaries required the imposition of direct taxation.[90]

The idea of direct taxation found a receptive audience among the northern District Commissioners. Indeed, by 1927 the main issue had become one of deciding on the form of the tax, not whether or not it should be implemented. In food-insecure Zuarungu, District Commissioner Rainsford argued for imposing a head tax paid in grain and the creation of chiefs' or "state" granaries. However, Rainsford wanted to leave this choice up to the people. "It would be better for them," he wrote, "to select a system of tribute suitable to themselves than to have a system forced upon them." Rainsford thus argued that British officials should meet with compound heads, who would select a form of tribute—grain, labour, cash, et cetera—by majority vote. The system would be enforced by criminal sanctions against chiefs who collected more than the prescribed amounts.[91]

Eyre-Smith argued against tribute on the grounds that it had produced "gross injustices" such as the Tugu incident. As a remedy, Eyre-Smith suggested converting labour and taxation into cash, recommending the conversion of all "free" labour to wage labour at 3d per day, and the imposition of a poll tax of 2/- per head on the male population. Headmen would collect the taxes and turn them over to the chiefs, who would in turn submit all of the money to the British administration. From the proceeds, the British would pay salaries to chiefs and use surpluses for local development.[92]

The colonial administration agreed with Eyre-Smith's position on taxation but rejected his suggestion to install the land priests as political rulers. However, the implementation of direct taxation was delayed by the Depression and a lengthy round of negotiations over indirect rule with the Colonial Office between 1930 and 1936. The

[90] A.J. Cutfield, 23/7/27, ADM/56/1/335, NAGA.
[91] W. Rainsford, 5/11/27, ADM56/1/87, NAGA.
[92] Eyre-Smith, 15/11/27, ADM56/1/87, NAGA.

implementation of indirect rule and direct taxation will be discussed in detail in Chapter Four. For now it is important to note that the system of chieftaincies and taxation sought to strengthen the communities of the Northern Territories without producing chiefly despotism and landlordism.

Conclusion

Guggisberg's LNRO laid the foundation for the adaptation of Henry George's ideas to the Northern Territories. The LNRO must be considered, however, in the context of Guggisberg's wider vision of development. Building on Clifford's ideas, Guggisberg's ten-year development plan represented the first programmatic development program in British West Africa. Under the program, Guggisberg planned to use surplus balances—mainly from cocoa production and mining—to develop infrastructure, health care and education. These state-provided works, Guggisberg believed, would in turn facilitate further economic, social and political development and thus provide the "Highway to Progress" leading to the "Cities of Final Development, Wealth and Happiness." As noted above, the Northern Territories figured prominently in the plan as a potential producer of groundnuts and shea-butter. More importantly, however, Guggisberg considered the north a clean slate for development along African lines, producing strong states in Gonja, Dagomba and Mamprusi that eventually would be stitched into the modern Gold Coast nation.

Given the Gold Coast's reliance on cocoa and mining, however, it was impossible to shield the north entirely from southern influences and the threat of "denationalisation." Guggisberg himself revived a labour recruiting campaign between 1921 and 1924.[93] The campaign pressured the chiefs to recruit migrant labour for the mines as well as communal labour for public works, which intensified commoner accusations of corruption and extortion. The growth of cocoa production, meanwhile, brought more and more northerners into the orbit of the migrant labour system between the north and the south. This process brought some cash back into the Northern Territories

[93] Jeff Crisp, *The Story of An African Working Class: Ghanaian Miners' Struggles, 1870–1980* (London: Zed Books, 1984), 46.

and in some cases facilitated the commercialisation of earth shrines. Lurking behind these developments was the perceived threat of African landlordism. Many influential Gold Coast officials had become worried about this possibility by the late nineteen twenties. Rattray, for instance, argued that private property would produce "a landless class, who would in time become African paupers—a section of civilised communities familiar to us, but hitherto unknown in Africa."[94] The Colonial Office shared this view, criticising Guggisberg's "inexpert handling" of the land issue in the south where he supported the development of private property. According to Fiddian of the Africa Department, Guggisberg left an "appalling mess" in the south due to his support of Surveyor-General Rowe, "whose ideas of land tenure were primarily those of a Land Surveyor."[95] The discovery of large chiefs' farms in the 1920s signalled that African landlords seemed to be developing in the north, and Guggisberg's successors stepped up their discussions of indirect rule and direct taxation in order to stem the tide of commercialisation.

The point here is that cocoa production and mining—so necessary for Guggisberg's surplus balances development programme—undermined his plan to build a Gold Coast nation from "traditional" roots and so avoid "too rapid an advance" up the "steep slope of civilisation." Faced with the perceived corruption of African development, the colonial administration drew on the familiar discourse of African evolution to set the Northern Territories back onto the path of authentic development. In the late 1920s, this colonial project sparked a debate over whether to install chiefs or land priests as trustees over their "tribal' communities. However, as Lentz demonstrates clearly, the debate was a false one because precolonial communities were not defined territorially, but rather by negotiable social networks based on patriclan and religion. In different ways, Lentz and Hawkins both show that the choice to ignore precolonial social structures was deliberate, in that colonial officers consciously imposed chiefs based on British ideas about evolution and development.[96] As we shall discover, this choice would feed into continued struggles over resources within the framework of indirect rule.

---

[94] Phillips, 122.

[95] Fiddian, n.d., CO96/700/8, PRO.

[96] Lentz, *Ethnicity and the Making of History in Northern Ghana*, 53; Hawkins, *Writing and Colonialism in Northern Ghana*, 122.

In the 1920s, however, the colonial officers believed that they could enhance chiefly authority though the indirect rule system, including salaried chiefs, paid labour for public works and direct taxation. This process was on the table in 1927 and it was very much accepted by most of the administrative staff. Also on the table was Guggisberg's draft Land and Native Rights Ordinance (LNRO) placing control over the entire Protectorate in the hands of the Governor. The LNRO, combined with the proposed political reforms, set the stage for the introduction of the Northern Nigerian system into the Northern Territories. Before the 1930s, colonial officials were unaware of the potential challenges to this system, especially by individuals such as Tengol and his control over the Yanii shrine. Instead, Guggisberg's policies seemed to be an important step in bringing "the ideal world of Henry George" to the Northern Territories. Chapter Four discusses the colonial state's implementation of this legislation in the Northern Territories between 1928 and 1936.

CHAPTER FOUR

DEVELOPING COMMUNITY: LAND, NATIVE ADMINISTRATION AND DIRECT TAXATION, 1928–1936

Introduction

Between 1928 and 1936, the colonial administration completed the work started by Clifford and Guggisberg by implementing indirect rule in the Northern Territories. The project carried forward the task of amalgamating the northern chieftaincies into native states and codifying the chiefs' powers as trustees of their communities. As part of this process, the administration implemented direct taxation for the first time since 1900. The end result was a formal system of Native Authorities, Native Tribunals and Native Treasuries under which the chiefs had responsibility for local administration as well as justice and tax collection. In the meantime, the colonial administration also implemented the Land and Native Rights Ordinance, which in its final form vested virtually all northern lands in the "people" through the chiefs, but with the Governor reserving the final authority over appropriation and land transfers.

Most scholars have characterised indirect rule in terms of its political and economic usefulness to the colonial powers. Faced with the mandate to extract colonial resources without Treasury support, and constrained by local resistance, the colonial state attempted to use the chiefs for its project of exploitation. On the surface this system resembled Mamdani's conception of "decentralised despotism," in that the colonial administration concentrated administrative, financial and judicial powers in the hands of the chiefs. In a slightly different context, Hawkins echoes Mamdani's notion of British-imposed despotism by arguing that colonial writing imposed "mimetic tryanny" on the African population. As we shall see, however, the colonial project was weaker than these images imply. First, indirect rule was not simply imposed by the colonial administration, but instead resulted from difficult negotiations with local rulers. Second, local authorities were competing for power within the colonial system, often successfully, and they took advantage of opportunities to subvert the system for their own ends. In this sense, the work by Lentz and Allman and Parker provides a better picture of indirect rule as a terrain of struggle, rather than a simple colonial straitjacket.

Beyond the outcomes of indirect rule, colonial intentions also were very important. Most significantly, the doctrine was framed by a philosophical program to protect African social cohesion from the disintegrating effects of westernisation. Land nationalisation was central to this vision, and in this sense indirect rule carried forward the Georgeist policies of the NNLC/WALC and the belief that it would be possible to extract raw materials without producing social changes and landlordism. Seen from this perspective, indirect rule was rooted firmly in colonial discourses of African tradition and modernity, protecting African communities as they travelled up the "steep slope of civilisation." But it was also fundamentally developmental in intent, in the sense that it sought to set the stage for the development of agriculture and livestock production after 1936. More to the point, indirect rule established a framework for development through African community. This desire built on the perceived need to ensure that communities rather than individuals benefited from the opening of the north to development. In other words, by 1936 the colonial administration believed that they had laid the basis for achieving Guggisberg's program of development without denationalisation.

Amalgamation and the Formation of Native Authorities, 1930–2

Governor Slater assembled a team of indirect rulers in the Northern Territories in the early 1930s after forcing the existing Chief Commissioner into retirement along with most of his staff. The new team included three passionate advocates of indirect rule, W.J.A. (Kibi) Jones, H.A. Blair and Duncan-Johnstone, all of whom possessed "an almost mystical devotion" to the doctrine.[1] Duncan-Johnstone emerged as the flag-bearer of indirect rule and brought the project of amalgamation to fruition in the Northern Territories. Retaining Guggisberg's vision of stitching "tribes" into a nation-state, he drew on the British experience as a model for the Northern Territories:

[1] Martin Staniland, *The Lions of Dagbon: Political Change in Northern Ghana* (Cambridge: Cambridge University Press, 1975), 79. See also Chief Commissioner's Report, 16 April 1935, Enclosure in Gold Coast #199, CO96/722/15, Administration/Taxation, Northern Territories, PRO.

> Quite so that is how Britain became a nation. First the little autonomous Saxon and Danish states then Saxon England with its independent Wales, Scotland and Ireland, and gradually we became a nation. So it will be here one day, the little local languages will die out and there will be one or two main languages; with intermarriage, education and intercourse made possible by modern transport conditions the tribal jealousies and differences will gradually disappear and the little states will come together and form one kingdom.[2]

Eventually, argued Duncan-Johnstone, a Gold Coast nation would form out of an amalgamation of the Northern Territories, Ashanti and the Colony.[3]

The indirect rule team believed that Native Authorities would be easy to construct in the centralised northern states of Dagomba, Gonja, and Mamprusi. These states appeared similar to the Emirates of Northern Nigeria, where the Colonial Office believed that "all that had to be done was to put into order and legalise the various taxes which had been levied by the rulers on the people, and turn them over to Government. Taxation was greatly reduced and everybody was happy."[4] It might not be so easy, however, in the stateless societies of the northeast and northwest. The Colonial Office itself argued that such societies were too "democratic" for the application of indirect rule and direct taxation. Anthropologist M.J. Field agreed, stating that indirect rule did not work well in "African democracies" without an "aristocratic" class. In such democracies, Field wrote, the chiefs derived their authority from their communities, "not from anything that sets them apart or implies any inherent claim to authority." In contrast, indirect rule removed these community rights, set chiefly authority apart from the subjects, and thus offended the "democratic instincts of the Africans." The doctrine only worked, argued Field, in cases where a hierarchical system already existed, such as Northern Nigeria, in which "the new authority, provided it is applied through the old channels, simply adds weight and volume to the old authority."[5]

---

[2] Quoted in James Merriman Lance, "Seeking the Political Kingdom: British Colonial Impositions and African Manipulations in the Northern Territories of the Gold Coast Colony" (Unpublished PhD. Dissertation, Stanford University, 1995), 167.

[3] Ibid., 169.

[4] Eastwood, n.d., CO96/693/2, PRO.

[5] M.J. Field, "Some Problems of Indirect Rule in the Gold Coast," typescript, n.d. Mss.Perham.390/5(ff. 1–68): 1938–43, Oxford University, Rhodes House Library (RHL), 2–5.

To resolve this problem Jones turned to the work of Donald Cameron, who had implemented indirect rule among the stateless peoples of Tanganyika between 1925 and 1931.[6] Cameron shared Guggisberg's belief that development should consist of amalgamating tribes into units capable of developing into nations. As Iliffe notes, Cameron's main contribution to the doctrine of indirect rule consisted of developing "conciliar systems" among stateless peoples. Under this program, Cameron attempted to federate scattered settlements under chiefs' councils rather than appoint single paramount chiefs.[7] This policy drew on Lugard's distinction between "homogenous" Emirates and "collections of chiefs" under native authorities. Cameron had developed the latter "district" system in Tanganyika by negotiating the federation of native authorities ruled by Chiefs' councils.[8]

The Colonial Office criticised the use of Cameron's model in the Gold Coast on several levels. First, unlike Tanganyika, chiefs in the Gold Coast possessed no statutory powers.[9] Second, Cameron himself had ended his Tanganyika service "a little shaken in his faith in, at all events, the indiscriminate application of indirect rule."[10] In his memoir, Cameron argued that the system ran the danger of devolving power to autocratic chiefs without popular support. "The allegiance of a people to a tribal head," wrote Cameron, "*freely and spontaneously, without external cause*, is the very essence of true indirect administration."[11] This goal, paradoxically, could only be achieved by firm state control over the development of the Native Authorities in order to guard against chiefly corruption.[12] This was an issue in the Northern Territories, where Chief Commissioner Walker-Leigh noted in 1929 that direct rule had severed many subordinate chiefs from popular checks and balances and given them a degree of independence from their subjects. Jones, however, convinced the Colonial

[6] John Iliffe, *A Modern History of Tanganyika* (Cambridge: Cambridge University Press, 1979), 319.

[7] Ibid., 323, 330.

[8] Quoted by A.C. Duncan-Johnstone, 21 November 1931, Southern Province Commissioner (CSP) Diary, Mss.Afr.s.593, Duncan-Johnstone Papers, RHL.

[9] Chief Commissioner's Report, 16 April 1935, Enclosure in Gold Coast #199, CO96/722/15: Native Administration/Taxation, Northern Territories, PRO.

[10] A.R. Slater, 15 December 1931, CO96/700/14: Indirect Rule, 1931, PRO, 6.

[11] Sir Donald Cameron, *My Tanganyika Service and Some Nigeria* (London: George Allen and Unwin Ltd., 1939), 95, italics added.

[12] Ibid., 76, 92.

Office of the feasibility of indirect rule in the north and Walker-Leigh reluctantly agreed that the chiefs would not object to resuming their proper places in the traditional hierarchy.[13] Between 1930 and 1935, the Colonial Office permitted Jones to federate the north's native states on the Tanganyikan model and to implement direct taxation in the Northern Territories.[14] With this blessing, Jones began to delineate the north's traditional boundaries and to amalgamate the colonial tribes into Native Authorities large enough for the efficient administration of local affairs.[15]

The North-west

In Lawra-Tumu, where "the people had not advanced beyond the patriarchal stage," the indirect rule team collected together the "heads of kindred families" and negotiated the process of amalgamation.[16] During this process some senior officials rejected the land priests as legitimate rulers. "It would be as logical," wrote Assistant District Commissioner H.A. Blair, "to search out Saxon, or even Celtic and Druidic families and set them up as local rulers in Britain."[17] The administration also rejected proposals to constitute each ethnic group as a single Native Authority because it contravened Cameron's model of amalgamation. In 1931, for instance, P.F. Whittal proposed to place the Sissala and Dagarti into autonomous divisions with separate elections for paramount chiefs. Duncan-Johnstone rejected the suggestion on the grounds that the "little states in the Lawra-Tumu District" would descend into "bickering and intrigue" if left as single chieftaincies. More importantly, however, Duncan-Johnstone argued that Whittal's idea was "directly opposed to the policy which has been so successful in Tanganyika."[18]

---

[13] Cited in Chief Commissioner's "Report on the Northern Territories," Enclosure in Gold Coast #199, 16 April 1935, CO96/722/15, PRO, 1.

[14] Minute, Calder, 18 February 1930, CO96/693/2, PRO; Minute, Malcolm MacDonald, 12 August 1935, CO96/722/15, PRO.

[15] Chief Commissioner's Report, 16 April 1935, Enclosure in Gold Coast #199, CO96/722/15: Native Administration/Taxation, Northern Territories, PRO.

[16] W.J.A. Jones, 25 January 1938, Enclosure in Gold Coast #13, Hodson to Ormsby-Gore, 12 February 1938, CO96/746/3: Direct Taxation, 1938, PRO.

[17] H.A. Blair, "Comments by Mr. H.A. Blair, Asst. DC (on the letters of St.J. Eyre-Smith, 2/3/30)," E.O. Rake (Acting Chief Commissioner) to Secretary For Native Affairs, 1 April 1933, ADM11/824, National Archives of Ghana, Accra (NAGA).

[18] A.C. Duncan-Johnstone, 21 November 1931, Southern Province Commissioner (CSP) Diary, Mss.Afr.s.593, Duncan-Johnstone Papers, RHL.

In the end it proved very difficult to achieve the level of amalgamation consistent with Cameron's model. The administration wanted to create an amalgamation of two divisions, Wala-Dagarti and Sissala, united under the paramountcy of the chief of Wa (Wa Na). When the Dagarti and Sissala refused, the District Commissioner proposed that Wa, Dagarti and Sissala form three independent paramountcies. But the chiefs and people would not divide themselves so neatly along ethnic lines. Among the Dagara, for instance, the divisional chiefs fought to protect their independence and refused to choose a paramount ruler.[19] This forced the administration to use Cameron's conciliar system to establish the Lawra Confederacy Native Authority, consisting of Lawra, Nandom, Jirapa and Lambussie, at a very low level of amalgamation. The task then became one of negotiating which settlements would be placed under each member of the Confederacy. Villages were given the choice of whether to follow Lawra, Nandom, Jirapa or Lambussie, and the resulting Native Authorities Ordinance of 1934 established the Lawra, Jirapa, Nandom and Lambussie Native Authorities as the "Lawra Confederacy."[20] Later the same year, Nandom took over Lambussie's responsibilities at the request of the latter's chief on his deathbed. As a result of this request, Lawra, Jirapa and Nandom controlled the Lawra Confederacy between 1934 and 1947. As we shall discover, this structure would feed into a major struggle between Nandom and Lawra over land rights and chiefly succession in the 1950s.[21]

In the Sissala areas, the administration faced the challenge of reconciling the territorial boundary between Lawra and Tumu and the "tribal" boundary between the Sissala and the "Wala-Dagarti". At first the administration wanted to unite the Sissala under a single paramount chief and Provincial Commissioner P.F. Whittal convened an "All-Issala Conference" towards this end in 1931. By this time, however, although ten Sissala chiefs belonged to the Tumu District,

[19] R.B. Bening, "Foundations of the Modern Native States of Northern Ghana," *Universitas* 5, No. 1 (November, 1975): 124.

[20] Chief Commissioner, Northern Territories to Commissioner, Northern Province, 11 February 1932, 13 June 1932, 7 June 1933, NRG8/2/52, National Archives of Ghana, Tamale (NAGT). District Commissioner, Lawra-Tumu to Commissioner, Northern Province, 21 April 1931, ADM56/1/309, NAGA. Lawra-Tumu District Commissioner, 4 August 1934, NRG8/2/65, NAGT.

[21] For an excellent and detailed discussion of the Lawra Confederacy and disputes among its members, see Lentz, *Ethnicity and the Making of History in Northern Ghana*, Chapter 4.

three belonged to Lawra and two belonged to Wa. None of the groups under Lawra and Wa agreed to leave their districts, partly because they preferred the location of the other Districts, partly because they had stronger ties to Lawra and Wa, and partly because they feared losing Sissala land occupied by non-Sissala settlers. As for the Sissala of Tumu, the chiefs refused to support the British plan for a Sissala union under Zini, Wallembelle, or Sekai.[22] Making matters worse was the fact that the chief of Zini, convinced that he would become the new paramount ruler, held a feast to celebrate the installation. Zini eventually agreed to serve under Tumu, and further negotiations produced a Tumu Native Authority containing six divisions, excluding the Sissala chiefs who lived in the districts of Lawra and Wa. The Native Authorities Ordinance of 1934 thus established the Tumu Native Authority as a single paramountcy overseeing divisions at Tumu, Wallembelli, Gollu, Kassena, Zini and Pulima.[23] Frankly admitting a lack of vision for the future, Duncan-Johnstone hoped that the system would evolve into one of true indirect rule where legitimate tribal chiefs would be elected from candidates who were village headmen.[24]

In sum, working from Cameron's model the indirect rule team attempted to amalgamate as many villages as possible in the northwest under each Native Authority. In the absence of clear traditional allegiances the process quickly became one of negotiations with chiefs and family heads over who would follow whom. The lists of chiefs and subjects were then assigned to specific boundaries, conflating personal networks with territorial rule. When the dust settled, therefore, the administration had simply fitted the existing chiefly hierarchy into the territorial framework of indirect rule. In the process, the earth priests lost power because their parish boundaries were ignored and their control over market fees was given to the chiefs of the native authorities.[25]

---

[22] Bening, "Foundations," 124.

[23] "Tumu Native Authorities," 12 June 1934, NRG8/2/65, NAGT. The Native Authorities were gazetted on August 4, 1934.

[24] A.C. Duncan-Johnstone, 29 September 1932, Southern Province Commissioner (CSP) Diary, Mss.Afr.s.593, Duncan-Johnstone Papers, RHL.

[25] Lentz, *Ethnicity and the Making of History in Northern Ghana*, 177–80.

The North-east

The situation was much the same in the Zuarungu District, where the colonial administration continued to believe that the population had been subject to Mamprusi rule before the slave raiding era. Working from this assumption, in 1932 the administration attempted to consolidate North and South Mamprusi. The District Commissioners travelled around the region to convince people of the far north to accept the paramountcy of the Mamprusi chief (*Nayiri*). In the east, Bawku agreed to submit to the *Nayiri's* authority in return for his elevation to a sub-paramountcy directly accountable to Mamprusi. In the west, the administration placed Kasena, Nankani and Builsa—who together comprised the Navrongo District—under the *Nayiri's* authority, despite the peoples' refusal to pledge allegiance to Mamprusi.[26]

The Talensi case was more complicated. Represented by Tongo, the Talensi were placed into a five-member Frafra Confederacy sub-Native Authority in 1932, which also included Zuarungu, Bongo, Nangodi and Sekoti, subsumed along with Kusasi under the Mamprusi Native Authority.[27] At first, the administration retained the *kunaab's* authority over Tongo, but it soon became clear that he would never gain enough authority to rule over the Talensi. In place of the *kunaab*-centred hierarchy, the colonial administration created a ten-member Talensi Federation that included seven Namoo chiefs and two *tengdaanas* representing four Tali settlements in the Tong Hills (Shia, Gorogo, Sipaat and Yinduri). The final member, representing the central settlement of Tenzugu, was the most controversial. By the 1930s, *kambonaaba* Tengol had manoeuvred himself into the position of chief of Tenzugu and *golibdaana*, keeper of the drums for the *Gologo* sowing festival centred on the earth shrine Ngoo. The *kpataarnaba* resisted Tengol's rise to power and the conflict burst into the open in 1935. Although the *kpataarnaba's* resistance was relatively weak, British officials were wary of Tengol and refused to give him sole power over Tenzugu. Instead, the settlement was to be administered jointly by the *golibdaana* and *kpataarnaba*, acting in turn according to a negotiated system of rotation. After this decision, the British sent

[26] Bening, "Foundations," 123.

[27] Paul André Ladouceur, *Chiefs and Politicians: The Politics of Regionalism in Northern Ghana* (London: Longman, 1979), 55.

the *kunaaba* back to his village and installed the Tongrana (chief of Tongo) as the first president of the new Talensi Native Authority.[28]

As Allman and Parker have shown, anthropologist Meyer Fortes supported the elevation of *Tongrana* Nambiong, a personal friend, to a position of power in place of the *kunaaba*. As a Namoo, the *Tongrana's* precolonial authority had not extended to the Talis, but Fortes nonetheless informed the administration that that the *Tongrana* had been "recognised as the man of highest rank in the district inhabited by the Talensi".[29] In particular, *Tongrana* Nambiong, who had been appointed in 1918, commanded the respect of most Talensi, unlike the *kunaaba* who was widely perceived as a stranger. Fortes thus marked out a position for Nambiong in the politics of Taleland, which he proposed in a memorandum that provided the framework for the federal Talensi Native Authority. The administration also put Nambiong temporarily in charge of Tenzugu, until the *golibdaana* and *kpataarnaba* settled a feud that had developed over the growing wealth from the pilgrimage trade to the Tongnaab shrine. Fortes much preferred Namboing in this position because he considered the *golibdaana* an illegitimate and corrupt "racketeer".[30]

During the Zuarungu negotiations, the Chief Commissioner proposed to split the District into three sections and hived each off to different districts on the basis of ethnicity. Under this scheme the Talensi would join Mamprusi, the Nankani (under Bongo) would join the Navrongo District, and the Nabdam (split between the villages of Bongo and Sekoti) would join the Bawku District. The Zuarungu District Commissioner opposed the scheme, pointing out that the three "tribes" were in fact indistinguishable from one another. Instead, the District Commissioner argued that the Zuarungu District should be absorbed into the Navrongo headquarters and serve Mamprusi as part of an enlarged Navrongo District.[31] Based on these negotiations, Duncan-Johnstone approved a plan in 1932 to amalgamate Southern Mamprusi, Kusasi, Zuarungu and Navrongo into the Mamprusi District with headquarters at Gambaga.[32]

---

[28] Jean Allman and Jonathan Parker, *Tongnaab: The History of a West African God* (Bloomington: Indiana University Press, 2005), 212.

[29] Fortes to CCNT, 1936, cited in Allman and Parker, 205.

[30] Allman and Parker, 197, 205–6, 212–13.

[31] Bening, "Foundations," 128–129.

[32] A.C. Duncan-Johnstone, 23 July 1932, 14 August 1932, Southern Province Commissioner (CSP) Diary, Mss.Afr.s.593, Duncan-Johnstone Papers, RHL.

Below the head chiefs, the issue of direct taxation sparked a debate over political authority at the village level. In 1935, Chief Commissioner Jones replaced the *kambonabas* with traditional family heads as local political authorities and tax collectors. This move was justified as a return to tradition. The *kambonabas* had no legitimate authority and relied on the threat of British power to maintain their rule and enforce their will; the family heads, by contrast, had the authority of tradition and would not have to rely on the direct power of the colonial government. District Commissioner Alan F. Kerr objected to the decision because it upset the existing channels of authority. Since the family heads did not have to rely on British power, when the administration abolished the *kambonabas* they also did away with the legal sanctions for disobeying headmen at the local level. Legal powers were codified only at the level of the chiefs of the Native Authority.[33] There seemed to be no "legal recognition" given to "anyone between the subordinate native authorities and the individual: that is to say, no powers or duties are given to the small chiefs, chiefs' sons, family heads, kambonabas, tengdaanas (land priests), compound owners etc. as such."[34] More importantly, the headmen may have been authentic and "traditional," but their traditional authority had disappeared with the rise of the *kambonabas*. It would be difficult if not impossible, Kerr believed, to recover the power that had been lost.

In Kerr's opinion the reform threw into chaos "the relationship between compound owners, family heads, headmen and smaller chiefs" at the precise moment—the eve of direct taxation—when the channels of authority needed to be clearly codified.[35] Without clear legal codification, Kerr feared the intensification of corruption by the family heads through the extraction of forced labour and payments for chiefs' messengers. This seemed more likely because the family-heads were hereditary leaders whose power was not based on the will of the people, whereas the *kambonabas* had been chosen by election after the initial appointments by the colonial administration.[36]

For these reasons, Kerr objected to the abolition of the *kambonabas*. While it was true that over time many *kambonabas* had usurped hered-

[33] See A.F. Kerr, 18 November 1935, 1/13/36, NRG3/2/11, NAGT.
[34] Alan F. Kerr, "Frafra Native Authorities," 1936, NRG3/2/11, NAGT, 3–4.
[35] Ibid., 6.
[36] Interview, A.F. Kerr, 3 October 1994. A.F. Kerr, "Frafra Constitutional Development," 18.

itary powers, Kerr believed that they could be reformed and would be more effective agents of indirect rule at the village level than the aging family heads. Seeking advice on this issue, Kerr wrote to Meyer Fortes, wondering whether "Ecclesiastical rule must give way to secular rule" under the *kambonabas*.[37] In September, 1936, Fortes wrote back, agreeing that "a strong case could be made out for the retention of at least one of the two types of Kambonabas found in this area."[38] In early 1937, however, Fortes drafted a memorandum that recommended replacing the *kambonabas* with family and clan heads, arguing that their traditional authority had survived underneath the veneer of the British-appointed *kambonabas*.[39] Kerr adopted Fortes' scheme, perhaps under the influence of Chief Commissioner Jones, who had decided in favour of the family heads in 1936. In his handing-over notes in 1940, Kerr informed his successor that the *kambonabas* had been "officially sternly abolished" and that only family heads should be recognised as local leaders.[40]

When the dust settled, the Native Authority system fell short of Jones' goal for amalgamation, establishing twelve Native Authorities where he had wanted only eight. But Jones could rationalise this apparent failure by appealing to tradition. The team created twelve Native Authorities, he argued, because the administration did not wish to coerce "any section of the people to join a group with which it had no kindred connection or traditional alliance."[41] As we have seen, the idea of traditional allegiance smoothed over the roughness of the negotiations over who would follow whom, some of which related to land rights and most of which fell back on "traditions" less than a generation old. Still, the administration believed that it successfully had established the foundation for Native Administration in the Northern Territories, based on traditional channels of authority.

---

[37] A.F. Kerr, 26 August 1936, 7–8, NRG3/2/11, NAGT.

[38] M. Fortes, 9 September 1936, NRG3/2/11, NAGT.

[39] Allman and Parker, 206.

[40] A.F. Kerr, "Handing-over Notes to I.S. Warren," 22/1/40, 13, personal papers, A.F. Kerr. Mr. Kerr generously provided access to this document.

[41] W.J.A. Jones, 25 January 1938, Enclosure in Gold Coast #13, Hodson to Ormsby-Gore, 12 February 1938, CO96/746/3, PRO.

Direct Taxation in the Northern Territories, 1930–1936

While he worked to construct the new Native Authorities, Jones championed direct taxation as the only mechanism for establishing Native Administration on a sure footing in the Northern Territories. Jones' taxation proposals drew on the example of Palmer's *biet-al-mal* to emphasise the importance of the "Independent Native Treasury" as the "cardinal feature" of "real local government with a measure of financial control."[42] According to Jones, without direct taxation it would be "impossible to establish 'Indirect Rule' on a sure basis" because "no system of rule can be effective unless it enjoys some measure of financial independence."[43] Governor Thomas agreed, drawing on Cameron's work to argue that the tax was "an outward and visible sign of the allegiance which a man owes to his state," and that "no administration can be of any use if it has not power, and power connotes financial control."[44]

Jones' argument was strengthened by the 1930 International Labour Organisation (ILO) Convention outlawing forced labour in the colonies, which threatened to undermine chiefly authority based on the extraction of communal labour. Politically, therefore, the colonial state felt an urgent need to rationalise the power of the chiefs in the absence of the legal right to extract labour from their subjects. As a substitute for chiefs' labour, the administration considered direct taxation a development of "tribute" in traditional societies. This new line of authority would be established by delegating the collection of the tax to family heads. As in Nigeria, Jones proposed to delegate tax collection to Native Authority leaders "and through them to village and compound heads who receive a commission on the proceeds."[45] "The interest of the individual taxpayer in the expenditure of revenue," he wrote, "will replace coercion as the means of ensuring the cooperation of the people in the general maintenance of the State."

[42] Ormsby-Gore made this argument in 1926. Duncan-Johnstone's source for Ormsby-Gore was Sir Anton Berton's "The Colonial Service." A.C. Duncan-Johnstone, 30 June 1930, Commissioner, Southern Province (CSP) Diary, Mss.Afr.s.593, Duncan-Johnstone Papers, RHL, 20/1.

[43] W.J.A. Jones, "Native Administration in the Northern Territories of the Gold Coast," 1930, in A.R. Slater to Colonial Office, 31 October 1931, Gold Coast Confidential (B), CO96/700/14, PRO, 8.

[44] T.S. Thomas, 21 February 1934, Sub-Enclosure 2 in Enclosure 199 of Gold Coast, 16 April 1935, CO96/722/15, PRO.

[45] Slater, n.d., CO96/693/2, PRO, 5.

Expenditure of tax revenue would promote community development. On this point, Jones reminded the Colonial Office of the recent British colonial strategy of "local taxation for local development."[46] This idea had taken root in England among Fabian socialists led by Beatrice and Sidney Webb, and in post-WALC West Africa it was twinned to land nationalisation and the idea of Henry George's single tax. Jones framed his taxation proposals in this environment, seeking to use direct taxation to achieve local development without producing landlordism or undermining African community. Collecting taxes from communities and depositing the proceeds into Native Authority treasuries would ensure that communities rather than individuals benefited from economic development.

The decision to impose direct taxation was also a matter of economic necessity. Under indirect rule, chiefs were to be paid salaries in order to demonstrate their authority as part of the government. In the wake of the Depression direct taxes offered one of the only means of subsidising these salaries. More practically, the colonial state needed direct taxation because the Depression had rendered indirect taxation inadequate for basic infrastructure needs, much less the estimated £150,000 per year needed to replace "communal" labour with wage labour for public works.[47] In this sense direct taxation was "the corollary to the abolition of forced labour."[48]

Beyond its practical necessity, it is important to recognise that Jones' proposed assessment policy reflected the influence of Henry George's single tax. Jones advocated a flat-rate taxation system, managed by the District Commissioners, for the first three or four years. At first the District Commissioner would collect the tax, then, when adequate training had been given, family heads would collect taxes from their compounds and pass the proceeds to village or section headman, who in turn would remit them to the sub-divisional chief for deposit into the Native Treasury. After a few years, Jones argued, the system should change to a lump-sum assessment in which an assessing officer took a "typical compound as the unit of assessment." Under this system the officer would note the acreage cultivated and

---

[46] W.J.A. Jones, "Native Administration in the Northern Territories of the Gold Coast," 1930, in A.R. Slater to Colonial Office, 31 October 1931, Gold Coast Confidential (B), CO96/700/14, PRO, 5–6.
[47] Ibid., 7.
[48] Ibid., 8.

value of produce and livestock (or profits of craftsmen/traders) and divide the figure by the number of taxable males in the compound to produce the "standard" amount for the village. This procedure would be carried out for each village in a given region and the mean of the sample compounds would be multiplied by the total number of males in the region to produce the lump-sum tax for the region. The village headmen and elders would be "given full discretion to distribute the burden according to the capacity as they alone have an intimate knowledge of the relative degree of prosperity of each individual. The communal but not the individual liability is made known."[49] Jones recommended that a 10% fee be paid to village chiefs, 15% to divisional chiefs, and 10% to the Paramount Chief which would be converted into a fixed salary "as soon as possible." Half of the estimated £400,000 would accrue to the Government and half to the Native Authorities.[50]

Jones' proposal clearly resembled the ideas of Henry George, filtered through the taxation policy of Northern Nigeria. The procedure would have amounted to a true devolution of tax collection, with half of the proceeds accruing directly to the Native Authorities. Such a devolution rested on the assumption that traditional chiefs would act in the interests of their communities in allocating the tax burden to their subjects. Jones followed the *Dual Mandate's* recommendation to set the assessment at the estimated "usufruct or yield of land if cultivated to a normal standard, inclusive of the consumption of the owner."[51] In working from this benchmark, Jones clearly set out to bring the idea of the single tax to the Northern Territories.

Jones rationalised the direct tax as an authentic development by emphasising that it was merely the conversion of traditional tributes into money taxes. This rationalisation served two purposes for Jones in the Northern Territories. First, it satisfied the British belief that Native Administration represented the true development of tribute-based African social systems. Second, as Jones had argued in 1930, portraying taxation as the development of tribute provided—at least

---

[49] Chief Commissioner's Report, 16 April 1935, Enclosure in Gold Coast #199, CO96/722/15, PRO.

[50] A.R. Slater, minute, n.d., CO96/693/2: Native Administration Ordinance, 1930, PRO.

[51] Chief Commissioner's report, 16 April 1935, Enclosure in Gold Coast #199, CO96/722/15, PRO.

theoretically—the means to reduce resistance to the policy. Invoking R.S. Rattray's *Ashanti Law and Constitution*, Jones argued that the African population would accept direct taxes if "careful propaganda" emphasised that they would be levied by their own Native Authorities, at "a fraction of their past obligations," with the intent of helping to "restore and preserve their nationality."[52]

The Colonial Office initially opposed direct taxation in the Gold Coast on the same grounds as their objection to Native Administration in general: that Gold Coast communities were too democratic for the tax, meaning that most people had never paid tribute to a suzerain. In 1935, however, convinced of the urgent need for direct taxes in the wake of the Depression and the ILO Convention on forced labour, the Colonial Office approved Jones' proposal. The approval came with several conditions. First, Jones could proceed only "on the understanding that a special note of warning should be sounded as regards chiefs (a) levying a higher tax than their people can afford and/or (b) using their tax-gatherers to oppress the people, e.g. in wiping out old scores."[53] The Colonial Office also warned that the implementation should be done gradually, in light of "the undesirability of putting these proposals into operation more quickly than is warranted by the progressive education of the native authorities and the development in them of a due sense of their responsibility in the utilisation of the revenue collected."[54] These warnings carried forward Thomas' fear, expressed in 1934, that direct taxation should be implemented only where villages expressed a consensus over the commutation of tribute into taxes.[55] Finally, the Colonial Office approved Jones' taxation proposal only insofar as it appeared as regularised tribute with the full support of the chiefs and people of the Northern Territories.[56]

Jones responded to these conditions by constructing the Northern Territories as a region whose history warranted the imposition of

[52] A.R. Slater, n.d. Slater to Passfield, 18 February 1930, CO96/693/2, PRO. Passfield agreed with Slater's argument.

[53] G. Creasy, 2 August 1935, Enclosure in Gold Coast #199 of 16 April 1935, CO96/722/15, PRO.

[54] Malcolm MacDonald, 12 August 1935, Enclosure in Gold Coast #199 of 16 April 1935, CO96/722/15, PRO.

[55] T.S. Thomas, 21 February 1934, Sub-Enclosure 2 in Chief Commissioner's Report, Enclosure in Gold Coast #199 of 16 April 1935, CO96/722/15, PRO.

[56] Malcolm MacDonald, 12 August 1935, minute on Chief Commissioner's Report, Enclosure in Gold Coast #199 of 16 April 1935, CO96/722/15, PRO.

direct taxes as part of its natural development. In the case of states like Gonja and Dagomba, Jones portrayed the tax as a revival of traditional "feudal dues" which had been destroyed by the ruthlessness of Samory, Babatu and the "direct rulers." Among stateless societies, where such a rationalisation was not possible, Jones simply invoked Cameron's model of a consensual federation of districts or divisions. Inasmuch as family members were subordinated to family heads through kinship ties, the tax could be construed as the development of traditional lines of authority. Inasmuch as the chiefs, though imposed by the British, had a history of acting as labour contractors, the tax could be construed as the development of chiefly authority. At the broadest level, Jones rationalised direct taxation in stateless areas as the development of tradition as long as the British believed that family heads and land priests would have developed into chiefs were it not for the destruction wrought by the slave raiders and British military activities in the late nineteenth century.[57]

After considering the taxation debate at length, the Gold Coast government passed the required legislation and the Native Authorities collected the first direct taxes, which the colonial state called "annual tribute," in August, 1936.[58] The Ordinances put chiefs on salaries as "staves of office" which demonstrated that chiefly authority was backed by the power of the colonial state. Thinking to the future, the colonial administration planned to convene regular chiefs' conferences in order to prepare the Native Authority federations for full amalgamation and eventual self-rule.[59] With the promise of revenues from the new tax, the Native Authorities also began working on local development projects, training clerical and medical staff and constructing, among other things, Native Authority schools and medical dispensaries.[60]

[57] Questionnaire, Chief Commissioner, Northern Territories to District Commissioners, 6 November 1934, Sub-Enclosure 1 in Enclosure in Gold Coast #199, CO96/722/15: Native Administration/Taxation, Northern Territories, 1935, PRO, 5.

[58] See CO96/727/12: Northern Territories: Direct Taxation, 1936, PRO.

[59] A.C. Duncan-Johnstone, 30 January 1932, Southern Province Commissioner (CSP) Diary, Mss.Afr.s.593, Duncan-Johnstone Papers, RHL, 10,36.

[60] Chief Commissioner's Report, Enclosure in Gold Coast #199 of 16 April 1935, CO96/722/15: Native Administration/Taxation, Northern Territories, PRO.

Land and African Community: The Land and Native Rights Ordinance, 1928–1932

Along with the direct tax, Native Administration in the Northern Territories revolved around land tenure and who would receive the "fruits of development." In 1928, Governor Slater and Gold Coast Colonial Secretary T.S.W. Thomas were forced to defend the LNRO against the African charge that it represented a "confiscatory measure" akin to the 1897 Lands Bill.[61] The resistance was not surprising considering that Guggisberg's LNRO vested northern lands directly in the colonial government without any reference to the people. Implementing the LNRO thus would be a tricky business. "Some uneasiness is being shown locally," wrote the Governor in August, 1927, "that this legislation heralds a departure from Government traditions of land policy in the Colony and I am anxious to issue explanatory announcement carefully drafted by the Attorney General to prevent recurrence of previous agitation."[62] Worried about African resistance, Governor Slater initially resisted the Ordinance. He also objected to its main features, including land nationalisation, registration of titles, and withholding rents from rural chiefs. Regarding nationalisation, Slater believed that vesting land in the Crown would provoke resistance as a reversal of Chamberlain's promise to abandon the policy after the withdrawal of Maxwell's 1897 land bill.[63] On this point Slater also argued that land nationalisation would "encourage subordinate chiefs to challenge the rights of their paramount chiefs to exercise control over the disposal of tribal lands."[64] Regarding land registration, Slater opposed Guggisberg's proposal to register titles for all claims of individual ownership of rural lands. Slater also objected to the provision to withhold rents from chiefs in rural areas, whom he felt should be the direct beneficiaries of land-based revenues as trustees of their communities.[65]

---

[61] R.B. Bening, "Land Policy and Administration in Northern Ghana, 1898–1976," *Transactions of the Historical Society of Ghana*, XVI(ii) (1995): 241.

[62] Telegram, Gold Coast Governor to Secretary of State for the Colonies, 5 August 1927, CO96/674/5: Gold Coast Land and Native Rights Ordinance, Great Britain, Public Record Office, Kew, London (PRO).

[63] B.G. Der, "Colonial Land Policy in the Northern Territories of the Gold Coast, 1900–1957," *Universitas (New Series)*, 4(2) (May, 1975): 137.

[64] L.E.V. McCarthy's summary of Slater's 1931 memorandum to the Colonial Office. McCarthy was a member of the African Crown Council. See CO96/700/8, PRO.

[65] See Slater to Cunliffe-Lister, Gold Coast 63 of 1932, CO96/702/4, PRO.

In the spring of 1930, however, Slater capitulated to the views of the Colonial Office. In doing so, he agreed to retain the registration requirement and grant the Governor the right to rescind land certificates and take land at will simply by posting a notice.[66] On the nationalisation issue, he offered to drop a concession to "non-natives" so that all titles to northern lands had to be approved by the Governor. Warming up to the Ordinance, Slater eventually wrote that

> the vesting in Government of lands in undeveloped territories is at once the simplest and surest way of preserving native rights, which are in essence community rights, and of securing for the native the fruits of development. The policy that has been pursued in the Colony (from which there can, of course, be no question of receding), while theoretically more equitable, has merely resulted—and is still resulting—in allowing the fruits of development to be monopolised, in all too many cases, by individual natives to the loss of the community.[67]

The Colony's policy allowed for government control only over non-native lands, leaving chiefs with a free hand to administer land tenure through by-laws based on customary law. This had not worked in practice because, in Slater's opinion, the chiefs were not capable of acting as proper trustees for their communities under conditions of rapid economic growth. In fact, the southern chiefs had developed a habit of alienating community lands to speculators for private personal gain. The only practical solution, Slater finally admitted, was for the colonial administration to exercise trusteeship through land nationalisation. This opinion came as a relief to the Colonial Office, who considered nationalisation both necessary and practicable in the Northern Territories. The Colonial Office believed that the northern population, unlike their educated southern brethren, could be made to realise that nationalisation was in the public interest.[68] Working from this belief, the Colonial Office approved an amended LNRO in 1931.

The *Gold Coast Spectator* responded vehemently to the new ordinance, claiming that the governor had elevated himself "to the position of agrarian lord paramount and dictator" keen on usurping "the

[66] P. Cunliffe-Lister (Secretary of State for the Colonies) observed that the new clause 8, might not actually permit the Govt to relinquish lands. See Cunliffe-Lister, 2 November 1931, Gold Coast #6 of 1931, in CO96/697/8, PRO.

[67] Slater to Passfield, 15 March 1930, Gold Coast #199 in CO96/694/7, PRO.

[68] See J.E.W. Flood, 29 August 1930, CO96/694/7, PRO.

natural rights of the African."[69] More than this, argued the *Spectator*, the Ordinance could be used to clear the Northern Territories for white settlement along East African lines.[70] To make matters worse for Slater, the Colonial Office also criticised the amended Ordinance because it was sloppily drafted. This criticism prompted several Colonial Office officials to support the Gold Coast elite's demand to incorporate the Northern Territories into the Gold Coast Legislative Council. The Colonial Office's reasoning, of course, differed from the argument of the African elite. Colonial Office staff wanted to avoid African misunderstandings of legislation imposed without debate, publicity or explanations from the Governor.[71] In the absence of such "understanding," Secretary of State Cunliffe-Lister advised the Gold Coast to drop land registration from the Ordinance in favour of allowing the question of titles to "evolve from within."[72]

Faced with renewed criticism, Slater amended the LNRO once again in 1932. This time he switched the Ordinance's wording from "public lands" to "native lands," which allowed him to vest the land in local communities through the Native Authorities. Land rents would not be withheld from chiefs because they could be deposited into Native Authority Treasuries, rather than the Crown, on behalf of their communities.[73] The LNRO established the Native Authorities as land granting bodies and land tenure devolved officially to the communities of the Northern Territories. At the village level, the land priests retained their role in granting rights of usufruct, but (at least theoretically) they could do so only with the approval of the appropriate Native Authority. At the national level, however, the governor retained the final authority to control land grants, concessions and appropriation.[74] The 1932 LNRO thus empowered the colonial state to appropriate land, if needed, for the purpose of development, while it transferred legal powers over local land tenure from the land priests to the representatives of the Native Authorities. This legislation reinforced the colonial policy of establishing the chiefs as the trustees over the development of their communities.

[69] *Gold Coast Spectator*, 9 January 1932, regarding Ordinance #9 of 1931, CO96/702/4, PRO.

[70] Ibid.

[71] Fiddian, 1 June 1932, Eastwood, 11 July 1932, CO96/702/4, PRO.

[72] Fiddian, 4 January 1932; Cunliffe-Lister, 4 January 1932, CO96/700/8, PRO.

[73] The Colonial Office agreed with this argument. See for instance Fiddian, 1 June 1932, CO96/702/4, PRO.

[74] Der, 139–140.

Conclusion

By 1936 the Gold Coast administration had imposed the necessary legislation and institutions for the implementation of Native Administration in a form similar to the Northern Nigerian system introduced in 1910. The new chiefdoms were territorially based and led by chiefs, rather than organised according to land priest parishes. Colonial officials believed that they had assigned the boundaries on the basis of tribe, which by the 1930s meant "a descent-based community with a common language and culture."[75] In reality, however, ethnic labels were applied *post-facto*, according to the personal networks controlled by the head chiefs based on the chiefs' lists developed before the 1930s.[76] Nevertheless, the colonial government believed that it had revived authentic tribal structures. From this base, northern administrators created Native Authorities large enough to function as economic units with chiefs responsible for administration, justice, finance and land tenure management. In a familiar phrase from the *Dual Mandate*, Slater considered this system capable of making the chiefs and their Native Authorities "a living part of the machinery of Government."[77] This phrase—popular among indirect rulers of this period—referred to the process of integrating the "spirit of the people," through indigenous institutions, into the program of creating and developing Native Authorities.[78] More than this, Slater portrayed indirect rule as a "barrier against (the) undue 'Westernisation' of native institutions" designed to "harmonise native institutions and law with the natural course of historical development."[79] But what was the "natural course of historical development?" The identification of indirect rule with Lugard[80] has obscured the fact that the idea of natural African development owed as much to the Georgeist philosophy of Charles Temple and the Nigerian single-taxers. Palmer's

[75] Lentz *Ethnicity and the Making of History in Northern Ghana*, 124.

[76] Ibid., 54; Lentz, Carola, "Contested Identities: the History of Ethnicity in Northern Ghana," in *Ethnicity in Ghana: the Limits of Invention*, ed. Carola Lentz and Paul Nugent, 144 (Houndmills: Macmillan Press, 2000).

[77] Slater's emphasis. A.R. Slater, *Native Administration in the Gold Coast and Its Dependencies* (Accra: Government Printer, 1930), 3, in CO96/700/14, PRO.

[78] Cameron, 94–5.

[79] A.R. Slater, "Native Administration in the Gold Coast and its Dependencies," 4, CO96/693/2, PRO.

[80] Sir F. Lugard, *The Dual Mandate In British Tropical Africa (3rd Edition)* (Edinburgh: William Blackwood and Sons Ltd., 1926), originally published 1922.

biet-al-mal was designed to tax away ground rents in order to block the formation of a landlord class in Northern Nigeria. The Nigerian connection suggests that, apart from its necessity in light of the Geneva convention, the direct tax must be considered in light of the debate over development and landlordism. Jones hinted at this context when he emphasised the devolution of direct taxation to the Native Authorities. "In the minds of the inhabitants of this and other West African colonies," wrote Jones,

> direct taxation is bound up with the ownership of land . . . The Africans therefore conceive tribute or tax to be the equivalent of rent for the land which they occupy and any attempt by Government to act independently of the Native Authorities in the matter of taxation will be regarded by them as tantamount to a claim to the ownership of the land.[81]

Jones' assumption that taxation was the equivalent of rent suggests a Georgeist thread to the indirect rule programme in the Northern Territories. In this vision the colonial state would appropriate rents through the Native Authorities and use the latter's share for community development. This larger development context is further illustrated by the fact that indirect rule and direct taxation in the Gold Coast were accompanied by a Land and Native Rights Ordinance similar to the Northern Nigerian legislation of 1910.[82]

In the minds of its architects Native Administration provided the tools for nation building. Indirect rule was not simply about preserving African community in the interests of political legitimation and control. It was also about the *development* of community as a basis for the political development of the Gold Coast nation and the economic development of the Northern Territories' natural resources. Politically, indirect rule continued the modernisation program laid down by Duncan-Johnstone in 1918 but not acted upon until his return to the north in the 1930s. Duncan-Johnstone's activities show that, contrary to James Ferguson's argument that development was "passive" before 1945, colonial development policy in the Northern Territories actively sought to build a modern nation-state. In the minds of the northern officials, however, this would be possible only

---

[81] W.J.A. Jones, 31 September 1931, in A.R. Slater, Despatch, Confidential (B), CO96/700/14, PRO.

[82] Anne Phillips, *The Enigma of Colonialism: British Policy in West Africa* (London: James Currey, 1989), 114,123.

after African community was put on a sure footing. As such, indirect rule rested on an agrarian doctrine of development concerned with preserving the social cohesion of traditional village communities. On paper this system resembled Mamdani's notion of decentralised despotism, where rural chiefs were given powers over their subjects in the areas of administration, finance and justice. Furthermore, as a mechanism for protecting the north from the individualism that had developed in the south, indirect rule also reflected the colonial opposition between civil society and community which Mamdani says characterised the African colonial experience. As Lentz argues, the evidence from Northern Ghana challenges Mamdani's argument. Chiefs might have been decentralised despots in theory, but in reality their power was less dominant than Mamdani would have us believe. The new chiefdoms provided opportunities for subordinate groups to challenge the power of the head chiefs.[83] Colonial officials, however, certainly thought they had achieved their goals. Indeed, by 1936 it appeared as though the indirect rulers had managed to drive a wedge between the rural north and urban south, thus blocking the development of "citizenship" in the Northern Territories. Having thus established the framework of African community in the north, the colonial administration turned its attention to the quest for agricultural development.

[83] Lentz, *Ethnicity and the Making of History in Northern Ghana*, 54.

CHAPTER FIVE

OVERPOPULATION, DEPOPULATION AND THE LOSS OF PRODUCTIVE POWER: DEVELOPMENT IN THE ZUARUNGU AND LAWRA-TUMU DISTRICTS, 1935–44

Introduction

Having set the framework for indirect rule, the colonial administration turned once again to developing the agricultural resources of the Northern Territories. The core of the project remained consistent in that the administration continued to pursue Guggisberg's vision of development without denationalisation, attempting to reconcile economic growth with the preservation of African community. By this time, however, Guggisberg's focus on exports had been dropped in favour of developing the north into a supplier of foodstuffs for the growing markets in Ashanti and the Colony.[1] The plan was to make the Northern Territories self-sufficient and then gradually develop its potential to supply grains, corn and meat to the south. This project rested on two important programs of social engineering. First, colonial officials wanted to reclaim large areas of the north locked up from development by trypanosomiasis, by clearing the land of tsetse flies and resettling communities onto the cleared areas. Second, the colonial administration hoped to revolutionise agricultural production by introducing mixed farming on settled farms, replacing the traditional rotational system of shifting cultivation.

The program in the Northern Territories unfolded against the backdrop of Colonial Office concerns over colonial welfare and environmental sustainability. Uncontrolled development in the colonies was producing unemployment and environmental degradation, which triggered a wave of labour resistance in the 1930s. As Cooper notes, the Colonial Office considered the protests a problem of development rather than a labour issue. What was new, however, was not

[1] Brenda Chalfin analyses this shift admirably in *Shea Butter Republic: State Power, Global Markets and the Making of an Indigenous Economy* (New York: Routledge, 2004), 22–8.

"development" as such but rather a preoccupation with colonial welfare and an emphasis on economic and social planning. The emphasis on welfare and planning manifested itself in the Northern Territories through new programs for tsetse eradication and mixed farming. Tsetse flies would be eradicated from infested regions of arable land, communities would be resettled from overpopulated areas where farming systems had collapsed, and farmers would be encouraged to increase their productivity and sustainability through mixed farming. The shell of indirect rule would guard against the development of capitalist agriculture—thus avoiding the experience of the south—and economic development would be made consistent with the preservation of African community.

Development and "Corruption" in the 1930s

Mixed farming and tsetse eradication in the Northern Territories emerged in response to the negative consequences of development in the south during the troubled times of the 1930s, which had produced empire-wide unemployment, producer/trader resistance to low producer prices, increasing costs of living, and the intensification of anticolonial nationalism. The protests of the 1930s occurred as colonial working populations reacted against the slow pace of the recovery from the Depression between 1930 and 1935. African resistance triggered a period of "reforming imperialism" between 1935 and 1940.[2] This approach began in earnest in mid-1938 when Malcolm MacDonald succeeded Ormsby-Gore as Colonial Secretary of State and began reworking the 1929 Colonial Development Act. In 1939, MacDonald announced a new Colonial Development and Welfare Act, effective from 1940, which provided up to £5 million per year for new programs in the colonies. The revised Act sought to attack colonial welfare concerns through economic and social planning.[3]

Many colonial officials emphasised the need for planning because they blamed the unrest of the 1930s on the uncontrolled development of cash cropping and capitalist agriculture, which produced

[2] Frederick Cooper, *Decolonization and African Society: The Labor Question in French and British Africa* (Cambridge: Cambridge University Press, 1996), 57,72. See also J.D. Hargreaves, *Decolonization in Africa* (London: Addison Wesley Longman Limited), 33–50.

[3] See Cooper, 65–68.

unemployment, declining living standards and malnutrition. This concern reached the highest level of the international community in 1936, when the League of Nations warned that increases in global agricultural production were producing malnutrition along with economic growth.[4] In Africa the worst case appeared to be the capitalist plantations of Kenya, where white settlers had forced the African population into subsistence-level wage labour. In West Africa, although some voices in the wilderness supported this model,[5] most colonial officials rejected it in favour of preserving the African peasantry. With the growth of cash cropping, some peasants would be expected to produce foodstuff surpluses to meet the growing demand for food in the cash crop areas. In the end, everyone would benefit from "the raising of the economic level of the general mass of the population", and the peasantry would be preserved.[6]

As the case of cocoa had shown, however, capitalist relations could and did creep into peasant production as well as plantation agriculture. Whereas E.D. Morel had praised the peasant basis of cocoa production in the early twentieth century, colonial officials in the 1920s and 1930s held its capitalist character responsible for unemployment, malnutrition, disease, deforestation and political protest. In a seminal study in 1926, Allen McPhee argued that the West African colonial states had a duty to intervene directly in African agricultural production, in order to "deal with native capitalists as they arise, as they will desire to oust the State from the control of industry."[7] Five years later, in the wake of the Great Depression, northern Provincial Commissioner A.W. Cardinall wrote that the rapid pace of economic progress in the south was "dangerous." Cocoa production had ushered in a "revolution" which triggered the growth of private property, absentee landlordism, and the rise of exploitative middlemen. According to Cardinall, "fresh problems of the gravest nature, such as preservation of forests, slum conditions, unemployed, spread of disease, transport and shipment, and a people

[4] See F.L. McDougall, confidential paper, sent to G.L.M. Clauson at the Colonial Office, 9 November 1935; C.G. Eastwood to F. Ashton-Gwatkin, 21 January 1936, CO852/19/14, PRO.

[5] Most notably Bourdillion of Nigeria. M.P. Cowen and R.W. Shenton, *Doctrines of Development* (London: Routledge, 1996), 294–5.

[6] Gold Coast, *Medical Department Annual Report, 1935* (Accra: Government Printer, 1936), 5.

[7] Allen McPhee, *The Economic Revolution in West Africa* (London: Frank Cass and Company, 1926), 280–1.

which has learnt to gallop before it could crawl have been set for Government to solve."[8] The Nowell Commission on the marketing of Gold Coast cocoa echoed Cardinall's fear of deforestation and extended it to cocoa growing areas themselves, arguing that the unregulated and uncontrolled clearing of forests for foodstuffs and cocoa had produced erosion on a scale which threatened the very crops being planted.[9] In 1941 Fabian Colonial Bureau Secretary Rita Hinden joined the chorus of concerned voices when she argued that the uncontrolled development of cocoa production as a migrant labour system produced workers dependent on buying food and absentee landlords unconcerned with environmental damage. To make matters worse, the privatisation of land attracted moneylenders who gained control over farms as landlords defaulted on loans after using the money for "unproductive" activities such as weddings and funerals. Unchecked by the British, the very "beneficence of nature", Hinden argued, produced an economic system which benefited indigenous middlemen (cocoa brokers) and moneylenders (often the same people) at the expense of the peasant producers, food production and capital formation.[10]

Environmental degradation was not the only concern facing the colonial state. By the mid-1930s the indigenous cocoa brokers also posed a formidable economic threat to the European firms active in the cocoa trade[11] as well as a major political threat to the colonial administration. The brokers had gained power after a slump in 1920–1 wiped out many of the producer/traders and producer associations who previously had dealt directly with the cocoa buying firms. Non-producing cocoa brokers profited by charging a commission per load and often adding an additional general commission for services rendered to the firms. In 1936–7, a sharp increase in the world cocoa price triggered intense competition between the European firms for cocoa purchases in the Gold Coast. The brokers took advantage of the competition to demand higher commissions, to the point where some firms complained that, in some cases, the

[8] A.W. Cardinall, *The Gold Coast, 1931* (Accra: Government Printer, 1931), 75, 84.

[9] Great Britain, *Report of the Commission on the Marketing of West African Cocoa* (London, HMSO, Cmd.5845, 1938), 25. Henceforth cited as the Nowell Report.

[10] Rita Hinden, *Plan for Africa* (London: George Allen and Unwin Ltd., 1941), 119–24, 161.

[11] J. Milburn, "The 1938 Gold Coast Cocoa Crisis: British Business and the Colonial Office," *African Historical Studies* 3, No. 1 (1970): 57.

producer price in the Gold Coast equalled the world selling price. In response, the major European firms co-operated in 1937 to draft an agreement to set prices and limit purchases in the Gold Coast and Nigeria. Through this monopoly on marketing, the European firms sought to reduce the costs which had spiralled upwards under conditions of free competition. As it happened, the firms implemented the agreement just as the world cocoa price plummeted. Cocoa producers in the Gold Coast blamed the drop in prices on the firms' agreement and reacted by holding up the cocoa crops. Many of the chiefs, being cocoa farmers themselves, supported the farmers. Faced with a direct attack on their profits, the cocoa brokers joined the hold-up and guaranteed its success over an entire season.[12]

The success of the hold-up prompted a Royal Commission into the marketing system of West African cocoa under the chairmanship of William Nowell. The Nowell Report noted the significant changes that had accompanied the rapid development of the Gold Coast cocoa industry, including an increased demand for imported foodstuffs, a growing need for wage labourers, and the development of land sales. The commercialisation of agriculture had opened the door for cocoa brokers to move in as middlemen and moneylenders, securing pledges of land in return for advances to cocoa farmers. Widespread indebtedness developed and the brokers gained control over crops and land. On the other end, the Commission noted the power exerted by the brokers over the European firms, as well as the attempt by the firms to suppress free competition in order to reduce the cost of buying cocoa in the Gold Coast. In drafting its recommendations the Commission sought a marketing structure that would satisfy the European firms and the peasant producers by strengthening the position of the producers against the brokers and the European firms, by promoting free competition in cocoa buying and by reducing the costs of marketing the crops. The only solution would be to establish a statutory farmers' association to bring all producers of a commodity such as cocoa under a single, state-controlled marketing system. These recommendations, pre-empted by the outbreak of World War Two, were designed to eliminate the middlemen and guarantee stable producer prices.[13]

---

[12] Ibid., 59, 61; Roger J. Southall, "Farmers, Traders and Brokers in the Gold Coast Cocoa Economy," *Canadian Journal of African Studies* 12, No. 2 (1978): 188, 209.

[13] Nowell Report, 16, 20–3, 149, 152, 157. Jan-Georg Deutsch, *Educating the Middlemen: A Political and Economic History of Statutory Cocoa Marketing in Nigeria, 1936–1947*

In Rita Hinden's opinion, the transformation of peasant production addressed by the Nowell Commission had produced numerous political, economic and environmental problems in the Gold Coast. The appearance of a class of "youngmen,"—non-chiefly, capitalist[14] cocoa farmers—as well as brokers produced a new political threat, especially when post-1930 conditions pushed the youngmen and brokers into an alliance with the chiefs and elite. Despite periodic declines in cocoa prices, producers steadily increased production. As farmers put more land under cocoa, levels of food production fell and the population became more reliant on food imports. The increase in production, however, failed to compensate for the declining cocoa prices (especially in the late 1930s); meanwhile, the price of imported food rose dramatically. In the face of rising inflation and stagnating real wages, this trend reduced living standards, produced malnutrition and fed into producer/trader resistance to the colonial state.[15] The political threat of produce hold-ups translated into a serious economic threat, because hold-ups threatened to reduce state revenues already suffering from falling cocoa prices. To make matters worse, the state's transport revenues also plummeted as farmers and middlemen switched from using the state's railways to the cheaper method of road transport.[16]

In the context of these developments, the Northern Territories moved into the spotlight as a potential supplier of grain and livestock to the food-starved cocoa belts. In 1936, Medical Director Duff expressed the consensus when he advocated mixed farming in the north to produce grain and groundnuts for both local consumption—needed to feed local communities and returning migrant workers—and sale to the Colony and Ashanti.[17] Duff's recommendations received

(Berlin: Das Arabische Buch, 1995), 111. Rod Alence, "Colonial Government, Social Conflict and State Involvement in Africa's Open Economies: The Origins of the Ghana Cocoa Marketing Board, 1939–46," *Journal of African History* 42 (2001): 402.

[14] On the development of capitalism in the cocoa areas, see Polly Hill's important studies, *The Gold Coast Cocoa Farmer: A Preliminary Survey* (London: Oxford University Press, 1956), and *The Migrant Cocoa-Farmers of Southern Ghana: A Study in Rural Capitalism* (Cambridge: Cambridge University Press, 1963). For an excellent recent study, see Gareth Austin, *Labour, Land and Capital in Ghana: From Slavery to Free Labour in Asante, 1907–1956* (Rochester: University of Rochester Press, 2005).

[15] Hinden, 161.

[16] Jonathan H. Frimpong-Ansah, *The Vampire State in Africa: The Political Economy of Decline in Ghana* (London: James Currey, 1991), 28.

[17] Director of Medical Services, Report, 20 December 1936, Enclosure in Gold Coast #760, CO852/59/5, PRO.

the support of the newly formed Gold Coast inter-departmental Standing Committee on Human Nutrition. In 1937 the Committee appointed a research officer, Dr. F.M. Purcell, who advocated mixed farming and livestock development to combat seasonal food shortages, vitamin A deficiencies and low meat consumption in the far north. In response to Purcell's report the Nutrition Committee recommended surveys on local foodstuffs and nutrition, the implementation of mixed farming and the development of the livestock industry.[18]

In developing these industries, however, the colonial administration did not want to undermine the African peasantry. In a plea to protect the peasants, Cardinall concluded his 1931 report with these words:

> The Gold Coast peasant farmer if he is to survive must remember and be taught always to remember that the crops which produce small but certain profits are those on which his existence depends, since they do not draw upon him the envious eye of the usurer or the greedy one of the capitalist.[19]

The development of smallholder agriculture could also, in McPhee's words, protect the peasantry against "the sudden uprooting of immemorial native customs and institutions."[20] Indirect rule provided an ideal model for such a project. Now that "the political framework of the Northern Territories" was "firmly based," wrote Colonial Secretary Gerald Creasy in 1936, the Gold Coast could begin to tackle the problems of sleeping sickness, mixed farming and the development of a livestock industry.[21] Delivered through indirect rule, colonial officials believed that foodstuff production in the north could be developed in a sustainable manner, while preserving the rule of the chiefs and guarding against the development of agrarian capitalism.

Development in North Mamprusi: Overpopulation and Mixed Farming, 1936–1940

The most important colonial development policy at this time was mixed farming, which focused initially on the densely populated areas

[18] K. David Patterson, *Health In Colonial Ghana: Disease, Medicine and Socio-Economic Change, 1900–1955* (Waltham: Crossroads Press, 1981), 98–99.

[19] Cardinall, 99.

[20] McPhee, 280.

[21] Sir G. Creasy, 22 November 1936, CO96/732/5, PRO. For notes on Creasy's 1935 visit to the Gold Coast, see CO96/722/15, PRO.

around Zuarungu in the North Mamprusi District. Having discovered agricultural collapse among the Talensi in 1932, the Gold Coast government posted a young agricultural officer, Charles Lynn, to Zuarungu to create a plan for the development of agriculture.[22] Lynn arrived in North Mamprusi to find a dense population practising fixed cultivation on a small area of land around the Tong Hills.[23] It appeared that population pressure, fixed cultivation and the absence of manuring had produced erosion and reduced the soil to a "basic minimum" level of fertility. Recurrent food shortages increased the population's susceptibility to disease, especially at the end of the dry season when they needed their strength to make their farms. Physical weakness fed into the decline of farming and produced a "vicious circle" of agricultural deterioration.[24] The Medical Department agreed with Lynn's assessment, reporting in 1935–6 that population pressure had reduced the peoples' ability to farm and left them in a "miserably under-nourished condition."[25]

Lynn discovered, however, that the under-nourished population was concentrated on only one-fifth of the land in the Zuarungu District, which turned him away from a purely demographic explanation of the collapse of agriculture in Zuarungu.[26] Instead, what appeared as a population-driven crisis of underproduction was in reality a social and cultural problem produced by historical forces. Lynn suggested that the slave raids of Samory and Babatu, combined with the subsequent invasion of tsetse flies into bush areas, had driven the farming populations into refuge in the less fertile Tong Hills. Arising out of this period of chaos, the custom of ancestor worship developed around the Tong Hills shrine. The power of sacred shrines like Tongnaab anchored the people to the land and produced "conservatism" and "apathy" towards improving farming methods or leaving the ancestral area to search out new farmland.

[22] C.W. Lynn, *Agriculture In North Mamprusi* (Gold Coast: Department of Agriculture, Bulletin #34, 1937), 3.

[23] Despite the dubiousness of the idea of carrying capacity, such high population densities certainly could have been problematic. See Keith Hart, "The Economic Basis of Talensi Social History in the Early Twentieth Century," in *Research in Economic Anthropology: Volume One*, ed. George Dalton, 194 (Greenwich: IAI Press, 1978).

[24] Lynn, *Agriculture In North Mamprusi*, 11,37.

[25] *Medical Department Annual Report, 1935* (Accra: Government Printer, 1936), 5.

[26] Gold Coast, *Department of Agriculture Annual Report, 1935–36* (Accra: Government Printer) 7. Lynn, *Agriculture in North Mamprusi*, 7.

In Lynn's words, the reliance on custom had "resulted in a system of farming which demands the minimum amount of labour from the farmer, and leaves the maximum to Nature; for Nature, in the shape of 'fetish', can be placated by the simple expedient of sacrifice." More importantly, the inertia of culture meant that custom was not adapting quickly enough in the face of environmental and economic change. Without the capacity to change, customary farming practices were losing the battle with ecological and economic forces.[27] As a result, the crowded areas around the Tong Hills suffered from land shortage, overgrazing and food insecurity.[28]

Acting on Lynn's advice the Chief Commissioner opened an agricultural station at Zuarangu to sponsor experiments into improving agriculture in the North Mamprusi District.[29] Based at the new station, Lynn began a series of experiments, drawing on the standard British model of the time for developing West African agriculture. The model took indigenous peasant techniques as its starting point. According to Agricultural Officer J.E. Symond, writing in 1932,

> (p)erhaps the most important lesson to be learnt from the experience available is that an agricultural policy which takes the local farmer as its starting point . . . is more likely to achieve success than a policy which starts with European ideals upon an expensive experiment station . . . It is only by a detailed knowledge of the farmer and his needs that results from experiments can be 'geared in' to local farming practices.[30]

From this base, agricultural officers attempted to apply scientific methods to local practices in order improve the productivity of peasant farming. According to a 1935 report on agricultural education, it was

> obvious that in these days of scientific farming and marketing it is essential that there should be farmers who have been educated to adopt the most modern methods of feeding the soil and of preventing its

[27] Ibid., 9–11, 35.

[28] P.M. Worsley, "The Kinship System of the Talensi: A Revaluation," *Journal of the Royal Anthropological Institute of Great Britain and Ireland* 86 (1956): 46.

[29] W. Collins, "Extension Work In Kusasi, 1932–1959," *The Ghana Farmer* 4, No. 2 (May, 1960): 64. R.B. Bening, "Colonial Development Policy In Northern Ghana, 1898–1950," *Bulletin of the Ghana Geographical Association* 17 (1975): 73.

[30] J.E. Symond, "Agriculture in the Northern Territories," quoted in R.B. Bening, "Land Tenure System and Traditional Agriculture of the Sissala," *Bulletin of the Ghana Geographical Association*, 18 (1976): 31.

> erosion, to combat diseases, and to sow, cultivate, pack and market on scientific and economic lines.[31]

Because of the novelty of "scientific" agriculture, the colonial state assumed firm control over its application to West African farming systems. In the spirit of trusteeship the application of science to peasant farming thus sought to fulfil Lugard's *Dual Mandate.* Increased peasant productivity would produce surpluses for southern markets, while farming systems would be carefully tailored to facilitate "the material and moral advancement" of the producers themselves. This "advancement" was not to be forced on the farmers. Instead, in the formulation of the influential Nigerian agriculturists O.T. Faulkner and J.R. Mackie, the improvement in peasant productivity through mixed farming was to be achieved through a careful, threefold process of experimentation, demonstration and extension.[32]

Between 1934 and 1936 Lynn conducted experiments with mixed farming in the Northern Territories along the lines developed by Faulkner and Mackie. Lynn's early work began on two farm plots near Zuarungu, then spread to farm sites in Navrongo, Bawku and Builsa which were opened in 1935 on the recommendation of Colonial Agricultural Advisor Sir Frank Stockdale.[33] On the experimental farms Lynn attempted to absorb indigenous techniques into the system of mixed farming. The goal was to enable single farmers to achieve sustainable cultivation on ten acre plots by using bullocks to draw ploughs and produce fertiliser.[34] A visit to Northern Nigeria convinced Lynn of the feasibility of this program. In Nigeria Lynn observed that a man with two bullocks could work enough land to produce subsistence for his family as well as "a handsome balance as recompense for his industry and as a return for the extra farming capital invested."[35]

After returning from Nigeria Lynn produced a program of mixed farming designed to "anticipate agricultural expansion to be in a

[31] Gold Coast, *Scheme for Higher Agricultural Education and Development of the Fishing Industry, 1935*, 1, CO96/724/18, PRO.

[32] O.T. Faulkner and J.R. Mackie, *West African Agriculture.* Cambridge: Cambridge University Press, 1933, 3–5, 77–8.

[33] S. Anyane, *Ghana Agriculture* (London: Oxford University Press, 1963), 86, 95.

[34] B.G. Der, "Agricultural Policy in Northern Ghana During the Colonial Era," *Universitas (New Series)* 8 (1979): 7.

[35] C.W. Lynn, *Report On A Visit To Northern Nigeria To Study Mixed Farming* (Accra: Department of Agriculture, Gold Coast, Bulletin #33, 1936), 2–3.

position to control its development."[36] Lynn's program called on the colonial state to develop the Northern Territories into a supplier of livestock and food to the Colony and Ashanti.[37] According to Lynn, it was "probably wiser to abandon for some years any attempt to make the Northern Province a producer of export crops, and to use every effort towards making them the suppliers of livestock and food for Ashanti and the Colony."[38] Given the lack of capital in the north, foodstuff production would have to be developed first in order to raise the surpluses needed for the eventual development of a livestock industry.[39] In Lynn's words, he would strive for "an increase of food supply per acre and per family by means of cattle-manure, quicker and more efficient methods of cultivation by the use of cattle-drawn implements, the use of sound rotations including green manures, and the improvement of the types of food crops employed."[40]

As more grain was produced food prices would fall, surpluses would be produced, and even the poorest farmers would be able to buy grain during famine periods. Where farmers had to buy grain they would be able to do so locally, since local grain production in North Mamprusi would replace imports from the Bawku District and the south. In the long run farmers would be able to invest surpluses into livestock production. The Agricultural Department summarised the entire process quite succinctly:

> The Department's trials (in North Mamprusi) are now aimed at a system whereby farmers might with bullocks and small ploughs cultivate an area of some ten acres as against the two or three at present hand-cultivated, maintain fertility on the area by the use of cattle manure, and feed the food-crops surplus to domestic requirements to stock bred especially for sale.[41]

By the time the North Mamprusi market became saturated, the producers would have been taught how to feed surplus grain to their livestock and rural development would be set in motion.[42] Livestock

[36] Ibid., 11.

[37] C.W. Lynn, 17 November 1932, quoted in Gold Coast, *Department of Agriculture Annual Report, 1932–33* (Accra: Government Printer, 1933), 12.

[38] C.W. Lynn, "Report on Zuarungu," *Gold Coast Farmer*, 1, No. 7 (1932): 112.

[39] Lynn, *Agriculture In North Mamprusi*, 11, 57.

[40] Ibid., 12.

[41] Gold Coast, *Department of Agriculture Annual Report, 1935–36* (Accra: Government Printer, 1936), 7.

[42] Lynn, *Agriculture In North Mamprusi*, 56.

exports would then be able to compete with French supplies, which at the time of Lynn's report significantly exceeded exports of livestock in the Northern Territories.[43]

Lynn's project rested on the belief that economic growth had proceeded far enough in the north to trigger a transition from "farming as a custom" to "farming as a business." That is, Lynn believed that agriculture in the north had become sufficiently commoditised to support a program of mixed farming. Most notably, at the time of Lynn's report (1937) local markets existed for the sale of surplus grain and small livestock. Farmers and traders imported grain "in large quantities" from Bawku and South Mamprusi, much of which was stockpiled in Bolgatanga sold during dry season shortages for 14s to 18s per 180 pound sack.[44] The growth of markets, argued Lynn and the Department of Agriculture, had triggered a rise in "money consciousness."[45] In Lynn's opinion, this development provoked a cultural shift away from submission to nature (through religious cults) towards control over nature. Agricultural policy thus should provide a "stimulus for development", in the form of producer prices and transportation, strong enough to complete this transition. Lynn did not believe that past failures to innovate necessarily precluded the possibility of future progress; he simply noted that the farmers lacked "sufficient incentive" for moving into new land and breaking new bush to develop better farms.[46]

Confident in the farmers' potential, Lynn proposed to create demonstration farms within the framework of indirect rule. Farm sites would be located on Native Authority land (including school land) and special sections of the Native Authorities would be created to focus on the development of mixed farming. Managed by the Native Authorities, the demonstration farms would be led by chiefs, headmen and school authorities.[47] The transformation of agriculture under this system would be slow but sure, as the people adjusted to the idea of farming "as a business" under the structure of indirect rule.

Lynn's programme of mixed farming was twinned with an emphasis on combating soil erosion. In a familiar colonial trope, the Gold

---

[43] Gold Coast, *Department of Agriculture Annual Report, 1935–36*, 7.
[44] Lynn, *Agriculture in North Mamprusi*, 56.
[45] Gold Coast, *Department of Agriculture Annual Report, 1934–35* (Accra; Government Printer, 1935), 13.
[46] Lynn, *Agriculture in North Mamprusi*, 56–8.
[47] Ibid., 58.

Coast laid most of the blame for erosion on shifting cultivation. Writing in 1940, for instance, Agricultural Officer Arthur Jones noted the accelerated erosion caused by the "indiscriminate" bush clearing for farms.[48] However, Jones also argued that fixed farming, practised without terracing or ploughing along the contour, produced sheet erosion as soil was washed away down unprotected slopes. Gully erosion followed sheet erosion as excess storm water, unabsorbed in the absence of vegetation, moved downhill and created rivulets which widened every time it rained. These problems were worsened by wind erosion, which Jones also attributed to local practices of "indiscriminate farming" and overgrazing. To combat these problems Jones recommended afforestation, terracing, contour ridging, strip farming along slopes, and maintaining a high humus content in farming soils.[49]

Mixed farming promised to solve these environmental problems as well as raising the productivity of agriculture in the Northern Territories. The use of bullocks would permit peasants to cultivate larger acreages as well as supply manure to fertilise the land and guard against soil erosion. In addition, conservation techniques such as terracing and contour ridging would protect the north against the forces of erosion and the appearance of the dust bowl on African soil. Once food security was established under sustainable conditions, cash crops could be grown in order to provide the surpluses necessary to capitalise the development of a livestock industry. The welfare problem of the overcrowded areas would be solved, productive power would be increased and the north would provide the foodstuffs and meat supplies necessary to combat deteriorating conditions—and political resistance—in the south.

As we shall discover below, the Gold Coast absorbed Lynn's programme, aimed at the "overpopulated" area of North Mamprusi, into its development doctrine for the Northern Territories between 1940 and 1944. Before discussing the implementation of mixed farming, however, we shall turn to the colonial state's efforts to reclaim, repopulate and develop the "depopulated" areas of the northwest.

[48] Arthur Jones, "Notes On Soil Erosion," typescript, n.d., 1. Mss.Afr.s.979: Arthur Jones Papers, Oxford University, Rhodes House Library (RHL).

[49] Jones, "Notes on Soil Erosion," 1–2.

Tsetse Eradication, Resettlement and Development in Lawra-Tumu, 1937–1945

In contrast to Zuarungu, the administration of Lawra-Tumu attributed the collapse of agriculture to historical forces which produced *depopulation*. Touring the Tumu District in 1940 District Commissioner Humphrey Amherst discovered the "depressing sight" of the village of Jeffisi, once famous for iron smelting but now littered with deserted compounds and a "tumble down mosque."[50] Jeffisi was not alone in its plight. Amherst found deserted settlements along the entire Kulpawn river valley, where villages seemed to be losing the battle against some of the thickest wild bush in the Northern Territories.[51] Nor was the problem confined entirely to Tumu. In 1937 Government Entomologist K.R.S. Morris,[52] noted a similar situation along the valley of the Kamba river, a tributary of the Black Volta which drained six hundred square miles of the Lawra District.[53]

Further investigations requested by Amherst confirmed population declines in the affected areas of between eight and one hundred per cent between 1931 and 1942. The Zini area, which had been surveyed for trypanosomiasis in 1938, 1939 and 1940, seemed particularly devastated.[54] According to Medical Officer Mark Hughes, this trend continued in Tumu well into 1947/8, where at least six villages between the Sissili river and Haute Volta, ten miles west of the heavily populated Navrongo area, had disappeared since 1907. The surviving population had been reduced to settlements of a few scattered huts barely able to fight off wild game and insect-borne disease, especially trypanosomiasis. Hughes focused on a surviving village, Vare, which had been reduced to thirty people living in five scattered compounds. Few people were old enough to remember the slave raiding era, and the headman was a boy of ten. Wild game grazed untouched among numerous belts of uncultivated bush around compounds and between Vare and the neighbouring village. A few

[50] William Humphrey Amherst, 11 January 1940, 26 January 1940, Mss.Afr.1207, Amherst District Diaries, Gold Coast, RHL.

[51] Amherst, 16 January 1940, Mss.Afr.1207, Amherst District Diaries, Gold Coast, RHL.

[52] London (Governor's Deputy) to Ormsby-Gore, 28 May 1937, CO96/741/8, PRO. A.O. Stanton, 11 November 1935, CO96/723/7, PRO.

[53] Amherst, 7 January 1940; NRG 3/13/21, NAGT. K.R.S. Morris, The Eradication of Sleeping Sickness, manuscript, n.d., 1, 3, RHL.

[54] Amherst, 21 January 1944, NRG 3/13/31.

people fished, wrote Hughes, but no-one had the energy to hunt the big game or the birds which ate the few crops under cultivation.[55] The people of the river valleys, it seemed, had lost their battle with the forces of nature, and most of the blame was placed on the spread of tsetse flies and trypanosomiasis.

The East African Debate

The spread of trypanosomiasis has been debated at length in the context of East Africa. The debate hinges on the work of Helge Kjekshus, whose argument revolves around the extent to which colonialism in Tanganyika undermined local peoples' abilities to subdue and control the forces of nature.[56] Kjekshus argues that ecological disasters incidental to colonialism—especially "tsetse-born sleeping-sickness epidemics"—upset a precolonial "agro-horticultural prophylaxis" and triggered a wave of depopulation.[57] This process reduced the African population to a "frontier situation" which forced the people to "recommence" their battle with the environment. According to Kjekshus, tsetse-borne disease outweighed slave raiding and "inter-tribal warfare" in disrupting the East African population at the turn of the twentieth century.[58] Kjekshus' argument implies that colonial pacification campaigns benefited from the ecological breakdown on the eve of the European scramble for Africa. This interpretation rests on Kjekshus' assumption that precolonial "ecology control" depended on the complete separation of people and tsetse flies. James Giblin criticises Kjekshus for misinterpreting his major source, John Ford's *The Role of Trypanosomiasis in African Ecology*. Like Kjekshus, Ford argues that African populations sustained ecological control by protecting themselves from the tsetse fly. Unlike Kjekshus, however, Ford maintains that indigenous peoples achieved immunity from trypanosomiasis through "light infection" gained by limited but necessary contact

[55] Mark H. Hughes, "Vare: A Study In Rural Decay," Spring, 1948, Mss.Afr.s.141, RHL, 27, 29, 30.

[56] For important contributions to the debate, see H. Kjekshus, *Ecology Control and Economic Development* (London: Heinemann, 1977), James Giblin, "Trypanosomiasis Control in African History: An Evaded Issue," *Journal of African History* 31 (1990): 59–70. Luise White, "Tsetse Visions: Narratives of Blood and Bugs in Colonial Northern Rhodesia, 1931–9," *Journal of African History* 36 (1995): 219–245.

[57] Kjekshus, 181. Kjekshus borrows the term "agro-horticultural prophylaxis" from John Ford, *The Role of Trypanosomiasis in African Ecology: A Study of the Tsetse Fly Problem* (Oxford: Oxford University Press), 1971.

[58] See Kjekshus, 181–184.

with the fly.[59] Thus framed, the debate is a normative one over the best method to eliminate or control human trypanosomiasis. On the one hand, Kjekshus' argument advocates the complete separation of human and fly. In contrast, Ford argues for the continued maintenance of enough contact to provide the human population with immunity to sleeping sickness.

The history of the Northern Territories reveals that colonial officials debated this very question in the 1930s and 1940s. Behind the normative problem of tsetse eradication, therefore, lies the more fundamental question of why these debates have appeared and reappeared over the past few generations. To shed light on this issue, we must understand *why* colonial states were interested in disease eradication, and how ideas about development informed their explanations and remedies. In the case of the Northern Territories, the tsetse control issue emerged during the colonial period at a time when uncontrolled development processes threatened the state with the loss of productive power.

Depopulation in Lawra-Tumu: Explanations, 1938–1944

At first glance Tumu's depopulation mirrors the Tanganyikan case analysed by Kjekshus. More than simply a welfare problem, however, Tumu's situation represented a much wider economic problem of the loss of productive power in Lawra-Tumu and, because of the spread of disease along migrant labour routes, in the mines and cocoa farms as well.[60] On a colony-wide level, the spread of disease appeared to have intensified along newly motorised trade and migrant labour routes during the economic recovery after 1930. The growth of trade, cocoa production and mining brought increased disease in their wake. According to the Medical Department, this was an "inevitable result of development" and required state intervention if it were to be overcome.[61] It was also a political problem, because of the consequent deterioration of health conditions and the urban threat of an unsettled surplus population comprised of migrants from the affected areas.

---

[59] Giblin, "Trypanosomiasis Control," 65, 67.

[60] Gold Coast, *Medical Department Annual Report, 1934* (Accra: Government Printer, 1935), 7. *Medical Department Annual Report, 1935* (Accra: Government Printer, 1936), 4.

[61] Gold Coast, *Medical Department Annual Report, 1935*, 4.

Colonial officials believed that the depopulation of the river valleys in Lawra-Tumu was linked to overpopulation in other areas. The process of outmigration occurred because, between the slave raiding era and the slump of 1929, the people of Lawra-Tumu had lost their ability to compete with their environment. Many of the inhabitants of the valleys of the Kamba and Kulpawn rivers left the area, and the survivors moved into settlements in the headwaters which became overcrowded. Overcrowding produced overfarming, erosion and a progressive cycle of impoverishment. The few people who remained in the valleys gradually lost the battle against nature and, especially, the struggle against the tsetse fly and trypanosomiasis.

In the opinion of entomologist K.R.S. Morris, the depopulated river valleys represented potential sources of cash crops and livestock which had been locked up from development by trypanosomiasis. In order to realise this potential the valleys simply had to be cleared of the disease. Known in West Africa since the 1300s,[62] human trypanosomiasis (sleeping sickness) affected slave supplies during the Atlantic slave trade and moved steadily in a westward pattern from Nigeria to Senegal between 1914 and 1918. The Gold Coast, having escaped the worst of the earlier epidemics, experienced a surge of the disease between 1930 and 1939. In 1938 Morris wrote of a trypanosomiasis pandemic along "two fairly wide bands" of the best land in the Kamba and Kulpawn river valleys, where medical cases had tripled between 1936 and 1937.[63] Because tsetse flies preferred riverine vegetation, Morris argued, the pandemic pushed the surviving human population onto the poor soils of the uplands and headwaters. This harsh new environment produced overpopulation, over-farming, over-grazing, deforestation, erosion, malnutrition and depopulation.[64] "The shallow soil," wrote Morris of the Kamba Valley, "impoverished by overcropping and erosion, can hardly be made to yield a living to the undernourished natives, *let alone allow of any export of foodstuffs*."[65] Having produced overpopulation in the headwaters and depopulation in the valleys, wrote Morris, "the presence of the

---

[62] A king of Mali reportedly died of trypanosomiasis in the 1300s. See J. Ford, "Ideas Which Have Influenced Attempts to Solve the Problems of African Trypanosomiasis," *Social Science and Medicine* (13B) (1979): 270.

[63] Morris, "Eradication of Sleeping Sickness," 1, 3.

[64] Morris, "Fighting the Fly," manuscript, Mss.Afr.1824, KM 1/2, 4, RHL, 9.

[65] Morris, "Eradication of Sleeping Sickness," 1, 3, italics added.

Tsetse fly" meant that the "most fertile land" in the Northern Territories was "often locked up from development."[66]

Investigations between 1938 and 1944 convinced Morris and agricultural officer John Hinds that while trypanosomiasis triggered depopulation in eastern Tumu, deeper historical factors had established conditions which had made the people particularly susceptible to the disease. First of all, Babatu's slave raids "severely weakened" the local population. Left to fend for themselves after the raids, the settlements around Tumu declined below the density necessary to support shifting cultivation. Low birth rates and high mortality eliminated the required supply of communal labour and produced population densities too low to fend off wild game from remote bush farms. Incapable of moving to bush farms, the people were forced into fixed cultivation on poor land, which in the absence of cattle quickly rendered their land infertile. Production declines caused further food shortages and depopulation until entire villages disappeared.[67] The abandonment of the Tumu District station by the colonial administration in 1920 sealed the fate of the villages. In sum, a cycle of decline prompted by the slave raids of the nineteenth century, and reinforced by the neglect of the colonial administration, set the conditions for trypanosomiasis to wipe out many of the settlements in the Kamba and Kulpawn river valleys.

Depopulation in Lawra-Tumu: Remedies, 1939–1945

To reverse this trend Morris set out to rescue the Kamba and Kulpawn valleys from the forces of nature and thus rebuild the productive force of the Lawra-Tumu District. The plan would attack depopulation by eradicating trypanosomiasis and managing economic growth to make it consistent with the prevention of disease.[68] Tsetse eradication, resettlement and the development of mixed farming formed the core of the program. According to the Medical Department,

---

[66] Ibid., 2.

[67] Gold Coast, *Northern Territories Welfare Committee, First Meeting, 1944,* NRG3/13/1, NAGT, 6.

[68] Gold Coast, *Medical Department Annual Report, 1933–4* (Accra: Government Printer, 1934), 4. K.R.S. Morris and D. Saunders, "Suggestions for the Control of Human Trypanosomiasis," Appendix D to "Report of the Committee on Human Trypanosomiasis," *Gold Coast, Medical Department, Annual Report, 1935*, Appendix IV, 85.

mixed farming would eradicate tsetse flies by reclaiming riverine bush, produce better diets and eventually facilitate the development of a cattle industry.[69] After surveying the problem, Morris produced a three-year, £15,000 plan to clear the Kamba and Kulpawn valleys of tsetse flies, treat all sleeping sickness cases and resettle the cleared areas with "an active farming community" of mixed farmers supervised by the Lawra Native Authority.[70] Once the settlers achieved subsistence production, Morris advised the colonial administration to encourage the production of export crops. Having reclaimed depopulated land, the Northern Territories would be able to compete with the French for the foodstuff markets of the Colony and Ashanti.[71]

Alarmed that "a large tract of useful country has become depopulated," the Colonial Office urged the Gold Coast to act on Morris' proposal as soon as possible.[72] In 1938 the Gold Coast administration submitted a tsetse control proposal to the Colonial Development and Welfare Committee (CDWC) and, with Colonial Office support, promised to include a "special clearing and resettlement scheme" for the Kamba valley in the 1940–41 estimates.[73] Morris reacted with relief to this decision, writing that his "prodigy" was finally to become a reality, though he privately criticised the state for acting in the interests of economic growth rather than science.[74] Morris of course was correct in attributing economic motives to the colonial state, for Governor Burns wanted to keep the migrant workers healthy. At the same time, Morris' program would guard against an oversupply of migrant labourers in the south by promoting rural development in

[69] Gold Coast, *Medical Department Annual Report, 1934*, 7.

[70] "Minutes of a conference held in Sekondi on July 7th, 1938 to review the situation with regard to trypanosomiasis and to discuss future measures to combat it," 11, CO96/747/1, PRO. Morris ignited controversy by sending his plan to the Colonial Office and the CDF before presenting it to the Sekondi Conference. See London (Acting Gold Coast Governor) to MacDonald, 28 September 1938, CO96/747/1, PRO.

[71] On this issue Morris noted the "succession of lorries passing southward from French country laden with food stuffs." Morris, "Eradication of Sleeping Sickness," 2.

[72] Minute, 29 June 1938, CO96/747/1, PRO.

[73] A.J. O'Brien, 22 September 1938, CO96/747/1, PRO. Hodson to MacDonald, 19 April 1940, Gold Coast #229, CO96/767/5, PRO.

[74] Morris believed that Accra supported him because his work benefited the migrant labour supply, "and that at least touches them." The Chamber of Mines indeed applauded Morris' work. See Morris, letters to mother, 28–9 September 1939, 12/11/39, Mss.Afr.1824, KM 1/2,4, RHL.

the north. Reducing rural poverty, that is, would provide a hedge against a flood of migrants arriving in the cities and towns to form a politically volatile mass of surplus labourers. Furthermore, tsetse eradication and rural development would combat the cycle of disease and poverty in the northern villages themselves, reducing social unrest and lowering cost of welfare measures.[75] For economic and political reasons, therefore, Governor Burns supported Morris' proposal and trypanosomiasis control figured prominently in his Development Plan of 1944.[76]

With indirect rule in place, the colonial state required Morris to work on tsetse eradication through the Native Authorities. Under the supervision of Morris and the chief of Jirapa, the team worked between 1940 and 1943, surveying twenty thousand square miles and eliminating tsetse flies entirely from one hundred square miles of cleared forest. After 1943 the administration combined tsetse clearing and resettlement with efforts to concentrate the people into populations dense enough to combat insect-borne disease.[77] "Sleeping sickness concentrations," attempted previously in East Africa and the Belgian Congo, built on the assumption that human survival in tropical disease environments depended on population densities of at least twenty people per square mile.[78] In north-west this goal was to be achieved by encouraging people in underpopulated areas to settle in higher densities according to ties of "clan and land." The Chief Commissioner approved the plan in 1944, to be implemented through the Native Authorities with the support of the administration with the possibility of issuing free livestock to the newly concentrated population.[79] Amherst attained few results, and, as we shall discover in

[75] Ibid.

[76] Governor Burns included Morris' tsetse control project in the Gold Coast Development Plan, drafted to solicit funds under MacDonald's 1940 Colonial Development and Welfare Act. Gold Coast, *General Plan for Development* (Accra: Government Printer, 1944), 1–2.

[77] Gold Coast, *Northern Territories Welfare Committee Meeting, 21 January 1944*, NRG 3/13/31, NAGT.

[78] See Marinez Lyons, "From `Death Camps' to *Cordon Sanitaire*: The Development of Sleeping Sickness Policy in the Uele District of the Belgian Congo, 1903–1914," *Journal of African History* 26 (1985): 69–91. Richard D. Waller, "Tsetse Fly in Western Narok, Kenya," *Journal of African History* 31 (1990): 81–101. Kirk Arden Hoppe, "Lords of the Fly: Colonial Visions and Revisions of African Sleeping Sickness Environments on Ugandan Lake Victoria, 1906–61," *Africa* 67(1) (1997): 86–105.

[79] See Gold Coast, Northern Territories Welfare Committee Meeting, 21 January 1944, NRG 3/13/1, NAGT.

Chapter Eight, the difficulties of resettlement would reappear in a major development initiative between 1948 and 1957.

The policies of Lynn, Morris and Amherst sought to reclaim the Northern Territories in the name of development, while guarding against the problems which had appeared in the south, especially deforestation and the growth of capitalist relations in the countryside. The programmes focused on improving welfare and increasing productive power in the stateless areas by eradicating tsetse flies, resettling surplus populations and developing mixed farming. Under such a programme, British trusteeship over development would reverse the destruction caused by the slave raids and the subsequent invasion of insect-borne disease. Economic incentives would reduce the inertia to change produced by culture, itself the product of an earlier period of development.

Morris and Lynn undertook their programmes under the shadow of past periods of development, framed according to the twin intentions of increasing agricultural production and preserving African community. The influence of past ideas worked to shut out alternative explanations of depopulation and overpopulation from the colonial doctrine of development. Such alternative explanations were in the air at the time of the mixed farming and tsetse eradication programs, the most notable of which was offered by Meyer and Sonia Fortes. Their analysis and recommendations, which were not taken up by the colonial administration, provide a useful counterpoint to colonial development doctrine as it emerged in the 1940s.

An Alternative Explanation of Agricultural Problems: Meyer Fortes, Culture and Food Security

Having arrived in Zuarungu a year after Lynn, Meyer and Sonia Fortes agreed that Talensi agriculture was quite precarious, that the "margin of security" was very small and that poor seasons caused much suffering and hardship. Talensi agriculture, they wrote, was a "hazardous business" because of the unpredictability of nature. "Primitive" methods resulted in extracting "only half as much out of the land as it is capable of producing."[80] This assessment was similar to

[80] M. and S.L. Fortes, "Food in the Domestic Economy of the Talensi," *Africa* IX, No. 2 (April, 1936): 252.

the interpretation which led Lynn to recommend the model of mixed farming.

However, the Fortes' interpretation of Talensi food insecurity differed from the accepted colonial wisdom about the collapse of agriculture in the overcrowded areas of the Northern Territories. Instead of focusing on peasant farms, Meyer and Sonia Fortes based their analysis on the view from the household. From this base they gathered data on household patterns of food production, distribution and consumption. Their primary concern involved the place of food in the social structure of the Talensi, specifically the issue of seasonal food shortages at the family level. In the Fortes' words, they were interested in "the principles according to which the domestic grouping of Tale society organise and sustain the social activities customary for the production of raw foodstuffs, their reservation and their conversion into and consumption as edible food."[81] Culture was important in Talensi agrarian systems, but it worked its way into food production and consumption at the level of the household rather than the village or region.

Food security varied between households depending on their position in a process later to be dubbed the "developmental cycle," a concept that referred to differentiation between households based on the ages of families living in individual compounds. Each compound (*yir*) contained a "joint family" consisting of groups of men related by patrilineal kinship ties, who lived with their wives and children. About one-third of the *yir* contained two or more separate entrance gateways which led into self-contained dwellings containing one or more households. This "plural entrance compound" represented families at different levels of segmentation in the developmental cycle. Within these compounds the main gate was controlled by the head of the joint family (*yirdaan*). Secondary gates were inhabited by cousins or nephews in addition to the *yirdaan's* first-born son, who was prohibited by taboo from sharing a gate with his father. Household autonomy increased gradually for married men over time. Within the household, each wife maintained her own quarters (*dug*) partitioned off from the other wives and mother-in-law, where she lived with her children. This unit was the "primary family."[82]

[81] Ibid., 273.
[82] Ibid., 238–239.

In 1934 Meyer and Sonia Fortes discovered food security gaps within compounds, where, they wrote,

> Every married man is a householder, but households vary greatly in status according to their degree of social and economic differentiation within the joint family. This is determined not only by the stage of development it has reached, but also by kinship factors and by those individual and social and psychological factors which we have referred to before.[83]

The "unit of food economy" consisted of a single entrance gateway and thus usually comprised more than one household. The senior male of the gateway, junior to the *yirdaan*, stood at the head of the unit of food economy. This man controlled a section of land and organised the production, distribution and storage of food by controlling the main gateway's "granary of granaries" from which he distributed foodstuffs to the women of the primary families. The primary families had autonomy over the food supplies once they were allocated by the unit head. The women added this allocation to their own food production (mainly vegetables), over which the unit head exerted no control, and used or sold the pool of foodstuffs according to their own preferences.[84] This analysis resembled Audrey Richards' analysis of the Bemba of Northern Rhodesia, where Richards found a relationship between "matrilocal kinship groupings and household consumption and production." This form of social organisation meant that the "food preparation group" corresponded neither to the individual household nor to the "unit of consumption." Senior wives carried the responsibility for preparing food for junior wives and families. According to Richards, this form of "joint housekeeping" contributed to food security by "tying together households at different stages in the developmental cycle."[85]

A similar structure existed among the Talensi, but food insecurity affected some compounds more than others according to their position in the developmental cycle; it was "a fluctuating compromise, slowly changing. Births, deaths, marriages and their social consequences, even the mere lapse of time reflected in the growing up

---

[83] Ibid., 239.

[84] Ibid., 242.

[85] Henrietta L. Moore and Megan Vaughan, *Cutting Down Trees: Gender, Nutrition and Agricultural Change in the Northern Province of Zambia, 1890–1990* (Portsmouth: Heinemann, 1994), 62–63.

of children and the ageing of parents, bring about changes which materially affect the food economy."[86] One important change was a man's seniority within the joint family, which determined the amount of farmland a man received from the *yirdaan*. *Yirdaan* typically possessed between six and eight acres while younger men might have only two acres or less. In addition, *yirdaan* often possessed large compound farms while younger men had to rely on less fertile bush farms. Thus elders were less prone to food insecurity than young men. Labour availability also differed according to one's stage in the developmental cycle, because each unit of food economy was responsible for cultivating its own food. On average, each unit used the labour of two men and comprised 1.4 households and two primary families. By implication, younger units of food economy would fall below this average and face a bigger threat of food insecurity.[87]

Facing greater food insecurity, the "younger units of food economy" had to rely on local and regional markets to make up foodstuff shortfalls. In fact, the market was the most important source of food next to a gateway's farms. If a granary became completely empty, the head of the food unit would sell livestock to buy grain. In order to avoid this crisis, the head would cut back on food rations and each primary family would be forced to make up deficiencies on its own. In this case, the "junior householders" and women would "exploit the resources of the grain market." Those with cash would travel to South Mamprusi to buy grain, keeping some for themselves and selling the remainder in the local markets. Most often the only profit from these trips consisted of the surplus grain set aside for the primary family. Some women would cook a portion of their grain, sell it at the local markets and use the profits to buy more grain. Most women and men, however, could only afford to buy small quantities of extra grain at local markets with proceeds obtained by selling a few items in their possession (chickens, groundnuts, vegetables, shea butter, bows, et cetera). Since family units rarely shared food with each other, a family's food supply depended on the wealth of women within the unit of food economy, and their access to local and regional markets.[88]

---

[86] M. and S.L. Fortes, 240–1.
[87] Ibid., 243–246.
[88] Ibid., 246. This was the case in other British African colonies, especially those with significant migrant labour economies. See Moore and Vaughan, 58.

Poultry was central to this market-driven source of food security among Talensi households. Culturally, poultry could be bought and sold without the consent of the unit head; household members relied on its sale in order to accumulate food for their families. Furthermore, because of its importance in Talensi economy, poultry ownership provided the most concrete expression of differentiation between households and individuals.[89] Echoing this argument, Lynn also noted that many compounds in North Mamprusi exported fowls to Kumasi, either personally or through middlemen in Bolgatanga (the closest market centre). The proceeds from these sales usually went into the purchase of grain for consumption. In some cases, however, wealthier compounds resold grain bought in Kumasi at higher prices in the local markets of North Mamprusi.[90]

This work, along with Lynn's investigations, provided concrete evidence of developmental cycles and the important relationship between cash, markets and food security. In fact, the north contained a patchwork of local markets connected to each other and to the larger southern market centred in Kumasi.[91] However, the colonial administration did little to investigate household-level production and consumption, or to determine the extent to which subsistence had become commodified in the Northern Territories. In part, this omission reflected the fact colonial officials considered individual accumulation a force which undermined African community. This belief pervaded colonial thinking about African kinship and development. Writing about Northern Rhodesia, for instance, Moore and Vaughn note that

> . . . women in Kungu in the 1930s were able to obtain food provided that they had money or goods to exchange. Cash was important to the food economy, even in the early 1930s. (Anthropologist Audrey) Richards noted this, but she could not integrate it into her analysis because she regarded cash as the source of the breakdown of kinship relations. Cash and kinship were, for her, almost mutually exclusive.[92]

Colonial officials in the Gold Coast also connected the development of a cash-based economy with the breakdown of kinship. The opposite

[89] M. and S.L. Fortes, 250.
[90] Lynn, *Agriculture in North Mamprusi*, 6–11, 21–24, 33.
[91] See J.S. Eades, *Strangers and Traders: Yoruba Migrants, Markets and the State in Northern Ghana* (Edinburgh: Edinburgh University Press, 1993).
[92] Moore and Vaughan, 58.

of the breakdown of kinship was, of course, the preservation and reproduction of community. In focusing on the gradual development of mixed farming through Native Authorities, the colonial state signalled its intent to reconcile agricultural development with the preservation of African community. With the Land and Native Rights Ordinance in place in the Northern Territories, colonial officials appeared confident that peasant farmers could increase their productivity on land held communally with the chiefs as trustees.

The colonial administration committed itself to this programme with the official adoption of mixed farming in 1940, when Lynn's program of mixed farming became official policy under Agricultural Director H.B. Waters. Waters proposed the program for the Northern Territories in order to "protect," "develop" and "improve" production. In Waters' opinion, Lynn's work had demonstrated that the technique was "better than the native methods in almost every way."[93] "In savannah areas," Waters continued,

> 'mixed farming' is considered to be the best method by which local famine can be overcome, nutrition improved, soil erosion in farms prevented, soil fertility maintained and improved, and surplus food produced for sale; the adoption of 'mixed farming' is regarded as the principle [sic] means by which the lot of the farmer can be improved and a firm foundation laid on which to build a sound rural economy.[94]

After securing producers with subsistence requirements, Waters hoped that Northern Territories farmers could be developed into producers of meat, milk, butter, cheese, rice, vegetables, edible oils, beans and peas. The development process would be a slow one, based on careful investigations of indigenous farming systems so that its "good features" could be retained while improvements were incorporated "gradually and only after full investigation not only by agricultural experiment and survey but also in the light of a comprehensive examination of the psychological and social effects of the changes contemplated."[95]

---

[93] H.B. Waters, "Review of Agriculture in the Gold Coast, 1940," CO96/773/19, PRO, 1,5,6. Waters wrote his report in 1940 and published it in 1944 as "Agriculture in the Gold Coast," *Empire Journal of Experimental Agriculture* XII, No. 46 (April 1944): 83–102. See also H.B. Waters, "Notes On Agriculture In The Gold Coast, 1940, in Gordon, J. and H.B. Daniel, "Notes on Gold Coast Crops and Agriculture," typescript, Accra, August 1947, Mss.Afr.s.977, RHL, 3.

[94] Waters, "Review of Agriculture," 5–6.

[95] Ibid., 6, 28.

Building mixed farming on indigenous roots formed the core of the Agricultural Department's approach. This approach required research into indigenous agricultural practices and improvements to those systems, effective propaganda to farmers, and gradual rather than revolutionary change. Through the Native Authorities, the state would supply bullocks, ploughs, training and financing to "progressive" farmers who had demonstrated a capacity to fertilise and conserve their land.[96] Through this process, the Gold Coast administration hoped to develop the productive power of the Northern Territories and transform the Protectorate into a food secure region capable of supplying surplus foodstuffs and livestock to the Colony and Ashanti.

Conclusion

Having established indirect rule to their satisfaction, colonial officials framed a development program for the Northern Territories between 1936 and 1940. Within this program, tsetse eradication and mixed farming sought to achieve the twin intents of development, producing surpluses while preserving African community. The strategy remained consistent with preserving African community as long as production could be reconciled with indirect rule. The project focused squarely on solving southern problems by developing the north, without triggering the development of agrarian capitalism. Charles Lynn admitted that foodstuffs and meat were needed to secure subsistence in the densely populated areas, as well as to stem the growth of surplus labour and satisfy the growing demand for food in the south. In developing Lynn's recommendations, however, the colonial administration passed over his evidence—and the evidence of Meyer Fortes—that household economics and local and regional markets were central to agricultural production and subsistence in the Northern Territories. Instead, the administration attempted to develop northern agriculture through indirect rule by establishing the Native Authorities as the units of agricultural production.

The Gold Coast based its plan on a certain reading of history, which carried forward the common European trope of interrupted African evolution. From Northcott's report in 1899 to the development policies of the 1930s, colonial officials believed that the north's

---

[96] Ibid., 22.

ascent up the "steep slope of civilisation" had been disrupted by the slave raiders of the nineteenth century. As a remedy, the intentional practice of development was needed to save the Northern Territories from itself. The agrarian doctrine of development, however, dictated that economic growth had to be made consistent with African community. This necessitated an approach that would protect northern communities from the development of capitalist relations and the "individualism" that had appeared in the south.

This threat was not yet a major issue in the north, although Lynn and Fortes presented evidence suggesting that northern communities were being integrated increasingly into the market by the 1930s. Scattered throughout their work, this evidence pointed to the impact of development on women, young men, chiefs, headmen, land priests and traders. Women in poorer households relied on selling goods and buying food to make up for shortfalls in agricultural production. Chiefs and headmen received salaries after 1935 for their role in the District Administration. Land priests and chiefs built up a pilgrimage industry. Traders from food secure districts regularly sold grain in the markets of Taleland. Increasing numbers of young men migrated south for wage work and often returned with consumer goods and remittances to their families.

The development policy of the colonial state worked to prevent these trends from developing to the extent that they had done in the south. Tsetse eradication and mixed farming were framed to make economic development consistent with African community by filtering them through the Native Authorities under the framework of indirect rule. Beyond the level of discourse, these programs represented an agrarian doctrine of development invoked in response to a previous period of development which had produced unwanted effects. This doctrine centred on indirect rule and as such threatened to reinforce decentralised despotism in the countryside of the Northern Territories. As Sara Berry has pointed out, however, hegemony on a shoestring worked better on paper than in practice and indirect rule was a leaky vessel at best for containing the colonial conception of African community. As we shall see in the next chapter, the failure of indirect rule as a tool for development without denationalisation would lead to its demise after 1945.

CHAPTER SIX

QUESTIONING MIXED FARMING, TSETSE ERADICATION AND INDIRECT RULE, 1940–1949

Introduction

The period 1940–1949 witnessed a shift away from indirect rule as colonial officials concluded that it was incapable of fostering rapid and sustained economic development in the Northern Territories. On the anti-tsetse campaign, Morris complained that having to work through Native Authorities slowed the progress of his clearing and resettlement program. Mixed farming fared little better, and technical officers such as Veterinary Director J.L. Stewart questioned its usefulness as a tool for agricultural development. Reflecting on the slow progress of the mixed farms, Stewart projected that it would take several hundred years to achieve any appreciable results. Stewart's criticisms reflected growing doubts about the ability of African peasants to improve their productivity within the system of indirect rule. Expressing a different concern, the Forestry Department warned about the environmental impact of tsetse clearings and mixed farming, complaining that indirect rule made it impossible to enforce forest conservation. Beyond these concerns, indirect rule also came under fire for failing to promote and preserve African community, as chiefs and land priests used the system for political and economic gain. Several chiefs amassed large farms, while some land priests dispensed their services for a fee and licensed their shrines to businessmen and women in the Colony and Ashanti. Although their numbers were few, these "accumulating authorities" worried the colonial administration and fed into criticisms of indirect rule.

African initiatives under indirect rule demonstrate that decentralised despotism was more effective in the Northern Territories on paper than on the ground. As Berry argues, indirect rule failed to contain the forces of accumulation. It also failed to promote sustainable production or African community, both of which were central to the colonial development program in the Northern Territories. Allman and Parker provide clear evidence for Berry's argument, showing that local actors accumulated wealth by controlling religious pilgrimages to the Tongnaab shrine. A similar process occurred in the Lawra District, evidenced by the sons of the chief of Birifu who parlayed the influence of their father's shrine into economic opportunities (see Map 5). Colonial officials bristled at this kind of "individualism" and the lack of broader development in the north. As a result, by 1949 the search was on for an alternative plan. Most colonial officers accepted that this would involve more state intervention into social and economic development and that it would necessitate some sort of communal production. The gradualism of indirect rule would be replaced by co-ordinated, programmatic development programs delivered under the watchful eye of the colonial state. With this shift, terms such as "planning" and "collectivisation" began to creep into the discourse of development in the Northern Territories.

Tsetse Control and Indirect Rule

As discussed in the previous chapter, from the late 1930s Morris' tsetse control scheme formed a central plank of colonial development in the Northern Territories. Under indirect rule, Morris faced a formidable challenge in recruiting workers for bush clearing, especially because the Geneva Convention of 1930 outlawed the use of forced labour. The Convention required the commutation of communal labour into wage labour, but the colonial government could not afford to pay adequate wages to labour gangs.[1] Morris thus had to rely on persuasion, working through the Native Authorities to entice chiefs' subjects to turn out for clearing operations for very little money. In 1934, the Medical Department expressed the hopeful view that Morris would be able to recruit labour through "propaganda and example."[2] Four years later, Morris had convinced the administration that he had succeeded. At the Sekondi Trypanosomiasis Conference of 1938, W.J.A. Jones, now Secretary for Native Affairs, praised him for avoiding "friction and misunderstanding" by

[1] Duff to O'Brien, 13 April 1935, CO96/723/7, PRO. Kelburne K. Grieve, Deputy Director of the Medical Service, to Medical Director, 15 March 1935, CO96/723/7, PRO, 5–6.

[2] Ibid., 10.

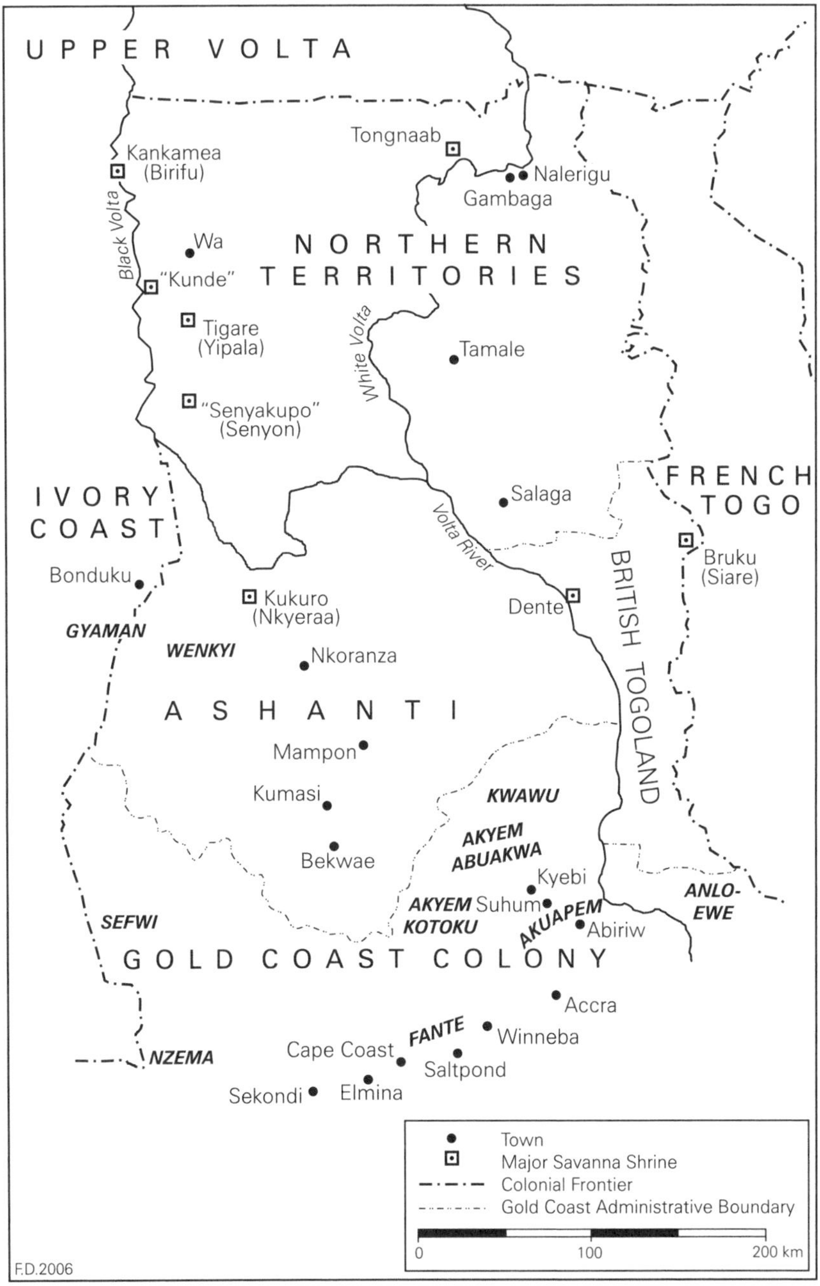

Map 5: Gold Coast, 1930, Including Religious Shrines
Source: Jean Allman and Jonathan Parker, *Tongnaab: The History of a West African God*. Bloomington: Indiana University Press, 2005.

obtaining labour through the Native Authorities instead of using direct compulsion.[3]

On the ground, however, Morris found it very difficult to recruit voluntary labour gangs. On an early clearing operation in South Mamprusi, for example, the team was hampered by "a great deal of delay in the carrying out of requests by the chiefs," despite "much persuasion by officers of the Administration."[4] This difficulty prompted Morris to change his tactics by 1938, when he admitted privately that

> these natives never know where they are and all this bloody humbug of laws and orders to protect them from exploitation and much meaningless verbiage. Given a good job of work and hit hard if they don't do it they know what to expect and remain perfectly happy. Thus we're having much success with our voluntary clearings against fly . . . The DC told the people straight out that they had to work on them, and gave the Chiefs powers to punish those who wouldn't turn out.[5]

As Morris revealed, the Chief Commissioner had empowered the chiefs to punish uncooperative "volunteers".[6] In 1940, supporting jail terms for offenders, Lawra-Tumu District Commissioner Humphrey Amherst wryly commented that "I am not sure whether this is sound native custom of collective responsibility, but I am sure it is practical!"[7] Two years later, writing of "leading by example," Amherst mused wryly that

> The salient feature of object lessons in this country . . . appears to be that they are never learnt, except bad ones such as English legal procedure, tin roof architecture, and religious intolerance. I'm not at all sure that the French method of forced agricultural improvement isn't the best.[8]

---

[3] "Minutes of a conference held in Sekondi on July 7th, 1938 to review the situation with regard to trypanosomiasis and to discuss future measures to combat it," CO96/747/1, PRO, 1.

[4] Gold Coast, *Medical Department Annual Report, 1933–34* (Accra: Government Printer, 1934), 9, 11–13.

[5] Morris, letter to parents, 10 February 1938, Mss.Afr.1824, KM 1/2, 4, RHL,. It should be said that, by the end of 1939, Morris had gained respect for his African staff, writing that his fly-boy knew more about tsetse than any Doctor on the Colony. Morris, letter to mother, 25 December 1939, Mss.Afr.1824, KM 1/2, 4, RHL.

[6] Morris, letter to parents, 10 February 1938, Mss.Afr.1824, KM 1/2, 4, RHL.

[7] At the same time, Amherst worked out a scheme for replacing communal road labour with paid gangs, but it meant closing everything other than the main roads. Humphrey Amherst, Informal Diary, 4 January 1940, Mss.Afr.1207: Humphrey Amherst District Diaries, Gold Cost, RHL.

[8] H.A. Amherst, 12 September 1942, ADM61/5/16, National Archives of Ghana, Accra (NAGA).

The Provincial Commissioner supported Amherst as long as improvements could be guaranteed.[9] The northern administration justified coercion in the interest of trusteeship, if it served the larger goals of tsetse eradication and development.[10] Stripped of the threat of force, indirect rule thus appeared incapable of delivering labour for Morris' scheme.

Beyond the labour issue, the colonial administration faced resistance from the local population over the clearings themselves, especially those that targeted sacred groves. Duncan-Johnstone encountered this problem in 1921 when, at the request of the Lawra chief, he decided not to build a dam close to the "king's pool" because it would disturb the sacred crocodile.[11] This sort of resistance continued into the 1930s. In 1938, for example, elders in the Lawra-Tumu District blamed a drought on the clearing of bush around a sacred pool. According to the elders, clearing the pool with paid labour made it a "white-man's pool" and drove away the god; subsequently, the construction of a wall around the pool blocked the god from returning.[12]

To combat this type of resistance, Amherst began to hold negotiations between the Administration and the chiefs and land priests before clearing land for tsetse control. This proved difficult, however, as Amherst found himself in the midst of complicated power structures which had emerged under indirect rule. In 1941, for instance, Amherst spoke to the chief of Jirapa about re-clearing the undergrowth around a fly-infested sacred pool near the village kraal. The land priest in question, Tobea, was a former chief whom the British previously had removed from office. Tobea had been appointed chief of Han by the Jirapa Federal Council in 1939 after declining a previous nomination because he was in line for the *tengansobship*. Shortly thereafter, the administration sacked him for refusing to cooperate with the Jirapa chief and the district administration.[13] In facing Tobea, Amherst thus confronted a disgruntled ex-chief as well as a land priest with ritual control over a shrine targeted for bush

[9] Provincial Commissioner to Amherst, 12 September 1942, ADM61/5/16, NAGA.

[10] Provincial Commissioner to Amherst, 12 September 1942, ADM61/5/16, NAGA.

[11] A.C. Duncan-Johnstone, Lawra-Tumu District Record Book, 1927–1938, ADM61/5/11, NAGA.

[12] H.A. Blair, 8 July 1938, ADM61/5/16, NAGA.

[13] Amherst, 2 February 1939, ADM61/5/16, NAGA.

clearing.[14] These kinds of histories made it difficult for Amherst and Morris now that they had to rely on the good graces of rulers who might have posed problems for the British in the past.

Beyond having to deal with uncooperative chiefs, Amherst also had to convince the chiefs' subjects of the benefits of the clearings. Once again, this was no easy task. In 1943 for example, Amherst tried unsuccessfully to persuade the inhabitants of Pudo—reduced by trypanosomiasis from forty compounds to three—to clear their sacred pools or move to another location. After the population refused to co-operate Amherst declared that "(a)s these (pools) are the chief source of trouble, and they won't fill them up, that seems to be that. I collected the entire population and went through the entire bag of tricks from Babatu's invasion to trypanosomes and malaria, and the present situation, and went on to Wuru leaving them to make up their minds."[15] The people refused Amherst's advice until the situation deteriorated sufficiently in 1944 to force them out of the settlement.[16]

Amherst's negotiations demonstrate the extent to which indirect rule complicated the implementation of development programs such as tsetse eradication. The Geneva Convention made the task even more difficult. In the absence of cash to pay the tsetse clearing gangs, voluntary labour became the only option for obtaining labour for bush clearing. Volunteers, however, rarely came forward, and chiefs failed to deliver workers through mere persuasion. Indirect rule thus frustrated Morris' scheme, and he resorted to the threat of punishment, backed up by the coercive power of the colonial state.

Coercion appeared to work. By 1947, Morris had cleared one hundred and fifty miles of the Lawra-Tumu District and reached, in his estimation, almost ninety thousand people.[17] Most notably, seventeen hundred people had resettled voluntarily into the cleared areas of the middle Kamba Valley, on fertile land along the river.[18] This success promised to produce a multiplier effect because the cleared areas were located along the trade and migrant labour routes.[19]

---

[14] Amherst, 21 June 1941, ADM61/5/16, NAGA.

[15] Amherst, 23 February 1943, ADM61/5/16, NAGA.

[16] Amherst, 22 February 1944, ADM61/5/16, NAGA.

[17] Gold Coast, *Department of Tsetse Control Annual Report, 1949* (Accra: Government Printer, 1950), 1.

[18] K.R.S. Morris, to Lawra-Tumu Land Planning Meeting, 15–16 August 1949, NRG8/5/36, NAGT.

[19] Gold Coast, *Department of Tsetse Control Annual Report, 1949*, 1.

For a permanent benefit, however, Morris believed that the cleared areas had to be carefully developed by concentrating the resettled populations into settlements of at least eight hundred people. At this concentration, roughly twenty people to the square mile, Morris argued that game tsetse (G.Morsitans) would be eradicated along with the riverine tsetse (G.palpalis and G.tachinodes) which had been eliminated by clearing. Spontaneous settlement thus had to be followed up by planned settlement to take full advantage of the gains made by 1949.[20] Lawra-Tumu District Commissioner G.N. Charles took up this advice by creating a committee to draft a resettlement scheme for seven hundred people. Charles hoped that, if the scheme were successful, it could be applied to other areas in Lawra-Tumu, which "cr(ied) aloud for planning if the people are not to die of starvation in a frighteningly short space of time."[21] Based on this vision, the administration created a Department of Tsetse Control in 1949, to secure the "complete control of sleeping sickness in the northern epidemic centres while simultaneously opening up well populated country for fuller agricultural development."[22]

Supported by the new Department, Morris established a development plan for the lower Kamba Valley, whereby settlers were offered "improved" compounds, cattle kraals, contour ridging and dams.[23] By 1950, two thousand people had resettled onto five thousand acres of farmland, encouraged by roads, dams, canoes, compounds and a pilot farm supplied by Morris' team. By 1951, tsetse control had been incorporated into resettlement schemes in other areas, including the Kulpawn river (Lawra-Tumu), Parago (South Mamprusi) and Damongo (Gonja), the latter of which was the site of a massive groundnut scheme (more of which in Chapter Eight). The resettlement schemes sought first and foremost to improve the health of the labour force. However, as Morris wrote in 1949, "incidental to this project are the benefits in health, agriculture, domestic economy, etc., to the people concerned and the demonstration that they will give to the surrounding population." Other benefits would include the growth of markets following road construction and the increased circulation of cash from the employment of tsetse

[20] Ibid., 1,4.

[21] G.N. Charles to Lawra Land Planning Meeting, 15–16 August 1949, NRG8/5/36, NAGT.

[22] Gold Coast, *Department of Tsetse Control Annual Report, 1949*, 1.

[23] Ibid.

clearing gangs. New markets would provide opportunities for the resettled farmers to sell their surplus produce, leading to further economic growth.[24] In Morris' opinion the colonial state could capitalise on these opportunities through co-ordinated programs to develop the resettled communities. In other words, a sustained process of development would depend on the replacement of the administration's piecemeal policies with a programmatic development plan.

Mixed Farming Questioned, 1940–44

Progress in mixed farming under indirect rule was even slower than the anti-tsetse program. Charles Lynn's approach to agriculture rested on a gradual process whereby individual farmers generated their own capital in small increments by establishing mixed farms. Working from the grassroots within the framework of indirect rule, Lynn envisioned his program as a slow but sure method of improving the productivity of the farmers. Between 1937 and 1951, Lynn built demonstration farms in the North Mamprusi and Lawra Districts and attempted to entice neighbouring peasant farmers to visit the sites and take up mixed farming. Considering the circumstances, the program produced good results in North Mamprusi, where the number of mixed farms increased from eighteen in 1940 to three hundred and thirty-five in 1951.[25] Progress was slower in Lawra-Tumu. In 1938, the Lawra Confederacy chiefs built a demonstration farm at the village of Dahele, which started well but faltered because of poor bullocks (which forced the farm to revert to hand labour), poor management and a remote location. It closed before the end of the year.[26] In 1940, Agricultural Officers E.R. Leach and James Broach

[24] Gold Coast, *Department of Tsetse Control Annual Report, 1950/51* (Accra: Government Printer, 1951), 2–7. K.R.S. Morris, *Fighting A Fly*. No date, Mss.Afr.1824, KM 1/2, 4, RHL, 17–18.

[25] Data from Gold Coast, *Agricultural Department Annual Report, 1940/1* (Accra: Government Printer, 1941), 5. *Agricultural Department Annual Report, 1944/5* (Accra: Government Printer, 1945), 5. *Agricultural Department Annual Report, 1947/8* (Accra: Government Printer, 1948), 11. *Agricultural Department Annual Report, 1948/9* (Accra: Government Printer, 1949), 3. See also Gold Coast, *Mamprusi District Annual Report, 1939/40* (Accra: Government Printer, 1940), 36/7, NRG8/3/91, National Archives of Ghana, Tamale (NAGT). See also B.G. Der, "Agricultural Policy In Northern Ghana During the Colonial Era," *Universitas (New Series)* 8(1979):10.

[26] A.B. Ellison, 29 December 1938, ADM61/5/16, NAGA.

built an agricultural station and a series of demonstration farms near Birifu with the permission of Chief Gandah.[27] The Agricultural Department also established farms in Wa, Nandom and Tumu, but as of 1951 there were only nineteen mixed farmers in the entire north-west.[28]

This slow pace of growth provoked criticism that mixed farming would never generate the surpluses necessary for the development of the Gold Coast. The critics, especially Fabian socialists, reserved most of their criticism for peasant production, which they considered incapable of meeting the production levels required to produce surpluses or increase African living standards.[29] "Peasant production has a romantic appeal," wrote Meyer Fortes in 1942, "and may have the political advantage of keeping the population fairly quiet. Economically it is not capable of providing a high standard of living."[30] In support of his argument, Fortes turned to Nigeria, where "at the present rate of progress it would take several hundred years for mixed farming in the style of the Department of Agriculture to become the dominant system in Northern Nigeria. Until it does become the dominant system it can't affect the general standard of living."[31] Gold Coast Veterinary Director Jock Stewart agreed, writing to the Fabian Colonial Bureau that mixed farming had been "a failure complete and absolute," producing a "life of perpetual toil and debt" for the peasant farmers.[32] "(I)n Nigeria," Stewart continued, "Lord Lugard had worked out a lovely programme whereby the African was to go from head loads to barrows then to ox-packing then to donkey carts then bullock carts then through horse gigs, phaetons and so on and about 2500 a.d. the first motor would arrive . . ."[33] In Stewart's opinion, agricultural development in West Africa could not afford to unfold so slowly.

---

[27] J. Hinds, 23 September 1943, ADM61/5/16, NAGA. J. Gandah, *Gandah Yir (House of the Brave)*. Unpublished manuscript, 143.

[28] Der, "Agricultural Policy," 11.

[29] Frederick Cooper, *Decolonization and African Society: The Labor Question in French and British Africa* (Cambridge: Cambridge University Press, 1996), 64.

[30] M. Fortes, "Comments on Mr. Cox's Notes on Plan for Africa," in letter, C.L. Cox to Rita Hinden, 2 September 1942, FCB81/1, ff7, Fabian Colonial Bureau Papers, Oxford University, Rhodes House Library (RHL), 1.

[31] Ibid., 2.

[32] J.L. Stewart to Fabian Colonial Bureau, 21 November 1945, FCB81/1, RHL.

[33] Ibid.

On a more practical level, Stewart also criticised mixed farming for conflicting with meat production, because the two activities required different breeds of cattle.[34] This conflict prompted Agricultural Director Jones to recommend a twofold cattle improvement scheme in which the Agriculture Department would develop cattle for mixed farming in the densely populated areas, while the Veterinary Department would develop cattle for the meat industry on large ranges in the uninhabited areas of the north.[35] In 1937 the Colonial Office approved the plan, convinced that a "modus operandi" had been established between the Veterinary and Agricultural Departments.[36] Stewart received permission to develop a series of Native Authority stock farms in order to supply beef cattle to the market in the south and bullocks to the mixed farmers of the north. By 1940 the Northern Territories was producing around ten thousand cattle per annum for the southern market and Stewart had allocated cattle to nineteen Native Authority stock farms.[37] Despite the withdrawal of Veterinary Officers for war duties, Stewart remained optimistic and in 1941 he reported that Native Authority cattle had caught the interest of the military, the mines and the United Africa Company. By 1943 Stewart had developed twenty-two breeding farms and eight bull farms. However, he still complained that the slow growth of mixed farming prevented the livestock scheme from meeting his expectations.[38]

Sustainability and Forest Conservation

In addition to blocking the progress of tsetse eradication and mixed farming, indirect rule also threatened to delay Governor Hodson's

[34] Observations on Nutrition, 1, Sub-Enclosure #2: Human Nutrition on the Gold Coast, CO852/59/5, PRO.

[35] J.L. Stewart, "Report on Gold Coast Cattle," Enclosure #2 in Gold Coast #70; W.J.A. Jones to Gold Coast Colonial Secretary; Auchinleck to Gold Coast Colonial Secretary, 16 January 1936, Enclosure #3 in Gold Coast #70, CO96/740/11, PRO.

[36] F.A. Stockdale, 24 May 1937; Ormsby-Gore, 14 June 1937, CO96/740/11, PRO. Gold Coast, *Veterinary Department Annual Report, 1937/38* (Accra: Government Printer, 1938), 25.

[37] Gold Coast, *Veterinary Department Annual Report, 1938/39*, 13. Gold Coast, *Department of Agriculture Annual Report, 1938/9* (Accra: Government Printer, 1939), 38, 60.

[38] Gold Coast, *Veterinary Department Annual Report, 1940/1* (Accra: Government Printer), 3, 7.

program of "active forest development in the Northern Territories."[39] Hodson's interest in forestry grew out of the threats posed by cocoa production in the south and desertification in the north.[40] The latter, according to Forest Conservator R.C. Marshall, threatened to produce "destitution and famine" in the Northern Territories.[41] In 1947, the Forestry Department announced a plan to evict 500,000 northerners for a series of forest reserves. This number included *all* of the people from the most populated and eroded area of North Mamprusi, and it brought the Forestry Department into a confrontation with the doctrine of indirect rule.[42] "The problem," Marshall had written in 1936, "is not, at bottom, a forestry problem at all. The problem is how to give forestry a chance to function . . . to put these fundamentally sound precepts into practice is, however, a very difficult question . . . the administration of the Gold Coast is no easy matter complicated as it is by the system of land tenure and the difficulties inherent in indirect rule."[43] This difficulty had been noted by Marshall's predecessor H.W. Moor in 1934, and it stretched back through the Forest Bill of 1911 to the Land Bills of 1894 and 1897. Moor argued that natural environmental problems, farming methods, land tenure and political considerations combined to complicate forest management in the Gold Coast. Making matters worse was the Gold Coast's dual system of managing forestry through both Ordinances and by-laws. Out of political considerations, argued Moor, the "stable administration" provided by the Forest Ordinance was "subordinated to an administration under defective and wholly inadequate by-laws passed by Native Authorities."[44]

Moor laid the blame squarely on the shoulders of indirect rule. "As an ideal," he said, "indirect administration is in line with general policy in West Africa. But it overlooks the fact that forestry is a technical and little understood subject, and in practice a difficult

[39] A. Hodson to Ormsby-Gore, Gold Coast #745 of 13 November 1937, CO96/735/2, PRO.

[40] H.W. Moor, *Report on Gold Coast Forests* (Accra: Government Printer, 1934), 3, CO96/715/8, PRO.

[41] Captain R.C. Marshall, *Report on the Gold Coast Forest Problem* (Accra: Government Printer, 1936), 32, in CO96/735/2, PRO. See also London (Acting Governor) to Malcolm MacDonald, 22 November 1935, in Gold Coast #591, CO96/721/6, PRO, Marshall, 20 May 1935, Gold Coast #591, CO96/721/6, PRO.

[42] Gold Coast, *Forestry Department Annual Report, 1947–8* (Accra: Government Printer, 1948), 4.

[43] Marshall, *Report*, 15.

[44] Moor, *Report on Gold Coast Forests*, 1.

problem has been created and, in existing circumstances, the Chiefs placed in an invidious position."[45] Marshall extended Moor's argument by criticising Guggisberg's policy of administering forest reserves in the south through the chiefs:

> As things stand it is a case of putting the cart before the horse. Trustees should manage an estate for heirs until such heirs become of age and the estate can safely be handed over to their management. Minors should not be allowed to ruin an inheritance through lack of understanding.[46]

In short, Government had a duty to supervise forest conservation until the chiefs were capable of administering it themselves. By-laws were insufficient, because they did nothing to protect reserve land from being sold by chiefs. The problem could be overcome only if an adequate policy were clearly defined and sufficient African and European staff put in place, supported by "a very firm hand by Government."[47] In 1937, Marshall still believed that by-laws could be retained, if they were supplemented by a Forestry Ordinance that could be applied if chiefs failed to enforce them.[48] By 1947, however, he had lost faith in the Native Authorities and recommended the forced removal noted above.[49] Once again, indirect rule proved incapable of providing the state with enough control to achieve its development vision for the Northern Territories.

Indirect Rule, Community and Individualism

The examples of mixed farming, tsetse eradication and forest conservation highlight the inadequacy of indirect rule as a framework for the productionist side of the colonial doctrine of development in the Northern Territories. On the other side of the development equation, indirect rule also failed to regenerate and preserve African community. If Stewart and Fortes criticised mixed farming for its lack of progress, Colonial Office experts feared the individualist implica-

[45] Ibid.
[46] Marshall, *Report*, 28.
[47] Ibid., 29.
[48] Ibid.
[49] See Minutes and Resolutions of Northern Mamprusi Forestry Conference Held at Navrongo, November 12th to 14th, 1947," NRG8/1/49, NAGT, 5. See also T.E. Hilton, "Land Planning and Resettlement in Northern Ghana," *Geography* 44 (1959): 232.

tions of its potential success. In 1936, economist Sydney Caine warned his colleagues that mixed farming might lead to profound "social changes" including "a change in the economic unit of farming, with the possible development of classes of 'farmers' and 'labourers.'"[50] The Colonial Office did not want to produce agrarian capitalism through its West African development policy. On the contrary, development was meant to guard against its appearance on West African soil. By focusing on the chiefs, Lynn's system ran the danger of transforming "family farming" into capitalist agriculture, albeit very slowly. In this sense, indirect rule threatened to undermine the African communities that the system was intended to protect.

These fears emerged during the 1930s and 1940s, when colonial officers confronted examples of individuals who appeared to undermine community by using the Native Authorities for individual accumulation. This process occurred in some cases among mixed farmers, fulfilling Sydney Caine's fears of individual accumulation through mixed farming. Individuals also accumulated wealth from Jock Stewart's communal cattle schemes. In Stewart's words, the Native Authority stock farms "stimulated local owners *of the more wealthy type* to think of making kraals for themselves and to take a greater interests in their methods of animal husbandry."[51] The wealthier local owners tended to be chiefs, who found avenues of individual accumulation within the structure of indirect rule. Their numbers might have been small, but the individual accumulators caught the attention of the colonial administration and affected the course of colonial development policy. We shall focus on two examples, one in the Lawra-Tumu District and another in Zuarungu.

The North-west

In the Lawra-Tumu District, Stewart's "owners of the more wealthy type" tended to be the Lawra Confederacy chiefs who had benefited from earlier policies of British rule. Chief Gandah of Birifu provides a case in point, having accumulated wealth through both mixed farming and animal husbandry.[52] Gandah's farm was very large,

---

[50] Sir Sydney Caine, minute, n.d., CO96/731/6, PRO.

[51] Gold Coast, *Veterinary Department Annual Report 1938/9* (Accra: Governnment Printer, 1939), 24, italics added.

[52] Several of Gandah's subjects also took up mixed farming, as did the Chief of Lawra. Gandah, *Gandah Yir*, 143.

peaking at close to eight hundred acres. In contrast, the average farm size in North Mamprusi according to Lynn was 7.98 acres per compound, or 2.49 acres per man.[53] The extent of Gandah's holdings permitted accumulation on a relatively impressive scale, which included by 1945 seventeen horses and over two hundred cows.[54] By 1947 Gandah had increased his cattle herd to five hundred and he had started to train his sons as mixed farmers. At the time of his death, Gandah's possessions included an equal number of sheep and goats.[55] Goody puts the extent of this wealth into perspective by noting that, during the period of indirect rule, the chiefs of the northwest became as wealthy as the leaders of the "older, traditional states" of Mamprusi, Dagomba and Gonja.[56] While perhaps not wealthy by European standards, Gandah nonetheless was able to use indirect rule for personal accumulation.

Chief Gandah used income from farming to diversify into trade and transport.[57] In 1949 several of Gandah's sons established a transport company, a shop and a corn mill with £2,000 of the family's capital. Market activity and opportunities for trade were not new to the Lawra District.[58] During the colonial period shops appeared in the bigger settlements, often controlled by the government, which paved the way for expatriate firms and traders from Nigeria (Yoruba) or the Colony and Ashanti.[59] The Gandah brothers tapped into this market by creating their transport company and opening shops in Lawra and Tumu. The enterprise was managed by S.W.D.K. Gandah, who had resigned from teaching primary school to travel to Obuasi, one of the south's major mining centres, for training as a driver and mechanic. Another son, who previously had worked for Chief Commissioner Tom Mead and a Lebanese trading firm, became the dri-

---

[53] Lynn, *Agriculture in North Mamprusi* (Gold Coast: Department of Agriculture, Bulletin #34, 1937), 19.

[54] Ibid., 124.

[55] Jack Goody, *Cooking, Cuisine and Class* (Cambridge: Cambridge University Press, 1982), 67.

[56] Ibid., 68.

[57] This supports Jonathan Barker's claim that farming could provide a springboard into other business activities. See *Rural Communities Under Stress* (Cambridge: Cambridge University Press, 1989).

[58] Cowries were still in use around Lawra as late as 1948. See J.H. Hinds, "A Currency Problem in the Lawra District," *The West African Review* December, 1947, 1428–30.

[59] Goody, *Cooking*, 94.

ver for the new company.[60] The Gandah Transport Company was quite successful, eventually becoming the sole shipper of goods bought in the south by the Lawra Confederacy Native Authority.[61]

Religion played an important role in the Gandahs' business fortunes. As in the Tong Hills, shrine pilgrimage in Birifu provided opportunities for accumulation by Gandah and his sons. In particular, the transport company grew out of contacts in Kumasi centred on Kwame Nti, an entrepreneur who had made a pilgrimage to Chief Gandah's shrine, *Kpengkpengbie*, in the 1920s.[62] Nti made his way to Birifu asking for spiritual help for his businesses in Kumasi. In 1932, Nti returned to Birifu and persuaded Gandah to travel south to install the shrine in Nti's home village of Kwapra, near Kumasi. It was believed that the Asantehene himself,[63] who knew of the shrine, intervened to convince the Chief Commissioner to grant Gandah a leave of absence to make the trip. Nti and his brothers soon became very wealthy, and their success prompted a "flood" of visitors from Ashanti to Birifu, including "barristers, civil servants of all ranks, headmasters and teachers, traders and drivers."[64]

Gandah benefited directly from the pilgrim traffic, receiving up to £400 for "licensing" the shrine to each pilgrim. The pilgrims also provided valuable business contacts in the south, especially for Gandah's sons. S.W.D.K. Gandah took the lead, travelling to Kumasi in the late 1940s. In 1948, the young Gandah—then a teacher at the Lawra Primary School—was granted leave to travel to Kumasi to see an eye specialist. After meeting the doctor he visited Kwapra, where he was received lavishly because of the good fortune bestowed by the shrine on the family of Kwame Nti. This initial meeting set the stage for a string of opportunities, which Gandah pursued after resigning from the Lawra School in 1948. Hoping to start a transport business, Gandah made a second trip to Kumasi to receive driving lessons from a friend of his father at the Government Transport Yard. The lessons never happened, but while in Kumasi Gandah

[60] Ibid., 49; Gandah, *Gandah Yir*, 162–74.

[61] Gandah, *Gandah Yir*, 187–8.

[62] Jack Goody had taken an interest in this phenomenon for his doctorate but only got as far as analysing funerals, published as *Death, Property and the Ancestors* (Stanford, Stanford University Press, 1962). See also Jack Goody, *The Expansive Moment: Anthropology in Britain and Africa, 1918–1970* (Cambridge: Cambridge University Press, 1995), 124.

[63] The paramount chief of Asante.

[64] Gandah, *Gandah Yir*, 85–90, 163–7.

met Owusu Ansah, the brother-in-law of one of Nti's brothers, who offered to teach him to drive in Obuasi where he worked as a businessman and entrepreneur. In Obuasi, Gandah managed one of Ansah's drinking spots while taking driving lessons after hours. Parlaying this experience into opportunity, Gandah eventually invested in a five-ton truck and the Gandah Transport Company was born. By late 1949, Gandah was making a healthy living from transport as well as a store and the grinding mill mentioned above. Gandah also opened a drinking spot in Tumu, where he relocated and played an important role in local and national politics between 1951 and 1957. S.W.D.K. Gandah's fortunes waxed and waned, although he eventually made his way to London where he worked as a statistician for Guiness breweries. A terrible car accident in Ghana forced him into retirement in 1982. However, with support from the British Social Services he led a productive life after the accident, writing a manuscript about his father and his own memoir before his death in 2001.[65] Although the rest of the Gandah family remains relatively poor today,[66] their experience nonetheless illustrates the opportunities for accumulation provided by indirect rule and shrine pilgrimages during the late colonial period.

The North-east

As in the north-west, shrine pilgrimages also opened the door to accumulation in the Zuarungu District. As we noted in Chapter Three, R.S. Rattray visited the Yanii Tongnaab shrine in 1928. In *The Tribes of the Ashanti Hinterland*, Rattray described the ceremony as "the most interesting and extraordinary of many curious rites which it has been my privilege to attend in the course of many years of anthropological fieldwork." Especially noteworthy were the professionals from Kumasi, Kwahu and Mampong, who consulted the shrine for help with their businesses. Many were well educated and wealthy, owning "well-furnished European houses" and cars. At the ceremony, the supplicants—including Rattray himself—stated their requests to Tongnaab, made a sacrifice and promised to return with payment if their wishes were granted. One trader asked for profits

---

[65] S.W.D.K. Gandah, *The Silent Rebel* (Accra: Sub-Saharan Publishers, 2004), 7, 128–40, 154–5, 284, Chapters 14–21.

[66] Carola Lentz, personal communication.

from his store and taxi service. Another asked for success in cocoa farming and trading. A third pilgrim who worked as a clerk simply asked Tongnaab to help him "get much money." Most of the requests were similar to these, Rattray wrote, in that "nearly everyone asked for "money" or "profit".[67]

As discussed previously, Tengol had used his power as a *kambonaaba* to develop the pilgrim trade to the Yanii Tongnaab shrine. Tengol rationalised his control over the shrine to Rattray by inventing a traditional pedigree, claiming descent from Sumri, a member of the Mamprusi ruling dynasty who had migrated from Nasia to settle at the base of the Tong Hills. Some time thereafter Sumri moved to the top of the Hills where he discovered a group of indigenous people whom Tengol called "Dagali." Sumri established himself as the ruler of the Dagali and he and his descendants intermarried with the original inhabitants. The Dagali recognised Sumri's rule by giving him the title of *golibdaana* (ruler of the drums), which conferred control over the Tong Hills shrine. Although this title did not mean "chief," Tengol told Rattray that one of Sumri's descendants, Kumalbeo, eventually travelled to Mampurugu to receive an official chieftainship from the Mamprusi dynasty. From this time until British contact, so the story went, the chiefs of Tenzugu traced their lineage to the Mamprusi Dynasty and received the Dynasty's official blessing by travelling to Mampurugu to perform the appropriate rites. In the precolonial period, therefore, Tengol claimed that his ancestors held the office of both chief and *golibdaana*. The colonial administration accepted Tengol's story when they recognised him officially as headman of Tenzugu and ruler over the Hill Talis.[68]

In providing his account to Rattray, Tengol legitimized not only his chieftaincy but also his control over the Yanii shrine and his religious status as *golibdaana*. The latter helped Tengol to capture and develop a lucrative pilgrim traffic to the Tong Hills.[69] By the mid-1930s the shrine had become famous across the Gold Coast and was attracting a steady flow of pilgrims from the Colony and Ashanti, most of whom came to ask for success in business. Tengol took advantage of the opportunity by advertising the Tong Hills shrine

---

[67] R.S. Rattray, *Tribes of the Ashanti Hinterland, Volume Two* (London: Clarendon Press, 1969, originally published, 1932, 361–5.

[68] Ibid., 342–3.

[69] Jean Allman and David Parker, *Tongnaab: The History of a West African God* (Bloomington: Indiana University Press, 2005), 101–4.

in the south and monopolising the profits. The venture made him a relatively wealthy man, investing his revenues in land, livestock and wives, and buying off supporters in order to keep the profits flowing. As we have seen, the *golibdaana's* wealth prompted resistance from the individuals and groups around Tenzugu who were shut out of the pilgrim traffic, claiming that he was exercising an illegitimate monopoly over the shrine and undermining the social cohesion of his traditional community.[70]

But was the *golibdaana's* role entirely illegitimate? Allman and Parker argue that Tengol's story reflected his mastery at manipulating British beliefs about tradition to his own advantage. In order to assess this claim, it is helpful to revisit the story of Tengol's rise to power after 1911 in more detail. Most observers, including anthropologist Meyer Fortes, would reject Tengol's claim of descent from the Mamprusi ruling dynasty, saying that he invented the story in order to receive the headmanship from the colonial administration. From Fortes' information it appears likely that Tengol did in fact invent a Mamprusi lineage to gain political power under the colonial system. While Fortes found a distinction in Talensi oral tradition between Mamprusi immigrants ("Namoos") and indigenous inhabitants ("Talis"),[71] he did not find any Namoo clans living in the Tong Hills. Instead, the Namoo clans lived in and around the settlement of Tongo, on the plains at the foot of the Hills. The Tong Hills themselves were settled exclusively by Talis ("Hill Talis"), with several Talis clans also settled on the plains in and around Tongo. Given this pattern of settlement, it appears likely that the *golibdaana* was a member of the Hill Talis rather than the Namoos, and as such his lineage would not have traced its origins to Mamprusi. Fortes' investigations indeed placed him in the Tali clan Bukiuk.[72]

From this information it is almost certain that the *golibdaana* did invent his Mamprusi origins in order to gain a level of political power he would not have possessed in the precolonial period. As headman of Tenzugu, the colonial administration gave Tengol political control over all of the Hill Talis settlements. As such he could

[70] Meyer Fortes, *The Dynamics of Clanship Among the Talensi, Being the First Part of an Analysis of the Social Structure of a Trans-Volta Tribe* (London: Oxford University Press, 1969, originally published 1945), 251–58.

[71] Meyer Fortes, "Festivals and Social Cohesion in the Hinterland of the Gold Coast," *American Anthropologist (New Series)* 38, No.4(1936), 591.

[72] Fortes, "Festivals and Social Cohesion," 591. Fortes, *Dynamics of Clanship*, 19, 21.

call up labour for public works projects, collect a tribute from all Hill residents, and judge all cases involving Tenzugu affairs.[73] This kind of power clearly was not "traditional." But as the head of a Tali clan, might the *golibdaana* still have had a legitimate claim to Tongnaab? In order to assess this question we must delve into Fortes' concepts of lineage and clan.

Fortes identified two types of lineages in Taleland, minimal and maximal. The minimal lineage consisted of the children of one father, while the maximal lineage consisted of all descendants of the male line of the earliest known patrilineal ancestor. The Talis' maximal lineages identified with five founding ancestors, Genat, Ba'at-Sakpar, Wakii, Degal and Ka'ar, who were the original *tengdaanas* at the time of Mosuor's[74] arrival in the area. Clusters of lineages made up sub-clans of the clan (the Talis as a whole). Every sub-clan therefore, was "a composite system of lineages." The clan system was very complex because each sub-clan contained members of more than one maximal lineage. There were authentic lineages (tracing direct agnatic descent from the founding ancestor of the clan), attached lineages (tracing descent through the male line of a female member of an authentic lineage) and assimilated lineages (outsiders absorbed into the clan, including slaves, pawns and refugees). A clan, in other words, was "a set of locally united lineages." At the most general level, therefore, Fortes concluded that "the clan organization as a whole consists of a series of interlocked chains of linked maximal lineages".[75]

The interlocking of maximal lineages in Hill Talis sub-clans meant that different lineages gathered together for different rituals. The rituals of the Hill Talis revolved around two distinct cults, the cult of the ancestors (External *bayar*) and the cult of the earth (*ten*). Before the first rain, the *ten* functioned as the shrine for the Sowing Festival, *Golib* or *Gologo*. At harvest time, the External *Bayar* was the focus of the Harvest Festival, *Bayaraam*.[76]

The unity of the Talis was achieved through the External Bayar, known generically as Tongnaab, which took the form of a sacred tree grove, a cave or another type of natural enclosure. In addition

---

[73] Fortes, *Dynamics of Clanship*, 250–57.
[74] The original Mamprusi settler according to oral tradition, discussed in Chapter Two.
[75] Ibid., 22, 30, 40, 45, 62.
[76] Ibid., 105–6.

to the External *Bayar* representing all Talis, every maximal lineage had its own *bayar* (*dugni bayar*), each of which had a specific name. Sacrifice formed the basis of External *Bayar* rituals and the cult had "tremendous magical power" that could be used for good or evil. In addition to its role in clan solidarity, the External *Bayar* of the Hills Talis also functioned as the site of initiation for boys into Tali society, as well as an oracle of sorts, especially in the realm of fertility.[77]

In precolonial times Tongnaab's reach spread beyond Talensi society, as the External *Bayar* had clients from regions outside the Tong Hills. Pilgrims from these regions would travel to the Tong Hills shrines, mainly in the dry season, often to ask for fertility. If the pilgrims were blessed with children they would return with the children to have them "ritually dedicated" to the shrine, named "and thus brought into communion with it". In return, the maximal lineage heads from the Tong Hills would visit the pilgrims' communities, to bless local shrines of the *Bayar* and to bring children under its spiritual guardianship. Through these reciprocal ceremonies the parents and children would develop strong religious bonds with the Tali *Bayar*. The pilgrims performed an important economic function for the Talensi, bringing gifts (salt, cloth, hoes, etc.—very valuable in the precolonial era) for the *Bayar*, which were shared secretly among the heads of the maximal lineages. According to Fortes, every External *Bayar* of the Hill Talis had a network of non-Tali client lineages from neighbouring areas (Mamprusi, Dagomba, Builsa, Gurunsi, Mossi). When they returned home the clients followed the ritual rules of the *Bayar*.[78]

Who controlled the Tongnaab shrine in precolonial times? From Fortes' investigations it appears that there was no single authority responsible for the Tongnaab as a whole. Instead, each External *Bayar* had a number of ritual functionaries who were the heads of the maximal lineages holding allegiance to that *Bayar*. Because of the overlapping nature of clan and lineage ties among the Hill Talis, the communicants for a particular *Bayar* usually included the maximal lineages of single clan as well as the maximal lineages of other clans linked by clanship ties and, to complicate matters further, the

---

[77] Fortes, "Festivals and Social Cohesion," 591, 599. Fortes, *Dynamics of Clanship*, 80–1, 106, 131–2, 252.

[78] Fortes, *Dynamics of Clanship*, 131–2, 252.

maximal lineages of adjacent clans not linked by clanship. The overlapping of maximal lineages in a given External *Bayar* meant that the ritual communities for a specific ancestor cult were not necessarily the same communities who sacrificed together at a given earth shrine.[79]

From Fortes' observations of the complex, overlapping ritual communities of the Tong Hills ancestor and earth cults, it is not very likely that the *golibdaana* could claim any sort of traditional right to monopolise the pilgrim traffic to a supposedly paramount Tongnaab shrine. As Fortes observed, and as Allman and Parker have verified, there were many Tongnaab shrines. In this complex, overlapping patchwork of ritual communities, no single lineage claimed ultimate authority over Tongnaab as a whole, and thus no-one could monopolise control over all of the Tongnaab ceremonies across Taleland. In Fortes' words, social cohesion depended on a "meticulous balance of local, clanship and ritual ties and cleavages focused on the politico-ritual offices vested in the heads of maximal lineages." These offices were distributed equally among the lineages so that no single lineage had more power than another. Allman and Parker are correct, therefore, in their assertion that the *golibdaana's* authority over Tongnaab grew out of his power as *kambonaaba*, provided by the British under indirect rule. British colonial officials appointed chiefs in Taleland based on stories of descent from the Mamprusi ruling dynasty. The British-imposed chieftaincies created a hierarchy of chiefs, which gave some chiefs and headmen more power than they had in precolonial times. This system tended to increase tension within and between clans, intensifying pre-existing forms of conflict. By far the most serious conflict centred around the *golibdaana*, whose control over the Yanii shrine, he claimed, gave him as much power as the chief of Tongo. Based on this claim, the *golibdaana* moved to monopolise the pilgrim traffic to the Tong Hills shrines.[80]

In the first decade of the twentieth century the pilgrimages to the Tong Hills took on a new character. Labour migrants from the Tong Hills began to advertise the Yanii shrine in the south, and southerners responded to the point where, as Fortes claimed, the pilgrim traffic was "a major industry of the Tong Hills." The southern

[79] Ibid., 78–81, 110–14.
[80] Ibid., 110–14, 251–7.

pilgrims asked mainly for success in family life and business, as well as "the privilege of ritual clientship of the *Bayar*" in which they would receive permission to set up Tongnaab shrines in their homes to protect them from witchcraft. For these services the southern pilgrims brought gifts of cash, often between £10 and £20, and paid "generously" for accommodation and animals for sacrifices.[81]

This "modernised" pilgrim traffic was monopolised from its beginning by the *golibdaana* and the Bukiuk clan. However, instead of sharing the profits with the other ritual functionaries of the Yanii shrine, the *golibdaana* kept the proceeds for himself and his supporters. Tengol used his supporters, paying them off with revenues from the pilgrims, to develop a sophisticated network connecting pilgrims from Ashanti and the Colony to the Tongnaab. It was a very lucrative business; Fortes estimated his income at several hundred pounds a year judging from his large farm, eighty wives and "sumptuous clothes." In this pursuit the *golibdaana* was supported mainly by members of his maximal lineage, but he also bought off representatives of the other lineages who by custom had to participate in the rituals.[82]

The *golibdaana's* actions triggered a shift in the politico-religious balance between the maximal lineages and sparked fierce resistance from rival lineages. As we have seen, the monopolisation of the Tongnaab by the head of a single maximal lineage was resisted especially by the Kpatar clan. Kpatar elders argued that they were primus inter pares in rituals among the Hill Talis and thus were entitled at the very least to a share of the profits. The conflict peaked in 1936 when the *kpatarnaab* withdrew his acknowledgement of the *golibdaana's* authority as headman of Tenzugu. In refusing to recognise the British-appointed chief, the *kpatarnaab* provoked a stalemate in which the colonial administration had refused to recognise either of the men as chief. Effectively there were two headmen trying to administer Tenzugu, each seeking to benefit from the commercialisation of the Tongnaab shrine. The struggle worked itself out along lineage lines, although some young men defected from their maximal lineages to support the *golibdaana*. The Sakpee *tengdaana*, for instance, sided with the *golibdaana* even though he was one of the ritual officers of the External *Bayar* over which the Kpatar lineage were the senior

---

[81] Ibid., 253–4.
[82] Ibid., 253–6.

custodians.[83] The extent of the struggle between the lineages of the Hill Talis demonstrates extent to which colonial rule triggered a transformation of political authority over the Yanii shrine as well as a change in the character of its supplicants.[84] Far from promoting the preservation of African community, indirect rule provoked an intense struggle between individuals in the Tong Hills over profits from the commercialisation of a sacred shrine.

The above discussion demonstrates that some members of Talensi society accumulated wealth and political power within the framework of indirect rule. The development of "shrine tourism" demonstrates the extent to which immanent forces of development could work to undermine the colonial state's attempt to preserve African community in the Northern Territories. The precise significance of these developments for Talensi social structure has been debated at some length. Fortes argued that changes to territorial political boundaries and economic accumulation did not affect the social structure of the Talensi. "The verdict of native custom is unequivocal," Fortes wrote, "social affiliation and not alleged territorial boundaries define the extent of the community."[85] Fortes argued that neither the *golibdaana*'s new wealth nor the resulting disputes had ripped apart Talensi social structure. Corporate groups remained aligned as before and the new "industry" deepened existing cleavages as well as reinforcing some of the traditional ties between clans.[86]

In a critique of Fortes, Peter Worsley emphasises that these developments reflected the integration of the Talensi into the world economy after 1937. Worsley argues that global integration provided opportunities for the appropriation of surpluses from trade and wage labour by elders, chiefs and land priests. As a result, differentiation had appeared among the Talensi based on access to economic resources rather than kinship ties. However, the transition was not complete. Migrant labour had not yet transformed kinship, and "nouveaux riches" such as the *golibdaana* tended to channel wealth into enlarging kinship networks by acquiring more wives.[87] As such, Worsley agreed with Fortes that kinship continued to dominate the social structure

[83] Ibid., 255–7.
[84] For an excellent recent account of this struggle, see Allman and Parker, 210–12.
[85] Ibid., 164.
[86] Ibid., 158.
[87] P.M. Worsley, "The Kinship System of the Talensi: A Revaluation," *Journal of the Royal Anthropological Institute of Great Britain and Ireland* 86 (1956): 72–3.

of the Talensi. However, where Fortes emphasised the stability of Talensi social structure, Worsley focused on its transformation.

For our purposes, it is most important that Fortes, Worsley and more recently Allman and Parker, provide evidence that economic and political accumulation did occur among the Talensi during the indirect rule period. Opportunities for accumulation depended on immanent processes of development, especially the growth of cocoa production and migrant labour, which pressed against the British intention to preserve and reproduce community in the Northern Territories. In the cases of the *golibdaana* and chief Gandah of Birifu, "shrine tourism" represented such a process. Accumulation was occurring, and, more to our point, it occurred outside the boundaries of the colonial state's agrarian doctrine of development and the preservation of African community. As in the north-west, the development of the shrine industry in the Tong Hills demonstrates the extent to which immanent forces of development could work to undermine the colonial state's attempt to preserve African community in the Northern Territories.

Alternatives to Mixed Farming

The problems outlined above with development under indirect rule prompted the colonial administration to search for alternatives in the late 1940s. As a basic principle colonial officials believed that the state would have to intervene more directly in the economic development of the Northern Territories. A precedent of sorts had been set during World War Two, when the colonial administration intervened more forcefully into the production of cash crops and foodstuffs. After 1939 the British government took control over the purchase and sale of cocoa from European firms, first through the Ministry of Food, then, after 1940, through the Colonial Office via the newly created Cocoa Control Board. In 1942 Britain expanded the mandate of the Cocoa Control Board to include vegetable oils and oilseeds and changed the Board's name to the West African Produce Control Board (more of which in Chapter Seven).[88] Between 1943 and 1946

[88] P.T. Bauer, *West African Trade: A Study of Competition, Oligopoly and Monopoly in a Changing Economy* (New York: Augustus M. Kelley, 1963), 199. J.F. Milburn, *British Business and Ghanaian Independence* (Hanover: The University Press of New England, 1977), 32.

Britain also created the West African War Council to co-ordinate price incentives and manage agricultural development in the Gold Coast, Gambia, Sierra Leone and Nigeria.[89]

Within this wartime structure of produce control the Gold Coast administration was asked to provide foodstuffs to troops at staging posts (for the Far East) established at Takoradi and Accra. With the Allied loss of Southeast Asia after 1942, the Gold Coast also was called upon to meet the wartime demand for rubber, palm oil and copra. Agricultural officers fanned out into the forest belt in search of rubber and other necessary wartime supplies, aided by price and distribution incentives offered by the Gold Coast Director of Supplies. As Frimpong-Ansah notes, these wartime developments provided a watershed in official thinking about development in West Africa.[90]

The wartime emphasis on development, however, did not focus exclusively on supplying foodstuffs and cash crops to Britain's war machine. On the contrary, the Gold Coast's effort to improve agricultural production during the 1940s also sought to counter the growing threat of African unemployment, deteriorating living standards and labour resistance. Once again, the problem initially focused on the cocoa industry. In the early 1940s, when France had fallen, Britain was in a state of siege and the German blitz had begun, the Gold Coast Agricultural Department focused its activity on swollen shoot disease and wartime disruptions to the cocoa industry. In March of 1940, Accra began to advise farmers closest to large towns and markets to increase their food production to compensate for decreasing wartime imports.[91] At the same time, the administration also appealed to the Northern Territories to raise its production of foodstuffs for southern markets.

Wary of agrarian capitalism, the colonial administration searched for an alternative form of agricultural production in the Northern Territories. After 1940 the search led to agricultural schemes variously described as "co-operative," "communal" and "collective" and influenced to varying degrees by Fabian socialism."[92] Co-operation

---

[89] Jonathan H. Frimpong Ansah, *The Vampire State In Africa: The Political Economy of Decline in Ghana* (London: James Currey, 1991), 29–31.

[90] Frimpong Ansah, 29–31.

[91] H.B. Waters, "Review of Agriculture in the Gold Coast, 1940," 8, CO96/773/19, PRO.

[92] For some examples, see R. Buell, *The Native Problem In Africa* (London: Frank Cass and Company, 1965, originally published in 1928), Allan McPhee, *The Economic*

was the most conservative of the three. Indeed, Lugard equated it with indirect rule in 1933, casting it as a tool for guiding Africans through a "critical stage of mental and spiritual growth" without producing "destructive individualism."[93] Colonial Office co-operation expert C.F. Strickland agreed. "Without tearing the social fabric," wrote Strickland, "the members adapt its texture to fresh needs, grafting the modern on the ancient and combining all that is vital in its inherited tradition with that which is now indispensable for survival in the economic world." "Beneficent" trusteeship, argued Strickland, was needed in order to prepare the "mould" for the "fusion" of African and Western cultures by inculcating thrift, foresight, "regularity and punctuality of action" into the African population. Aimed at the peasantry, Strickland's proposals for marketing co-operatives did not necessarily imply "communalism." However, co-operative agriculture certainly appeared capable of guiding Africans from tribe to nation without producing western individualism. This project was especially important to colonial officials in the cocoa-growing areas, where co-operatives were first introduced systematically in the early 1930s. At the time, colonial officials turned to marketing co-operatives in order to curb the direct export of cocoa to the United States by African producer-traders, and to eliminate a growing class of non-producing brokers acting as middlemen in the cocoa trade.[94]

African direct exporters developed significantly after 1917, in the wake of a wartime crisis in cocoa exports in 1916–17. Due to the war, shipping for cocoa was scarce in 1916 and became worse in 1917 when the British Government further restricted space for cocoa to make room for palm oil shipments, which were more urgent for the war economy. By 1917 the space available for cocoa exporters was half of the amount available in 1916. This resulted in oversupply in the Gold Coast and the price fell dramatically, from 18/-per load in 1916 to about 5/-per load in 1917. Cutting costs in response to the crisis, European merchant buyers began to dismiss their African buying clerks. In 1917, however, shipping space opened up after the

Revolution in British West Africa (London: Frank Cass and Company, 1971, originally published in 1926).

[93] C.F. Strickland, *Co-operation For Africa* (London: Oxford University Press, 1933), 2. Anne Phillips, *The Enigma of Colonialism: British Policy in West Africa* (London: James Currey, 1989), 90.

[94] Strickland, 9–14, 41–60, 85–95.

USA entered the war. Former clerks now had the opportunity to ship cocoa direct to the American market, as ships could transport cocoa to the United States and then bring soldiers from the United States to Europe. Presented with this opportunity, African traders bought cocoa voraciously as the price rose immediately following the war. A boom in 1919–20, however, was followed by a major slump in 1920–21 and, although the major European firms survived, many of the African sellers went out of business.[95]

The larger European buying firms responded to the unpredictability of the local cocoa market by buying up smaller firms and negotiating pooling agreements. Farmers knew full well about this monopolisation of cocoa buying and began to co-operate to hold up cocoa sales whenever prices were low (hold-ups occurred in 1921–2, 1922–3, 1930–1, and most famously in 1937–8). Farmer-traders formed associations to co-ordinate the hold-ups, which they used to gain direct access to American markets, bypassing the European firms and indigenous brokers.[96] In an important early development, the Chiefs of the Eastern Province sent delegates to the World Cocoa Conference in England in 1924. After their return the delegates formed the Gold Coast Farmers' Association in order to ship cocoa direct to the USA. Direct shipments in 1924–5 were large enough to threaten the business of the European firms, but misappropriation of funds ended this experiment. In 1930–1, the Gold Coast and Ashanti Cocoa Federation was formed in response to a European buying pool prompted by the slump in world prices for primary commodities. The Federation organised the holdup of 1930–1.[97]

At this time the Colonial Office discussed the implementation of a Co-operative Societies Ordinance in the Gold Coast. Co-operation had been suggested by the Gold Coast's Director of Agriculture as early as 1925,[98] but it was not applied widely in the Gold Coast until the Ordinance was implemented in 1931. The 1931 Ordinance was intended as a hedge against the growth of direct sales to the United States by indigenous trader-producer associations. "Leading

[95] Roger J. Southall, "Farmers, Traders and Brokers in the Gold Coast Cocoa Economy," *Canadian Journal of African Studies* 12, No. 2 (1978): 194–6.

[96] Ibid., 203–4.

[97] David Kimble, *A Political History of Ghana: The Rise of Gold Coast Nationalism, 1850–1928* (London: Oxford University Press, 1965), 51.

[98] C.Y. Shephard, *Report on the Economics of Peasant Agriculture in the Gold Coast* (Gold Coast: Sessional Paper I of 1936), 26.

Africans," reported the Gold Coast's Director of Agriculture, had been trying to take the trade away from the "local European firms."[99] In addition, the Gold Coast government also intended to use Co-operation to abolish the advances made by European merchant firms to cocoa growers, which had been leading to the pledging and mortgaging of farms to local cocoa brokers.[100] The Co-operative Societies were to replace the brokers who acted as moneylenders to the cocoa farmers.[101] Through the Ordinance, the administration implemented marketing co-operatives in the cocoa growing areas in the 1930s.[102]

The Co-operation Ordinance of 1931 implied colonial trusteeship over the development of the cocoa industry, but did it necessarily imply the preservation of African community? In itself, of course, co-operation did not necessarily imply large-scale collectivisation schemes or even smaller programs of communal farming. Indeed, although some commentators recommended the extension of co-operatives to fermentaries,[103] co-operation in the cocoa growing areas was confined to marketing and credit. In this way co-operation was quite consistent with individual peasant holdings. On the other hand, co-operatives clearly could be used towards communal ends. In 1932–3, on the recommendation of a District Agricultural Officer, at least two co-operative societies bought farms, worked them collectively (without pay) and paid the revenues into the society.[104] In general, however, the cocoa co-operatives of the 1930s were intended to remove the middlemen from a system based on individual peasant holdings, not to promote agricultural collectivisation. But colonial administrators easily could have reconciled individual peasant holdings with the preservation of African community. If a land market could be blocked, and the chiefs supported as trustees over communal land, then individual peasants could live and farm as part of a larger, traditional community. This idea no doubt was difficult to sustain in the cocoa growing areas. The north, however, provided a clearer opportunity to reconcile co-operation with community and

---

[99] Colonial Office, Correspondence on the Gold Coast Co-operative Societies Ordinance, 3, CO96/698/16, PRO.

[100] Ibid. See also Gareth Austin, "The Emergence of Capitalist Relations in South Asante Cocoa-Farming, c. 1916–33," *Journal of African History* 28 (1987): 272.

[101] Shephard, 44–5.

[102] Austin, 272–3.

[103] Shephard, 68.

[104] Sheperd criticised this practice at the time on the grounds that profit-making should not form the primary goal of co-operation. Ibid., 58.

to expand the vision to encompass a broader program of communal farming.

The communal variant of co-operation provided an ideal strategy for developing agriculture in the Northern Territories in the 1940s. Some colonial officials, as we shall discover in Chapter Seven, extended this idea to formal collectivisation. In most cases, however, the term was used more loosely to describe strategies for combining individual producers on communal lands in order to raise their productivity and output. Jock Stewart epitomised the new thinking with his ideas about collective farming, envisioning "combined mixed farming on a co-operative or communal basis which fits in with native custom."[105] Stewart expanded on this theme in a series of letters to the Fabian Colonial Bureau during the 1940s. In 1944, he wrote that mixed farming failed

> because it is framed thus instead of on collectivist lines . . . Then the half baked idea that the African must go slowly, "must learn to walk before he can run," a favourite cliche of governors means that they must have bullock ploughs and implements which are slightly better than the hand-hoe; this is accepted as a law of the Medes and Persians by officialdom but the African jumped straight from head loading goods to the motor lorry . . .[106]

In place of the slow development of individual mixed farms, Stewart recommended an immediate jump to mechanised agriculture organised co-operatively along communal lines.

Stewart believed that he had implemented the spirit of collectivisation in his Native Authority Stock farms developed between 1933 and 1938. Governor Arnold Hodson supported Stewart's scheme, mainly because the Gold Coast had seen a decline in French cattle imports after the construction of a meat processing plant in Dakar in French West Africa. To protect the domestic supply for the plants, French colonial authorities stepped up border patrols to catch traders attempting to evade French cattle taxes. Writing in 1935, District Commissioner Humphrey Amherst noted that the movement of cattle from French areas into the Gold Coast had ceased almost completely. This development made livestock development in the Gold

---

[105] Gold Coast, *Veterinary Department Annual Report, 1942/3* (Accra: Government Printer, 1943), 1–4. On Stewart's dissatisfaction with mixed farming, see Gold Coast, *Veterinary Department Annual Report, 1937/8* (Accra: Government Printer, 1938), 4. See also Gold Coast #633 in CO96/750/1, PRO.

[106] Stewart to Fabian Colonial Bureau, 21 November 1945, FCB81/1, RHL.

Coast "imperative" in light of the growing demand for meat in the mining and cocoa areas in the Colony and Ashanti.[107]

In structuring his scheme Jock Stewart flatly rejected the peasantry as a vehicle for the program, writing in 1937 that it was "necessary not to confuse the large scale cattle improvement scheme for meat production, where large herds are dealt with, and the peasant 'mixed farming' scheme, which is quite different and aims at arable improvement." It was "difficult," he continued, "for the peasant individualist to develop a meat industry" because "under peasant conditions, cattle always tend to get smaller." Instead, he argued, "the development of meat and working bullocks is a matter for the large herd of the country under range conditions."[108] This could be accomplished by developing communal cattle farms managed by the Native Authorities.

In reality, Stewart's stock farms were neither as successful as he claimed in producing marketable cattle, nor did they succeed in promoting communalism. The Native Authorities, which Stewart tended not to support directly, rarely possessed the means to re-stock their farms with cattle from local markets. As a result the farms did not become successful breeding sites and depended on supplies from the north's veterinary station. The biggest complaint against the Native Authority stock farms, however, was that they quickly became "chiefs' farms" used for building personal fortunes. In some cases, chiefs—with the support of District Commissioners—forced their subjects to hand over cattle to the farms.[109] Once again, a supposedly communal development project had produced individual accumulation within the framework of indirect rule. Reacting to this trend Stewart's successor S. Simpson gradually abandoned the Native Authority stock farms after 1950.[110] At the time of the Cattle Scheme's demise, the stock farms had failed to produce either beef cattle or bullocks in any appreciable quantities. Regarding the latter, Stewart's refusal to co-operate with the mixed farming programme meant that the Native

---

[107] A. Hodson to Ormsby-Gore, 4 August 1936, Gold Coast #544, CO96/732/5, PRO. Humphrey Amherst, 7 November 1935, 20 December 1935, Mss.Afr.s.1207, Amherst Papers, RHL.

[108] J.L. Stewart, "Report on Gold Coast Livestock," Enclosure #1 in Gold Coast #70 of 1937, CO96/740/11, PRO.

[109] Der, "Agricultural Policy," 13–14.

[110] W.J.A. Jones, Enclosure, Gold Coast 13, 25 January 1938, CO96/746/3, PRO.

Authority cattle farms barely influenced the development of agriculture in the Northern Territories.[111]

The lack of co-ordination between development programs drew criticism from the Colonial Office, which was moving towards programmatic and planned development in the late 1940s. Citing the lack of inter-Departmental planning in the Gold Coast, Colonial Office Agricultural Advisor F.A. Stockdale labelled Stewart's cattle program "half-baked" because it addressed only "one stage (one compartment, in fact) of development." "They will fail in their objective," Stockdale continued, "unless they are linked up with other measures in which the Medical and Agricultural departments—as well as the Administration—are concerned."[112] The Gold Coast administration levelled a similar criticism at Morris' anti-tsetse work, despite its success by the 1950s.[113] The stage was set for a shift away from indirect rule as the framework for development in the Northern Territories.

Conclusion

By the end of the 1940s indirect rule came under criticism by the colonial administration as an inadequate vehicle for economic and social development. Operating through the Native Authorities, mixed farming progressed far too slowly for the wishes of the colonial officials in Accra. Tsetse eradication schemes suffered a similar fate, succeeding only where Morris could pay his workers or use a thinly disguised version of forced labour. Forestry policy not only contradicted tsetse-clearing operations, but it was ineffective in itself as long as it lacked the coercive powers of state-backed central legislation. To complicate matters, the African population did not adhere to the communal ideal so dear to the British. Instead of promoting a return to community, indirect rule prompted struggles over individual strategies of economic, political and social accumulation. Chiefs and land priests took advantage of opportunities in farming, livestock husbandry and "shrine tourism" to accumulate wealth and political

[111] Der, 13.

[112] F.A. Stockdale, 30 November 1936, CO96/740/11, PRO.

[113] Gold Coast, *Department of Tsetse Control Annual Report, 1949* (Accra: Government Printer, 1950), 1.

power. Prominent examples included the Gandahs' foray into trade and transport, and the *golibdaana's* monopolisation of the pilgrim traffic to the Tong Hills. These examples support the arguments Berry, Lentz and Allman and Parker, that indirect rule provoked struggles over resources, rather than imposing hegemony based on British versions of African tradition.

Taking the story further, African struggles within the framework of indirect rule led colonial officials to question its usefulness as a strategy for development. Of course the British ideal of African tradition did not die easily, indeed the administration fought to preserve indirect rule in the Northern Territories as long as possible. After 1945, however, forces beyond the administration's control made it necessary to seek alternatives, which eventually took the form of economic and social planning. As we shall discover in Chapter Seven, this shift in thinking eventually led to the emergence of Land Planning as the new paradigm of development in the Northern Territories after 1948.

CHAPTER SEVEN

LAND PLANNING, LOCAL GOVERNMENT AND PARTY POLITICS, 1940–1957

Introduction

In the 1940s, dissatisfaction with indirect rule prompted colonial officials to question its usefulness as a development strategy in the Northern Territories. In particular, two underlying pressures stretched the doctrine to the breaking point between 1945 and 1953. First, Britain's post-war Labour Government faced a serious shortage of raw materials and US dollars, which intensified the pressure to increase cash crop production in the African colonies. Second, a steady decline in African producer prices and the spread of unemployment provoked labour resistance and anticolonial nationalism. These pressures prompted the colonial administration to create a new development strategy based on land planning and local government. In a sense, the pressure for rapid development triggered a return to Chamberlain's project of developing the African estates. Unlike Chamberlain, however, colonial officials in the 1940s remained concerned with the preservation of African community and clung to the idea of economic development without social transformation. This was a formidable project of economic and social engineering, and it required a more centralised and programmatic development program than had been pursued in the past. In the Northern Territories, the colonial administration turned to the policy of land planning, which would (they hoped) revolutionise agricultural production while maintaining environmental sustainability and preserving the social structures of African communities.

Frederick Cooper has shown that the turn towards development planning after 1945 was generalised across the British and French African colonies.[1] However, Cooper fails to observe that the shift occurred in response to a previous period of development centred

[1] Frederick Cooper, *Decolonization and African Society: The Labor Question in French and British Africa* (Cambridge: Cambridge University Press, 1996).

around indirect rule. By 1945, the forces of accumulation and economic development had reached the breaking point in the Northern Territories, at least in the official mind, and indirect rule was jettisoned from the colonial doctrine of development. But the focus on African community outlived the demise of indirect rule. In other words, the agrarian doctrine of development remained consistent after the war, but it assumed the guise of local government rather than indirect rule.

Local government was designed to absorb school leavers into village politics and prevent them from joining the nationalist politics of Ashanti and the Colony. The administration also encouraged local government authorities to participate in community development activities through local development committees. In this way, not only would potential nationalists be absorbed safely into community politics, but they also would contribute to economic and social development and thus help to raise living standards and improve social welfare in the north. Development thus would be achieved in the Northern Territories without producing the politically volatile social groups that had emerged in the Colony and Ashanti.

As it turned out, however, land planning and local government proved no more capable of reconciling economic development and African community than had mixed farming and indirect rule in the 1930s. Land planning was hampered by the reluctance of the colonial administration to use centralised legislation to force compliance on the local population. Local government failed to contain the educated elite safely in their village communities. In particular, political reforms failed to block the movement towards anticolonial nationalist politics, and by 1956 the Northern Territories had become politicised along party lines. However, as Lentz clearly shows in her recent work on Nandom,[2] party politics reflected local disputes over land and chieftaincy as much as ideological commitments. In this sense, political modernisation simply created another framework for local struggles over power and the spoils of office. As in the past, local actors continued to assert their agency against the colonial doctrine of development.

[2] Carola Lentz, "The time when politics came": party politics and local conflict," Chapter Eight of *Ethnicity and the Making of History in Northern Ghana*, manuscript, forthcoming as *Ethnicity and the Making of History in Northern Ghana* (Edinburgh: Edinburgh University Press, 2006).

Productionist Development Revived, 1945–47

The drive towards local government and land planning unfolded during the resurrection of Chamberlain's productionist agenda after 1945. This turn towards Chamberlainism can be attributed to two main factors. First, anticolonial resistance intensified during World War Two, prompting colonial officials to counter with new schemes of social and economic development. Faced with declining wages and poor working conditions, colonial workers rose up in a wave of strikes across the African colonies, including Kenya (1939, 1942), the Gold Coast (1941), Northern Rhodesia (1941) and Nigeria (1945). As Frederick Cooper observes, the Colonial Office refused to treat these protests as a labour problem. For instance, the Head of the Colonial Office Economics Department, Sydney Caine, refused to address the problems through wage hikes and other forms of worker amelioration. Instead, Caine blamed the unrest on uncontrolled "detribalisation" and argued for increasing African productivity as a means towards raising African living standards and thus solving social and political problems.[3] Framed in these terms, economic development sought to curb labour unrest and unemployment in the African colonies.

But there was a more direct reason for the colonial push for African development in the post-war period. Immediately after World War Two, Britain faced a crisis of production and finance which turned Clement Attlee's new Labour Government towards rapidly developing the African estates. The war left Britain with a £10 million current account shortfall and debts to America and sterling area countries of £18 billion. This posed a major problem for Attlee, who had promised to deliver a strong welfare state for British workers. To make matters worse, the war left Britain's economy shattered and unable to produce sufficient food and raw materials, much less dollar-earning commodities. Turning to Washington and Ottawa for help, Britain received a write-off of its Lend Lease debt and a loan for £5 billion on the condition that the British government would make the pound fully convertible within twelve months. Far from solving the crisis, the implementation of convertibility in 1947 provoked a run on the pound that exhausted most of the North American loan. During this time the United States intensified Britain's dollar

[3] Cooper, 115–123.

crisis by insisting on debt payments in dollars. Meanwhile, conditions in the colonies worsened as resistance increased, prompting Britain to withdraw from India in 1947.[4]

Desperate for dollars and raw materials—and having shed an important part of its empire—the Labour Government turned to Africa as a source of non-dollar markets and dollar-earning commodities. In the words of Chancellor of the Exchequer Sir Stafford Cripps, "the whole future of the sterling area and its ability to survive depends in my view upon a quick and extensive development of our African resources."[5] This possibility was expressed in moral terms by the Colonial Office Reference Section (CORS), who asked "what contribution (to world food shortages) is being made by the 63,000,000 people of the Colonial Empire occupying about one-twenty-fourth of the World's surface?"[6] Chamberlain's policy of developing the estates, it seemed, had been resurrected out of the debris of World War Two.

This project hinged on the Chamberlainite belief that the British Empire could be rationalised as an integrated economic system. Speaking of the expansion of colonial production, Sir William Maclean of the CORS emphasised that "by careful planning and by the interplay of what is produced by the industries old and new being developed in all parts of the Colonial Empire with what can be produced in the United Kingdom to help forward these new industries, a new era of trade and commerce with the Colonies can well be established."[7] Calling up the image of Chamberlain's undeveloped estates, the CORS outlined a plan for the colonies to fill their fair share of the world food shortage.[8] Before World War Two, expanding markets had provided sufficient demand for colonial production to be carried out by private capital, leaving the state to provide public works. International markets shrank, however, during the decade before the war, forcing post-war development programs to focus on

---

[4] Wm. Roger Louis and Ronald Robinson,"The Imperialism of Decolonization," *Journal of Imperial and Commonwealth History* 22, No. 3 (1994): 464–66. Cooper, 203–4.

[5] Cooper, 204.

[6] Colonial Office Reference Section (CORS), "Notes on Colonial Food Production," Memo #16 of May, 1947, i, Mss.Br.Emp.s332, Box 44, File 1, Oxford University, Rhodes House Library (RHL).

[7] Sir William MacLean, "Economic Development in the Colonies," notes prepared for an address at Chatham House, 21 November 1946, 7, Mss.Brit.Emp.s332, 44/1, Arthur Creech-Jones papers, (RHL).

[8] CORS, "Notes on Colonial Food Production," i.

the colonies' internal markets. Development would focus on secondary industries and import substitution, with an eye towards increasing purchasing power to enable colonial subjects to buy consumer goods from Britain. To this point the argument mirrored Joseph Chamberlain's program for developing the colonial estates. Unlike Chamberlain, however, the CORS argued for direct state intervention into colonial production and trade. To this end the Colonial Office formed three organisations—the Colonial Development Corporation, the Overseas Food Corporation and the Primary Products Committee—to supplement private enterprise in facilitating the post-war development programmes.[9]

Furthermore, the post-war Labour government clothed its development vision in the rhetoric of colonial welfare and social advance. This approach reflected global trends. In 1947, for instance, the United Nations proposed a twofold mandate for agricultural policy in the colonial world. The plan included, first, "the preservation and improvement of the productive powers of the basic natural resources of the country concerned" and second, "the social welfare and advancement of the people and the economic use of the land and labour available—their use in such ways as would produce the maximum return of real and permanent power."[10] Reacting to the UN proclamation, the CORS stated that Great Britain sought more than colonial contributions to its "larders." Instead,

> production is being developed in the general design of long-term policy aimed at raising the economic stability of dependent people to a standard sufficiently high to enable them to reap as much benefit from the industrial enterprise of our factories as we can reap from the primary production of their soil, and with the ultimate mutual sharing of the benefits of both as equal partners in the British Commonwealth of Nations.[11]

This mutually beneficial rationalisation of Empire demanded immediate local increases in colonial foodstuff production. According to the CORS, "freedom from want" at the local level formed the first priority in the Empire's development plan because "(t)he higher standards of living enjoyed and the measures adopted to prevent famine

---

[9] Colonial Office Reference Section (CORS), "Notes on the Expansion of Colonial Production," Memo #17 of June 1947, 1, Mss.Br.Emp.s332, 44/1, RHL.

[10] CORS, "Notes on Colonial Food Production," 20.

[11] Ibid., 21.

all involve a bigger consumption of products locally."[12] The grow-more-food campaigns of World War Two provided a base for this project, having produced agricultural surpluses and "dietary reform" by expanding the production of vegetables, rice and livestock.[13]

> Thanks to propaganda, education in new farming and agricultural methods, improved methods of marketing and distribution, improvement of stock breeding, and soil conservation, immunisation against cattle disease, and successful campaigns against tropical pests, such as the locust, and tsetse fly, and above all, by a great measure of inter-territorial co-operation, not only had the African on the whole achieved a higher standard of living in many regions but by local production has largely disposed of the needs for food imports.[14]

Having secured local foodstuff production, the wartime campaigns had been useful in supporting the continued expansion of export agriculture in the Gold Coast.

In the realm of finance, the wartime colonial agricultural campaigns also provided a model for extracting hard currency from the West African colonies through marketing boards. In 1942, against the wishes of the Nowell Commission,[15] the British government created the West African Produce Control Board (WAPCB) as a monopoly to buy produce from West African producers at fixed prices under a quota system. The WAPCB intended to stabilise producer prices and stimulate the production of groundnuts and oil-palm products, while keeping West African produce out of enemy hands.[16] Before the war, the Cocoa Control Board (the predecessor of the WAPCB) allocated shipping quotas for cocoa to merchants who purchased and shipped West African cocoa to Britain at fixed prices. After 1942, the WAPCB took over shipping directly and the merchants became licensed buying agents. The WAPCB's activities extended to oilseeds in 1942 and oil-palm products in 1943, which previously had been controlled by the Association of West African Merchants and the Ministry of Food (MOF). Between 1942 and

[12] Ibid., i. CORS, "Notes on the Expansion of Colonial Production," 4.

[13] CORS, "Notes on Colonial Food Production, 1, 2, 7, 8. MacLean, 1–2.

[14] CORS, "Notes on Colonial Food Production, 8.

[15] The Nowell Commission had not recommended fixed prices for producers or quotas for merchant firms. David Meredith, "State Controlled Marketing Boards and Economic Development: the Case of West African Produce During the Second World War," *Economic History Review (2nd Ser)* 34, No. 1 (1986): 80.

[16] P.T. Bauer, *West African Trade* (Cambridge: Cambridge University Press, 1954), 257.

1947 the WAPCB sold the West African produce at cost exclusively to the Ministry of Food. This system not only provided cheap food and raw materials supplies to Britain, but it also produced steadily rising surpluses for the WAPCB. Motivated by the Board's success, as noted in Chapter Six, the British government moved to make statutory marketing a permanent feature of the West African produce trade. A White Paper of 1944 announced the formation of local marketing boards. After a three-year delay due to objections from the UK cocoa brokers and the American government, the WAPCB was converted into a group of local marketing boards in the West African colonies in 1947.[17]

In the face of the sterling crisis after 1947, the Gold Coast Cocoa Marketing Board (CMB) provided much-needed dollar earnings, especially through sales to the USA. As the leader in West African cocoa sales, the CMB accumulated a surplus of £76 million between 1947 and 1951.[18] At the same time, low prices to producers decreased the demand for imports from the United Kingdom, thus lowering Britain's need to export vital commodities and send foreign exchange overseas. Although this might not have been intentional, the West African marketing boards did serve, in P.T. Bauer's words, "to minimise West African demands on sterling area resources and foreign exchange reserves."[19] Politically, the local character of the marketing boards also served as a hedge against nationalist resistance, inasmuch as African representation deflected political activity away from anti-colonial nationalism. The CMB, for instance, included an equal number of African and European members. More importantly, the West African boards generated badly needed surpluses while contributing to the smooth devolution of power by opening up opportunities for local political representation.[20]

If the West African marketing boards eased Britain's postwar fiscal crisis, their activities in non-cocoa exports also addressed the desperate need for oilseeds and proteins. In 1949, the Gold Coast Cocoa Marketing Board was augmented by the formation of a broader Agricultural Products Marketing Board.[21] By this time the colonial

[17] Meredith, 81–6. Bauer, 247–51.
[18] Bauer, 285.
[19] Ibid., 342.
[20] Ibid., 277–99. Meredith, 78–9.
[21] Bauer, 271.

administration had set its eyes on the Northern Territories as an undeveloped estate with the potential to become a significant player in the production of groundnuts for export. As a basis for the development of agriculture in the north, Gold Coast Agricultural Director D.H. Urquhart created a ten-year plan to increase the agricultural productivity of the Northern Territories. It is to Urquhart's plan that we will now turn.

Agricultural Modernisation and Land Planning in the Northern Territories, 1940–49

Urquhart's ten-year plan centred on replacing traditional agricultural techniques and mixed farming with modern farming methods under the rubric of land planning. Emphasising the need to feed the colony's growing urban population, Urquhart argued for state intervention to achieve an agricultural revolution. "Fortunate and peculiar circumstances," wrote Urquhart,

> have allowed production and therefore revenue to increase in the past with a minimum of guidance and very little expenditure. These fortunate circumstances cannot be expected to continue indefinitely and it is already apparent that, with the changes taking place within the country, and the rapid growth of the urban population, steps must be taken to safeguard production and guide development.[22]

For Urquhart, "guiding development" meant facilitating the transition from traditional to modern farming, a transition which cocoa production had failed to achieve because it simply "fitted into, without altering, the traditional farming system."[23]

Urquhart emphasised modernisation because he considered traditional farming incapable of generating the necessary productivity increases. Most farmers still practised shifting cultivation, which he considered "inefficient per unit of labour and land employed," "wasteful of natural resources," and subject to "inevitable productivity declines." "In short," Urquhart wrote, "an increased standard of liv-

---

[22] Gold Coast, *Department of Agriculture Annual Report, 1948/9* (Accra: Government Printer, 1950), 1.

[23] Gold Coast, *Department of Agriculture Ten Year Plan, 1949/50–1959/60*, Accra: mimeo, 18 February, 1949, 3, Mss.Afr.s979, 44/1, RHL.

ing cannot be developed upon it."[24] Traditional social structures also worked against agricultural innovation. Matrilineal inheritance patterns meant that farming groups included nephews and nieces rather than sons and daughters, which discouraged farmers from accumulating capital. The development of a livestock industry was blocked by communal livestock grazing, traditional attitudes towards cattle and the lack of money to purchase animals and feed. Communal land ownership, "mutual family aid" and a lack of marketing knowledge blocked individual capital accumulation and produced indebtedness and exploitation at the hands of irresponsible middlemen. "The result at present," wrote Urquhart, "is that the farmer is dependent for the disposal of his surplus produce upon the whim of a rising class of inexperienced brokers intent only on maximum profits."[25]

In order to overcome these obstacles, Urquhart believed that agricultural development had to rest on a rural structure mirroring Europe's prior to its takeoff into modern agriculture, that is, patrilineal social organisation and fixed cultivation. In Urquhart's opinion, the "patrilineal, hardworking, food-producing Northern Territories" possessed the ideal social foundation for this program.[26] More specifically, Urquhart modelled his plan on the north's most densely settled areas, where families had replaced shifting cultivation with settled farming but had not developed the techniques for sustainable farming under the new conditions. Drawing on Lynn's report on North Mamprusi, Urquhart argued that the farmers practised an unsustainable form of settled farming wherein traditional religious beliefs and land tenure arrangements anchored kinship groups to overpopulated ancestral lands. Lacking the will to move, the knowledge to maintain soil fertility and the credit to innovate, the farmers locked themselves into the cycle of poverty described by Lynn in 1937.[27]

Unlike Lynn, however, Urquhart advocated the rapid development of agriculture through the injection of western knowledge and technology. In Urquhart's opinion, Britain's centuries-long history of rural development provided the knowledge needed to "short circuit" the

[24] D.H. Urquhart, "Memorandum on Agricultural Policy," 9 December 1947, 1, Mss.Afr.s.979: Arthur Jones Papers, 44/1, RHL.

[25] D.H. Urquhart, "Existing Maladjustments and Undesirable Practices in Land Use," n.d. but 1949, 6, Mss.Afr.s979, 44/1, RHL.

[26] Ibid., 7.

[27] Ibid., 2–5.

historical process in the colonies. "The time taken to reach the most modern standards," he wrote, "can be reduced to the relatively few years required to work out the application of known principles to local conditions in their varying forms."[28] Because traditional practices had ossified and were incapable of self-generated change, the ten-year plan required state intervention to remove the obstacles to development.[29] The state would educate the farmers to change "their way of thinking and farming methods," consolidate holdings, and provide agricultural credit and technology inputs to encourage innovation and productivity increases.[30]

In 1947, Urquhart summarised his development goals as seeking "the maximum efficient production and distribution of those foods and raw materials most suitable for the improvement of nutrition and increase in standard of living of the people consistent with the preservation of the natural resources of the country."[31] In the short-term, Urquhart conceded that his program would have to begin with the modernisation of mixed farming, the model preferred by the United Nations for West Africa.[32] In the long-term, however, the only solution would be the complete replacement of the current system "by one using every modern development."[33] This vision hinged on the development of land planning, under which the Agricultural Department would work with other Departments to classify lands according to their suitability for farmland, pasturage, tree plantations and forest reserves. Soil surveys would determine the best program for each area of farmland and indigenous farming techniques would be studied in order to develop suitable local variations of western techniques.[34]

Medical Officer Mark Hughes defended the new vision as an important hedge against overpopulation and ecological collapse, writing that "on the edge of an overpopulated area, it is impossible to

---

[28] Urquhart, "Memorandum on Agricultural Policy," 3–4.

[29] D.H. Urquhart, "Agriculture in the Gold Coast," talk given to the British Council, Accra, 13 February, 1946, 11–12, Mss.Afr.s.979, 44/1, Arthur Jones Papers, RHL. See also Urquhart, "Existing Maladjustments," 15.

[30] Urquhart, "Existing Maladjustments," 7. In 1947, Urquhart wrote that "the application of existing technical knowledge is all that is required to ensure extensive development of Gold Coast agriculture." See Urquhart, "Memorandum on Agricultural Policy," 3.

[31] Urquhart, "Memorandum on Agricultural Policy," 1.

[32] CORS, "Notes on Colonial Food Production," 11, 20.

[33] Urquhart, "Memorandum on Agricultural Policy," 4.

[34] Urquhart, "Agriculture in the Gold Coast," 11–12.

view with complacency the steady retreat of man before the unbridled forces of nature. A halt must be called somewhere."[35] In Hughes' opinion, this project required a variation of the American Tennessee Valley Authority (TVA), which had reclaimed a vast area for settlement and development through the use of public funds and public management.[36] Using the TVA model, Hughes argued, the colonial administration should send in a team of doctors and agricultural experts, an entomologist and a forestry officer to reclaim the land of the north from the forces of nature. "The suggested team," said Hughes,

> should start by concentrating the people of these dying places into compact villages, where provision can be made for sanitation and social amenities. At the same time people should be freed of propozoal and helminthic parasites, and attacks should be made upon the insect carriers of disease. Concentration of the people will involve great changes in farming customs, and expert assistance will be required to teach new ways. The abandoned areas may usefully be turned into forest game reserves. Such a scheme will need a certain degree of compulsion, for the people are too far gone in their misery to be capable of much initiative. The opportunity for active measures of rehabilitation must be grasped before political changes render such actions nugatory. The process of decay has been watched for forty years, and it is now our plain duty to take steps to reverse it without further delay.[37]

The Administration agreed with this view and rejected the Forestry Department's mass eviction proposal (discussed in Chapter Six) in favour of Land Planning Areas in the "overpopulated" regions of North Mamprusi, Kassena-Nankanni and Lawra, which would provide for the "better preservation and utilisation of land.[38] This compromise, approved by the Chief Commissioner, recommended designating as "Planning Areas" the Forestry Department's proposed Headwaters Reserves.[39]

In 1948, the Chief Commissioner announced a new policy to "plan the development of agriculture, forestry and water supplies in the

[35] Mark H. Hughes, "Vare: A Study In Rural Decay," Spring, 1948, 34, Mss.Afr.s.141, RHL.

[36] Mark H. Hughes, "Depopulation Among the Sissili," Navrongo, August, 1947, 28, Mss.Afr.s.141, RHL.

[37] Hughes, "Vare," 34.

[38] H.A. Amherst, 24 June 1949, NRG8/1/49, NAGT.

[39] Gold Coast, *Department of Agriculture Annual Report 1947/48* (Accra: Government Printer, 1949), 11–12.

area to ensure the maximum conservation of water supplies and to prevent soil erosion."[40] In support of the policy, Lawra District Commissioner G.N. Charles emphasised the need to eliminate farming techniques which encouraged erosion, undermined soil fertility and produced the low standards of living which plagued the District. At a District meeting in 1949 Charles informed the chiefs of his desire to apply mechanisation "sooner than later" to the Kamba resettlement scheme.[41] In addressing the meeting, Charles put the case for land planning as follows:

> My point is this—the need for land planning in this area is evident to all who are familiar with it. It is necessary in order to prevent the position deteriorating, in order to ensure that the next generation do not die of starvation. But I submit that this is not sufficient—our aim must be, not merely to maintain the status quo, but actually to raise the standard of living by the increased production of food . . . And this I think cannot be done except by the introduction of the most modern methods.[42]

Agricultural Director R.D. Linton approved this vision in 1949, allocating £1 million to the land planning scheme.[43]

Land Planning and the Debate over Central Legislation, 1949–1953

The magnitude of Linton's allocation sparked a debate over whether to employ centralised control over land planning. On the one hand, the Northern Territories Forestry Conservator argued that the programmatic nature of land planning made a Central Committee essential.[44] Veterinary Director Simpson agreed, arguing that the Gold Coast's and Kenya's experience proved the inadequacy of implementing land planning through Native Authorities. "The legislation," concluded Simpson, "must be made by Central Government, but propaganda can be made in advance to prepare the Native Authorities for the enforcement of the legislation.[45] Agricultural Officer Rowland Smith supported centralisation after touring East and Southern Africa

---

[40] Ibid.
[41] G.N. Charles, n.d., NRG8/1/49, NAGT, 38–9.
[42] Lawra-Tumu Land Planning Meeting, 15–16 August 1949, NRG8/5/36, NAGT.
[43] R.D. Linton, 8 July 1950, NRG8/1/49, NAGT.
[44] Northern Territories Forest Conservator, 28 August 1949, NRG8/1/49, NAGT.
[45] Simpson, 11 July 1950, NRG8/1/49, NAGT.

in 1950. Once the state's emphasis shifted from conservation to land planning, central governments had to take control of development programs.[46]

Against these arguments District Commissioner Humphrey Amherst fought for a decentralised system in which District Committees would control land planning programs, with sub-committees at sub-stations and project committees for specific areas. In Amherst's opinion, native authority participation at the Project Committee level would be essential since any "compulsion" would have to be achieved through native administration soil conservation rules.[47] The Acting Secretary for Rural Development supported Amherst's stance on the grounds that centralised coercion would not work in the Gold Coast's political climate. "Owners and lessees of farms," he wrote in 1950, "can only be controlled in this matter to the extent that Native Authorities are willing and able to enact and enforce legislation under the Native Authorities Ordinance."[48]

The colonial administration supported decentralisation and worked to establish local development committees responsible for assisting the Native Authorities to develop the land planning areas. The committees were to be adapted to local conditions and were to include the District Commissioner as chairman, the officers of the Native Authorities, colonial technical officers and "representatives of all sections of the community" comprised of "other local bodies which have a special interest in the area." The local committees were to undertake Native Authority development work that the Native Authorities could not afford to carry out themselves.[49] Successful development under this scheme would be a sign of the community's commitment to progress, and community commitment would elicit state support. The scope of that support would depend on the extent to which local communities appeared willing to help themselves:

> If, as is hoped, these committees are successful in stimulating initiative, enterprise and the spirit of self-help, much can be achieved with

[46] In February and March, 1950, Roland Smith visited Kenya, Tangangyika, Nyasaland and Basutoland. See Roland Smith, "Report On A Visit To Eastern and Southern Africa," NRG8/1/68, NAGT, 22.

[47] Humphrey Amherst, 19 August 1949, NRG8/1/49, NAGT.

[48] Acting Secretary for Rural Development, 30 June, 1950, NRG8/1/49, NAGT.

[49] Robert Scott (Gold Coast Colonial Secretary), "Community Development and Local Development Committees," 19 September 1949, Annexure II, NRG8/1/49, NAGT.

> comparatively slender funds and the extent of such achievement will be the measure of the people's genuine desire for advancement to improved standards of living. Self-help will beget, and will deserve, help from external sources.

Colonial Secretary Robert Scott hoped that this scheme would release the creative energies of rural communities and enable them to "make one pound do the work of two or three."[50]

In this manner, land planning quickly became hitched to community development, which Scott portrayed as a "movement to secure the active co-operation of the people of each community in programmes designed to raise the standard of living and to promote development in all its forms."[51] What this meant in reality, however, was a program designed to maintain British control over development programs at a time when previous strategies had failed and where indirect rule had produced few if any of its intended results. For Scott, this did not mean a rejection of trusteeship but rather the *appearance* of its rejection. As in the case of community development in Tanganyika, wrote Scott,

> Emphasis should be placed on (the indigenous people's) knowledge more on that of the officer, surprise should be shown from time to time at the information elicited and an atmosphere of friendly discussion induced until the more enlightened members begin to discuss the idea which has been put into their heads as if it were their own.[52]

Scott betrayed the political nature of the committees by stating that they would bring together "local advocates of advancement whose enthusiasms and energies, unless they are harnessed in the common cause, are likely to be deflected to unconstructive criticism."[53]

Scott argued for the immediate implementation of this strategy, even in the face of a shortage of technical experts. "It is quite impracticable *and would be politically disastrous*," he wrote, "to wait until there is a sufficiency of experts."[54] In response to Scott's arguments the Gold Coast government advised its District Administrations to establish local development committees as soon as possible—despite the fact that community development teams would not be available for

---

[50] Ibid. 6.
[51] Ibid.
[52] Ibid., 1.
[53] Ibid., 2.
[54] Ibid., 3, emphasis added.

some time. This decision signalled a victory for decentralised land planning. The central government allotted £100,000 to District Commissioners in 1949 and gave the local committees discretion to spend the money as they saw fit.[55]

In Lawra-Tumu, District Commissioner Charles created the North-Western Land Planning Committee, focusing initially on Morris' tsetse clearance scheme in the Kamba Valley. At a land planning meeting at Lawra in August, 1949, Charles created a sub-committee of the Lawra District Council to develop a scheme to settle seven hundred people along the Lawra-Nandom road. Charles intended to incorporate "every possible form of development" into the scheme and to make it a model for land planning in the Northern Territories. Outside the Kamba Valley the District Administration advised the chiefs to encourage their Native Authorities to enforce soil conservation by-laws and promote mixed farming.[56] In Zuarungu, the District Administration formed the North-Eastern Land Planning Committee, attempting to incorporate Native Authority soil conservation rules into a more programmatic land planning strategy.[57] The Zuarungu Land Planning Committee built on an extension of Morris' tsetse clearance project to North Mamprusi. In April, 1949, Medical Officer David Scott began a trypanosomiasis survey at Shiaga, with the intention of working eastwards to Bawku.[58] In the initial phases, the District Administrations delegated the major tasks to the Native Authorities, who were expected to create and enforce a series of land planning by-laws.

By 1950 it was clear that decentralisation provided inadequate control over land planning, indeed the administration deemed it a dismal failure.[59] Although thirteen out of seventeen Native Authorities had made rules, they proved impossible to enforce.[60] In response, Chief Commissioner T.A. Mead created a non-statutory Central Land Utilisation Committee (CLUC), which eventually could be

[55] Ibid., 2.

[56] Lawra Land Planning Meeting, 15–16 August 1949, NRG8/5/36, NAGT.

[57] Zuarungu District Commissioner, 11 September 1949, NRG8/1/70, NAGT.

[58] David Scott, 27 April 1949, NRG3/15/4, NAGT.

[59] The investigation grew out of a request for information from the Director of the Inter-African Information Bureau on the Conservation and Utilisation of the Soil. Gold Coast, memorandum, 31 July, 1950, NRG8/1/70, NAGT.

[60] Gold Coast, memorandum. Mamprusi District Commissioner, 11 September 1950, NRG8/1/70, NAGT. Lawra District Commissioner, 12 September 1950, NRG8/1/70, NAGT.

turned into a statutory board under the control of the government.[61] Agricultural Officer D.J. Billes applauded this idea as a critical step in facilitating "what would amount to a social and agricultural revolution, materially altering the status of the Northern Territories."[62] However, the Gold Coast Executive Council rejected Mead's request because the board's functions would overlap with Departmental tasks. Instead, they asked Mead to adopt a "fresh approach" based on "the development of existing organisation," that is, development by local committees.[63]

In March, 1952, Mead reached a compromise with the central administration, calling for the creation of a Soil Conservation branch under the Department of Agriculture.[64] Within this structure, land planning activities would be developed by a network of project committees who would submit projects to the CLUC.[65] This move only solved half the problem, however, for there existed no legislation "to maintain and develop what is being done." To make matters worse, non-statutory status of the CLUC meant that land planning financial management fell to the already overburdened departmental staff. As a result of this stalemate, the recently constituted land planning committees sat in limbo awaiting an adequate organisational framework.[66]

These persistent problems provoked a proposal for a statutory land planning board in 1952.[67] The CLUC and CLUC sub-committee both agreed that legal land planning powers would be crucial to the success of the programme and that they should be given to the Ministry of Agriculture. D.J. Billes and F.E. Hughes argued for the delegation of legal powers to a Northern Territories Land Utilisation Board as a statutory body. In their opinion, the land planning committees should not be forced to refer to Accra for every decision. The Board, argued Billes and Hughes, had to have enough "teeth" to apply a "Northern Territories outlook" to its land planning activities.[68] Billes clearly wanted enough authority and autonomy to create and enforce legislation prohibiting cultivation in overcrowded areas

[61] T.A. Mead, 22 September 1951, NRG8/1/68, NAGT.
[62] D.J. Billes, 3 March 1952, NRG8/1/93, NAGT.
[63] Gold Coast Executive Council, 21 January 1952, NRG8/1/68, NAGT.
[64] D.J. Billes, 3 March 1952, NRG8/1/93, NAGT.
[65] Chief Regional Officer, 27 June 1952, NRG8/1/93, NAGT.
[66] T.A. Mead, 20 February 1952, NRG8/1/93, NAGT.
[67] The debate and proposal can be found in NRG8/1/93, NAGT.
[68] D.J. Billes and F.E. Hughes, 3 March 1952, NRG8/1/93, NAGT.

and forcing resettlement where necessary.[69] The Ministry of Agriculture agreed to enact an ordinance along these lines, stressing that it would apply only in the Northern Territories because it would "raise serious opposition from the Ashanti and Colony members and thus frustrate our good intentions for the Northern Territories."[70]

The proposed land planning ordinance, enacted in 1953, provided for the designation of land planning areas by Order-in-Council and the establishment of land planning committees as executive bodies subject to policy direction from the Ministry of Agriculture. Representatives from local and district councils (more of which below) could be appointed to the land planning committees, but only on the specific recommendation of the Ministry of Housing and Local Government.[71] In 1953, the North-East and North-West Land Planning Committees were abolished in favour of a central committee, the Northern Territories Land Utilisation Committee, and subordinate area committees for Dedoro-Tankara, Wiaga, Bumbugu, Frafra, Tamne and Sielo-Tuni. Lawra-Tumu was not included, because of the District Administration's reputation for ignoring instructions from the colonial state to make its development plans more programmatic. With this decision the Lawra-Tumu District, which the Provincial Commissioner a few years before had declared "the centre of activities on the Northern Territories," was written out of the development program in the north.[72]

Despite the centralisation of power under the new ordinance, the colonial state continued to make local participation the cornerstone of the new plan. The state also shied away from evicting existing peasant producers to make way for land planning areas. This hesitation appeared partly due to a lack of funds, staff and political dominance with which to implement Ordinance-based coercion. But the government's caution also reflected the administration's balancing act between indirect rule and the coercive measures that characterised many post-war colonial development schemes. Factored into the calculation was the fear of African resistance to foreign exploitation.

---

[69] D.J. Billes, 29 September 1952, NRG8/1/93, NAGT.

[70] Gold Coast, Ministry of Agriculture, 25 November 1952, NRG8/1/93, NAGT.

[71] Gold Coast, Ministry of Agriculture, 16 June 1953, NRG8/1/93, NAGT.

[72] Provincial Commissioner, Northwest Province, 22 May 1943, ADM61/5/16, National Archives of Ghana, Accra (NAGA). Chief Regional Officer, Northern Territories, memorandum, NRG8/1/113, NAGT.

As Forest Conservator R.L. Brooks noted, the Gold Coast land planning schemes threatened to undermine the spirit of indirect rule by granting coercive powers to the central government.[73] The state needed to use coercion, however, to guarantee the enforcement of the land planning programme. How could this be achieved? Simply put, it could not. Although the possibility of central coercion presented itself with the abandonment of indirect rule after 1952, the administration continued to frame development policy mindful of African resistance. In the field of land planning, therefore, the colonial administration continued to struggle with the contradiction between agricultural development and the preservation of African community. As we shall discover below, the implementation of local government produced a similar struggle.

Political Reforms and the Northern Territories, 1946–50

In 1951, while the administration laid its plans for economic development and land planning, the Gold Coast moved to internal self-government under Kwame Nkrumah. This shift occurred despite the attempts of colonial officers to fend off nationalist resistance. During World War Two, for instance, Governor Alan Burns attempted to defuse political protests by Africanising the colony's political system. In 1942, Burns opened the administration to African Assistant District Commissioners and Executive Council members. Two years later he strengthened the local powers of the Native Authorities, and in 1946 he introduced a new constitution bringing Ashanti and the Colony together into the Legislative Assembly. In Austin's words, Burns' reforms solidified a "triple ruling elite" for the Gold Coast, consisting of the British officials, the chiefs and the "intelligentsia."[74] In 1947, the southern intelligentsia took advantage of the political opening by forming the United Gold Coast Convention (UGCC), a reformist political party seeking independence through constitutional means. Later that year the UGCC Working Committee invited a young political activist named Kwame Nkrumah to return home

[73] R.L. Brooks, 26 August 1950, NRG8/1/49, NAGT.

[74] Dennis Austin, *Politics in Ghana, 1946–1960* (London: Oxford University Press, 1964), 8–9.

from England to become the UGCC's General Secretary.[75] With the formation of the UGCC and the arrival of Nkrumah, the stage was set in the south for the development of nationalist party politics.

The same could not be said of the Northern Territories, where the colonial administration attempted to block the development of nationalist politics by excluding northerners from direct representation in the Legislative Assembly. Instead, the administration created a non-statutory chiefs' association, the Northern Territories Council (NTC), in 1946. The idea for a northern chiefs' council dated back to 1938 when the northern administration convened the first meeting of all paramount chiefs, and it was reinforced by Lord Hailey's 1941 recommendation to introduce the chiefs to politics without undermining their identity as traditional rulers.[76] Drawing on these precedents, the administration created the NTC as an advisory body without legislative authority, introducing chiefs into national politics without giving them any real power.[77] The Council would come to be dominated by chiefs and their sons and relatives educated at the Government Training College in Tamale.[78] Built in 1944, the Training College provided a meeting place for a nascent elite with aspirations of forming a political association. This possibility worried the colonial administration, which had quashed an earlier association of teachers and civil servants because it threatened to become a northern ARPS. With the NTC, the administration hoped to direct the activities of the emerging northern elite away from anticolonial nationalist politics. Its main role therefore was to advise the Chief Commissioner on matters relating to the Native Authorities.[79] In this sense the Council can be seen as an extension of indirect rule, under which the colonial administration attempted to work with the chiefs and their sons within the framework of Native Administration.

Meanwhile, political events in the south outpaced Burns' plans for gradual reform and rendered the 1946 constitution obsolete. In 1948–9, rioting in Accra prompted a constitutional enquiry that

[75] Ibid., 53–4; Paul Andre Ladouceur, *Chiefs and Politicians: The Politics of Regionalism in Northern Ghana* (London: Longman Group Limited, 1979), 80.

[76] R. Bagulo Bening, *A History of Education in Northern Ghana, 1907–1976* (Accra: Ghana Universities Press, 1990), 193.

[77] Ibid., 75.

[78] The College was opened in 1944 to provide teacher training in the Northern Territories See Ladouceur, 70.

[79] Ladouceur, 72, 79.

moved the colony towards internal self-government. In early 1948, after police killed several ex-servicemen at a peaceful rally in Accra, rioting spread quickly across the Colony and Ashanti. In response, the colonial government declared a State of Emergency, arrested the UGCC leadership and detained them in the Northern Territories, and created a commission to investigate the causes of the disturbances. The Watson Commission traced the roots of the problem to two issues: the administration's anti-swollen shoot campaign, aimed at cutting out diseased cocoa trees, and the decline in purchasing power due to rising import prices and stagnant wages. According to the Commission, these problems had provoked resistance among the population at large, but especially among unemployed school leavers. In light of the report, the colonial state commissioned an all-African committee under the chairmanship of Henry Coussey to discuss the Watson Commission's recommendations and formulate a blueprint for a new constitution.[80]

The Coussey Committee reported in October, 1949, recommending a bicameral or unicameral system of semi-responsible government including an Executive Council and a Legislative Assembly, and reserve powers vested in the Governor. The Assembly was to be a mix of modern and traditional politics, with two-thirds popularly elected and one-third chosen by traditional authorities.[81] In the north, however, the Coussey report rejected the popular franchise entirely. Instead, the Northern Territories' nineteen legislative seats (out of eighty-four) were to be elected indirectly by a Northern Electoral College, composed of the sixteen members of the NTC and 104 delegates from newly formed District Councils. The District Councils would be part of a new three-tiered system of local government consisting of regional, district and local councils, two-thirds directly elected and one-third appointed by traditional authorities.[82]

The idea of District Councils owed much to the championing of local government by colonial governors in Africa after 1945. For example, during a conference at Cambridge University in 1947, the governors concluded that village councils should form the "foundation of all local government in Africa." The edifice of local government would be constructed on the framework of the existing Native

[80] The Coussey Committee sat from December, 1948 to August, 1949. See Ladouceur, 74.

[81] Austin, *Politics in Ghana*, 86.

[82] Lentz, *Ethnicity and the Making of History in Northern Ghana*, 294.

Administration system, amalgamating small units into a web of connected, secular political units "with a chain of responsibility through district councils to the central native administration." In order to "develop" and "strengthen" African government, the District Councils would be open to "progressive" members of African society, "including the middle class." This move would guarantee the representation of the educated elite. It also meant that African local government would be based on elections, either directly through the ballot box or indirectly through a series of electoral colleges appointed by the colonial states.[83] Colonial Secretary of State Arthur Creech Jones also believed strongly in local government, which he considered a key element in Britain's "whole policy for the development of the African Territories" because it would introduce democratic representation into the African colonies.[84]

In the Northern Territories, local government reform sought to control the growth of African nationalist politics, which colonial officers considered premature. "Premature" nationalism was dangerous, because modern politics would produce corruption if it developed too early in the transition between tradition and modernity. The Acting Assistant CCNT expressed this sentiment especially clearly in 1948, wiring that

> unscrupulous politicians are not of course confined to Africa, but the African scene provides at this moment and at the present stage of development an unusually promising field for them in the breakdown of religious sanctions and of traditional power structures.

The solution was to design local government reforms around existing traditional institutions. The Acting Assistant CCNT continued:

> It is for this reason that, at any rate in the field of local government I feel that traditional forms which have evolved their own sanctions and which are still respected should be developed, altered and strengthened rather than that political forms that may have proved suitable in some other areas with a completely different history, climate and social structure be imposed on grounds of ideological principle.[85]

---

[83] "Conference of African Governors, 1947, Local Government in Africa," Confidential AGC #12, Enclosure to the Secretary of State's Confidential Despatch date the 13 January, 1948, NRG8/2/96, NAGT.

[84] A. Creech Jones, "The Secretary of State to the Officer Administering the Gold Coast," 13 January 1948, NRG8/2/96, NAGT. "Conference of African Governors," 152, NRG8/2/96, NAGT.

[85] Acting Assistant Chief Commissioner, Northern Territories to Gold Coast Governor, 17 January 1948, NRG8/2/96, NAGT.

One of the goals of local government, therefore, was to prevent nationalist organisations from developing on northern soil. This could be accomplished by channelling the north's educated elite into a political system that meshed with the British doctrine of colonial development, and thus did not threaten to undermine the power of the colonial state.

In 1949, Burns' successor Charles Arden-Clarke approved the Coussey report in principle and thus committed the government to the balancing act between modern and traditional politics. At the national level, Arden-Clarke opted for a unicameral legislature, partial suffrage, and reserve powers for the governor. The UGCC also supported the Coussey report's recommendations, with the exception of a minority report objecting to the Governor's reserve powers. Nkrumah, however, resisted. By this time, he had split from the UGCC and formed the more radical Convention People's Party (CPP), which rejected the moderate, constitutional road to independence under the slogan "Self-Government Now". The CPP quickly gained a following among unemployed school leavers, the so-called veranda boys, and began to plan for a Gandhian campaign of Positive Action to press for immediate independence. Excluded from the Coussey Committee because of their radicalism, Nkrumah and the CPP drafted an alternative plan calling for immediate independence and universal suffrage. When Arden-Clarke rejected the plan, Nkrumah's followers launched Positive Action in early 1950. In the face of boycotts and a general strike in 1950, Arden-Clarke declared a State of Emergency. Nkrumah was imprisoned, along with the leaders of the CPP and the Trades Union Congress.[86]

Politics and the Northern Territories, 1951–3

The national election went ahead in February, 1951, with Nrkumah and his inner circle in jail. In a profound development, the CPP won a landslide victory and Nkrumah was released from prison to become Leader of Government Business. As planned, the NTC sent nineteen delegates to represent the Northern Territories in Nkrumah's new parliament. As Lentz observes, at this time the northern par-

[86] Austin, 86–90. Hargreaves, 127.

liamentarians were "decidedly politically-unaffiliated in the CPP-dominated Legislative Assembly." Most of them were chiefs' relatives who had been educated together in Tamale and shared a strong sense of identity as northerners rather than sympathy to particular political parties.[87] In Saaka's words, the northern members operated as "a non-aligned bloc in a CPP-dominated Assembly," an observation confirmed by S.W.D.K. Gandah's recollection that very few people had party membership cards before 1954.[88] Once in government, some of the northern representatives, including J.A. Braimah and J.H. Allassani, accepted ministerial posts in the new government, taking advantage of the opportunity for national power.[89] However, as we shall see below, party politics would not emerge in the north until the election of 1954, and not fully until 1956. For the time being, northerners attempted to press for northern concerns as a collective bloc.

In the meantime, the administration implemented local government in the form of the Local Government Act of 1951. Drawing on the Coussey report, the Act divided the former Native Authorities into traditional State Councils and elected District and Local Councils. The State Councils were run by chiefs, whose authority was confined to traditional constitutional affairs. As recommended by the Coussey report, chiefs were guaranteed one-third of the seats on the Local and District Councils, the remaining two-thirds elected by popular franchise.[90] This stipulation fell short of the wishes of some NTC members, such as Duri chief and Lawra M.L.A. S.D. Dombo, who wanted more positions reserved for chiefs. In 1951, Dombo went so far as to introduce a motion in the NTC to raise the chiefs' representation to one-half. Dombo's motion was defeated ten to five, but many NTC members still worried about the reforms, one even suggesting that the bill should be postponed for further study.[91] In the

[87] Carola Lentz, "'The Time When Politics Came': Ghana's Decolonisation from the Perspective of a Rural Periphery," *Journal of Contemporary African Studies* 20, No. 2 (2002): 251.

[88] Yakubu Saaka, "Some Linkages Between the North and South in the Evolution of National Consciousness in Ghana," *Journal of Black Studies* 18, No. 1 (1987): 13–14. S.W.D.K. Gandah, *The Silent Rebel* (Accra: Sub-Saharan Publishers, 2004), 221.

[89] Saaka, 13–14.

[90] Ladouceur, 74.

[91] Lentz, *Ethnicity and the Making of History in Northern Ghana*, 298. *Record of the Tenth Session of the Territorial Council held at Tamale*, 31 October–2 November, 1951, 11, 15, Balme Library Collection, University of Ghana.

event, the elected majority mattered little in the 1950s, because almost all local government positions were filled by chiefs or their relatives.[92] Moreover, the council boundaries mirrored the boundaries of the old Native Authorities, and British officers remained in place, although their titles were changed to Chief Regional Officer (replacing the CCNT) and Government Agent (replacing the District Officer). In this sense, the local government system preserved important elements of indirect rule.[93]

At the same time, the councils were placed under central control through a new Ministry of Local Government. In the Governor's opinion, this safeguard preserved the authority of the central government while devolving power to locally elected officials. The government would continue to control "the main lines of policy," leaving "as much of its execution as possible to the initiative and discretion of locally elected people." In its own words, the Act had "laid down . . . one system for all Local Authorities and controls them all, but still permits local choice and local variations *within certain defined limits*. Anything done by a Council beyond those limits is '*ultra vires*.'"[94] In this manner, by establishing local government and opening it to the educated elite, the colonial state attempted to channel nationalist political activities into safer avenues of community development, over which the state retained firm legal control.

Local Government and Colonial Development Doctrine

The creation of District and State Councils reflected the administration's desire to substitute a modern political system for indirect rule without undermining the essence of African community. Colonial Secretary of State Creech Jones epitomised this need with a dispatch to the African governors in 1947 tying local government to economic and political development. According to Ursula Hicks, as a Labour Party member Creech Jones believed that local government would enable the British to implement a form of "local socialism," absorbing the unemployed "educated classes" into community-driven

[92] Lentz, *Ethnicity and the Making of History in Northern Ghana*, 298.
[93] Staniland, 128.
[94] Local Government Ordinance, 1951, typescript, 382, NRG8/28/23, NAGT. Italics added.

development programmes.[95] The aims of local government were thus similar to those of indirect rule, especially the emphasis on local treasuries and taxation.[96] If community formed the root of both systems, however, its basis had changed from heredity to popular election. Framed in these terms, local government sought to subsume the troublesome members of civil society (the educated elite and unemployed school leavers) under the umbrella of village community, with one foot firmly planted in tradition.

On the surface this project appeared to work, as many District Councils reflected the boundaries of the old Native Authorities. The north-west provides a clear example, where the administration created three District Councils for Wa, Lawra and Tumu. Underneath the Lawra Confederacy Council were the four Local Councils of Lawra, Nandom, Jirapa and Lambussie, which mirrored the old subordinate Native Authorities. The link between local government and older chiefs' boundaries was intended to reflect "units of co-operation and common interest."[97] This cloak of continuity, however, concealed deeply rooted differences between chiefs, which reflected the complex interaction between traditional authority, colonialism and the development of modern politics and civil society. Simply put, the chiefs did not conform to the colonial ideal of the modernisation of African community. Using the modern framework of the local government system, chiefs fought for autonomy and the right to tap into government resources earmarked for community development. Focused on controlling the institutions of civil society (local councils, village development committees, et cetera), these struggles also were rooted in earlier battles over traditional authority.

Birifu provides an excellent example. During the colonial period, the chief of Birifu had been subordinated to Lawra, and there ensued a long period of political struggle. Although the chiefs had reconciled by the late 1940s, relations deteriorated after the death of the Birifu chief in early 1950. In 1951, the new Chief, Nonatuo Gandah,

[95] Ursula K. Hicks, *Development From Below: Local Government and Finance in Developing Countries of the Commonwealth* (Oxford: The Clarendon Press, 1961), 4–6.

[96] Hicks notes that the finance committee formed the backbone of local government in nineteenth century England. See Hicks, 23.

[97] *Report of the Commission of Enquiry Into Representational and Electoral Reform* (Accra: Government Printer, 1953), 17, cited in Lentz, "'The Time When Politics Came'", 257.

requested independence from Lawra on the grounds that Birifu had been subordinated to Lawra by political force during the colonial era.[98] As a result, Gandah argued, Birifu received no funding for local development. Gandah blamed this state of affairs on former District Commissioner W.J.A. Jones, whose subordination of Birifu caused the village to be "plundered" by Lawra. The Assistant District Commissioner dismissed Birifu's request out of hand, arguing that the Government's resources were insufficient to focus local development on any single village.[99] Nonatuo Gandah then submitted a petition to the Minister of Local Government requesting his own Local Council. Once again the government rejected Gandah's request. For his part, the chief of Lawra tried to defuse the situation by offering Gandah the Chair of the Lawra District Council. However, after his term in office, Gandah made yet another attempt, again unsuccessful, to secede from Lawra. By this time, party politics had arrived in the north and Gandah shifted his tactics by joining the CPP instead of the NPP (more of which below).[100] In fighting for control over local development, Gandah's illustrates the complex ways in which civil society (the new Birifu chief was an educated elite) pressed against the colonial ideal of modernising African community.

Local Government and the Land Priests

If local government fed into chiefly rivalries, on paper it nonetheless supported chiefs more than land priests. The State Councils established the chiefs as trustees over community traditions and customary law, including matters of land tenure. This decision occurred despite the attempts of some colonial officers to revive the authority of the land priests. For instance, in 1948 Commissioner of Lands R.C. Stacpoole tried to have them reinstated as political authorities, in the spirit of the Land and Native Rights Ordinance (LNRO) of 1931. Stacpoole worried that the chiefs would become corrupt landlords, unable to manage "economic pressure on an ancient system of land tenure arising from the change to permanent crops and the

[98] Lentz provides an excellent discussion of this event in her study of colonialism and ethnicity in the north-west. See Lentz, *Ethnicity and the Making of History in Northern Ghana*, 305–7.

[99] Birifu Na to Chief Commissioner of the Northern Territories, 9 July 1951, Assistant District Commissioner to Birifu Na, 3 August 1951, NRG8/2/110, NAGT.

[100] Lentz, *Ethnicity and the Making of History in Northern Ghana*, 307.

general alienation of land." In Stacpoole's opinion, the rapid development of a modern land market controlled by the chiefs would undermine the spirit of the West African Lands Committee (WALC) "to the detriment of the old system of land tenure until at last will arrive a time at which a new system of tenure will be evolved *based on complete fallacy and without definition.*" In response, Stacpoole proposed to revive the LNRO of 1931. All land would be held communally rather than individually, and the land priests would be empowered as legal trustees over land transactions on behalf of their communities.[101]

In making this suggestion, Stacpoole consciously wanted to take the north back to 1912, before economic progress had undermined the "purely native system of land tenure". Quoting the WALC, Stacpoole wrote that "land is God-given like air or water, and every single individual is entitled to a share. But land is not simply the property of the living, it belongs also to the ancestors and to future generations." This system had been preserved by the LNRO, allowing the land priests to adjudicate applications for usufructary rights. The authority of the land priests protected the "welfare of the community" by channelling the benefits from increasing land values, which were "due to communal efforts," into the community rather than lining the pockets of greedy individuals such as the chiefs. Reviving the land priests would stop "the unhindered deterioration of native land tenure to a point at which greed and the lack of informed forethought lead native communities to part with the land upon which their prosperity, and very livelihood depends."[102] For Stacpoole, therefore, the office of land priest was crucial to the preservation of community against the forces of landlordism.

Although Stacpoole's ideas were not new, they revived the debate among northern political officers over how to bring traditional land tenure arrangements into line with the new system of Native Administration. Stacpoole argued, correctly, that the land priests still wielded some power despite the fact that official business was carried on through the chiefs. For example, land priests were involved in the approval of land rights for shops, and they exercised significant authority in matters of land tenure.[103] However, most northern officials

[101] R.C. Stacpoole, May, 1948, 5–12, 159, NRG8/1/51, NAGT.
[102] Ibid., 2–9.
[103] See for example Lentz, *Ethnicity and the Making of History in Northern Ghana*, 348–9.

rejected the land priests in favour of the chiefs, whom they considered worthy successors in the modernisation of land tenure. For example, the Acting Chief Commissioner argued that the land priest was "becoming an anachronism and is being replaced by the Native Authority; but the Native Customary system of land tenure should not be upset even if the tengdaana himself does descend to the status of an interesting anthropological relic."[104] District Commissioner Gass portrayed the process as the natural secularisation of land tenure:

> To my mind the power and influence of Native Authorities over land has been a logical development from the old system of land tenure and one that economically and politically has been natural and inevitable. To regularise this position now will surely lead to an improved system and allow it to develop consistently with modern conditions. To try to enforce a religious control of land against existing trends is rather the way to stultify development and install (sic) chaos.[105]

Salaga District Commissioner Crabb argued that although the north's land tenure was moving towards private property, its negative effects, which had posed serious problems for colonial rule in the south, could be avoided in the north by proper control. In the Northern Territories, argued Crabb, the development of land tenure had been "worked out by the people themselves to their own satisfaction without our direct intervention and indeed without our noticing what has been going on." The colonial administration simply needed to regularise what had been happening "in fact if not in law," that is, the development of Native Authorities as land authorities with land priests as consultative figures without statutory powers.[106] This would place the control over land in the chiefs, acting as trustees for their communities through the Native Authorities.

The preference for the chiefs was enshrined in the Local Government Act of 1951, which empowered the chiefs to control traditional matters through the State Councils. On paper, this decision once again undermined the authority of the land priests against the chiefs. As in the past, however, official support for the chiefs simply established new terrain for longstanding struggles over land and power. Lentz provides an excellent example in a conflict between the chief and

[104] Memorandum, Chief Commissioner, Northern Territories, n.d., but 1948, NRG8/1/57, NAGT.

[105] M.D.I. Gass, n.d. NRG8/1/57, NAGT, 5.

[106] Crabb, 16 August 1948, NRG8/1/57, NAGT.

earth priest of Nandom in the 1950s. The conflict was related to another struggle, between the chiefs of Nandom and Lambussie, over two villages along the border between the two divisions. As noted earlier, Lambussie had been subsumed under Nandom when the colonial state created the Lawra Confederacy. In 1948, the administration reversed this decision and granted autonomy to Lambussie. This decision fuelled conflict over farming rights and taxation. The villages in question belonged to Lambussie and they were mainly Sissala, but many Dagara farmers had settled from the Nandom side of the border. However, because of their colonial tribal identity the Dagara farmers paid taxes to the Nandom Local Council rather than Lambussie. In 1955, the chief of Lambussie threatened to evict the farmers unless they joined the Lambussie Local Council. To justify his case, he reminded the Lawra Confederacy State Council that Lambussie had gained autonomy from Nandom in 1948, and that the Dagara farmers had received the right to farm from a Sissala earth priest. The State Council ruled in favour of Lambussie, saying that the Dagara farmers who had settled permanently across the border should join the Lambussie Local Council.[107]

The Nandom chief opposed the ruling and petitioned the Chief Regional Officer for an autonomous Nandom State Council, independent of the Lawra Confederacy Council. In response, the Lawra chief attempted to have the chief of Nandom removed from office. To this end he enlisted the support of the Nandom land priests, who had been fighting with their chief for some time over income from market fees, rents and building permits. When local government was introduced, the earth priests successfully had demanded representation on the Nandom Local Council. As members of the Council, they demanded an annual commission on a new United Africa Company store. The Nandom chief objected, with the support of the Government Agent, on the grounds that the land priests were entitled only to "customary sacrifices," not commissions. Stung by this rejection, one of the land priests refused to support Nandom in the conflict over the Dagara farmers in Lambussie.[108]

On the surface, this example illustrates that land priests continued to exercise power despite the colonial bias in favour of the chiefs. However, it also demonstrates the extent to which "traditional"

[107] Lentz, *Ethnicity and the Making of History in Northern Ghana*, 345–7.
[108] Ibid., 348–9.

matters such as land had become transformed and modernised by 1950s. Using the institutions of local government, land priests fought not only over customary rights, but also over the lucrative proceeds from economic development. Furthermore, these struggles weaved their way through complex political machinations within the local government system. As we shall see below, the situation became even more complex with the arrival of party politics in the north in 1954.

Party Politics, 1954–57

The new terrain of struggle between political actors in the Northern Territories was complicated further by the development of party politics on the eve of the election of 1954. Before the election, the government extended the franchise to the north and allocated twenty-six Legislative Assembly seats to the Northern Territories. Responding to this development, a faction of northern chiefs connected to the NTC and the colonial administration created the Northern Peoples Party (NPP) in 1954. The party was started by two members of the 1951 Legislative Assembly, S.D. Dombo and Mumumi Bawumia, who believed that the north could influence national policy with a united front in parliament.[109] Both men had connections to chieftaincy. Dombo was a sub-divisional chief in the Jirapa Division.[110] Bawumia was a close associate of the *Nayiri*, the paramount chief of Mamprusi, and became the clerk of the Mamprusi District Council.[111] On paper, the formation of the NPP by these men signalled a major political cleavage in the Northern Territories. On the one hand stood the NPP with its roots in the NTC and the politics of indirect rule. On the other hand stood the CPP, which had attracted a group of northerners opposed to the domination of the northern political scene by the chiefs empowered by the colonial administration during the period of indirect rule.[112] As we shall see below, however, the situation was rather more complicated.

[109] Gandah, *The Silent Rebel*, 221.
[110] Lentz, *Ethnicity and the Making of History in Northern Ghana*, 342.
[111] Christian Lund, "'Bawku is still volatile': ethno-political conflict and state recognition in Northern Ghana," *Journal of Modern African Studies* 41, No. 4 (2003): 590. Dennis Austin, "Elections in a Rural African Area," *Africa* 31, No. 1 (1961): 10.
[112] Ibid., 115, 121, 145.

In the south the CPP leaned heavily on the support of non-royal "youngmen" rather than chiefs and their royal relatives.[113] Against the UGCC, which had the support of several major chiefs in the south, Nkrumah raised enough mass support to win the election of 1954, which granted the Gold Coast an all-African Legislative Assembly. A wave of political opposition, driven by the formation of an Asante-based political party, the National Liberation Movement (NLM), provoked Britain to demand a third election in 1956.[114] Once again, the CPP won the election and the Gold Coast became the independent nation of Ghana in 1957, under the leadership of Kwame Nkrumah.[115]

Meanwhile, the NPP emerged as the strongest party in the north, winning the majority of seats in both 1954 and 1956. Some authors have attributed the victories to the party's character as a British-backed movement of chiefs who mobilised their subjects against the "commoner" upstarts of the CPP.[116] However, NPP candidates did not dominate all northern campaigns completely, and the CPP's ranks included chiefs and their relatives as well as elite "commoners". In fact, voting patterns were complex and reflected local rivalries between chiefs and even within chiefs' families as much as the "chief-commoner" divide. They certainly were not driven simply by the conservative intentions of the colonial administration. Subordinate chiefs joined the CPP in the hopes of unseating paramount chiefs, and candidates for paramount chieftaincies joined to strengthen their candidacies. In addition, many political candidates ran as independents in 1954, eschewing any party affiliation whatsoever. Cleaner party divisions emerged in 1956, but the campaigns remained anchored in local and regional affairs. As Carola Lentz has shown, it is very

---

[113] Richard Rathbone, *Nkrumah and the Chiefs: The Politics of Chieftaincy in Ghana, 1951–60* (Athens: Ohio University Press, 2000), 23–25.

[114] See Jean Allman, *The Quills of the Porcupine: Asante Nationalism in an Emergent Ghana* (Madison: University of Wisconsin Press, 1993), for an analysis of Asante nationalism after 1945.

[115] The decolonisation process has been covered in many studies, the best of which remain those of Dennis Austin. See for example Dennis Austin, "Elections in a Rural African Area," in *Independent Black Africa: The Politics of Freedom*, ed. William John Hanna (Chicago: Rand McNally and Company, 1964), 341–63 and Austin's excellent *Politics in Ghana*. See also David Apter, *Ghana in Transition* (Princeton: Princeton University Press), 1972.

[116] See for example Saaka, "National Consciousness," 11–12.

difficult to determine any simple patterns of political affiliation.[117] In very general terms, the core of the NTC supported the NPP and dissociated itself from the CPP and Nkrumah's "Freedom Now" campaign. In contrast, the CPP often attracted the educated elite, as well as "lesser" chiefs who had lost power during indirect rule. The NPP also argued against independence on the grounds that the north was not ready for self-government and thus ran the risk of domination by the southern political elite. Some of the less powerful northern chiefs disagreed with this sentiment, and a significant number of them joined the CPP.[118] In many cases, however, their dissent reflected local disputes over power rather than commitments to rival ideologies.

This trend was illustrated especially clearly in the Lawra-Nandom constituency of the north-west, where party affiliation closely followed chiefly rivalries. In 1954, the main contenders were Abayifaa Karbo, son of the chief of Lawra, and Nonatuo Gandah, the chief of Birifu. As noted above, when Karbo came out in support of the NPP, Gandah decided to join the CPP in the hopes of obtaining the coveted Local Council for Birifu. Karbo won a very close race, polling 27.6% against Gandah's 24.2%, which produced a victory of only 330 votes (2,674 versus 2,434). The remaining votes were divided mainly between two of three independent candidates. The same two men ran in 1956, but there were fewer independent candidates and Karbo was able to rally more support, winning a decisive victory for the NPP with 73.3% of the vote.[119]

The hardening of party lines in 1956 further cemented the connection between local conflicts and party politics. For example, during the campaign, Polkuu, a cousin of the Nandom chief, publicly supported Gandah and the CPP. Although he had run as an independent in 1954, against the NPP's Abayifaa Karbo from Lawra, Polkuu in fact was supported by the CPP. This allowed the CPP to run two candidates, Gandah and Polkuu, against Karbo. The CPP

[117] See the excellent analysis in Lentz, "'The Time When Politics Came," and Lentz, *Ethnicity and the Making of History in Northern Ghana*, Chapter 8.

[118] Gandah and Lentz provide excellent material on the complexities of party affiliations in the north-west. See Gandah, *The Silent Rebel*, Chapters 19–21 and Lentz, "The Time When Politics Came." For other areas, see Austin, *Politics in Ghana*, 185–6 and Ladouceur, 92.

[119] Gandah, *The Silent Rebel*, 224; Lentz, *Ethnicity and the Making of History in Northern Ghana*, 343.

hoped that Gandah and Karbo would split the vote and that Polkuu would come through the middle to victory. The strategy failed, so Polkuu and Nandom chief Imoro decided to support the CPP openly in 1956. As noted above, by this time the Lawra State Council had decided against Imoro in the Lambussie case and warned him not to interfere with the rights of his land priests. During the election the struggle became politically charged, with the Nandom chief allying with the CPP and the Nandom earth priests joining the Lawra chief and the NPP.[120]

Karbo's election as an NPP member within a CPP government fed into the politicisation of the conflict after 1956. In early 1957, the NPP-friendly land priests and headmen from fourteen villages in the Nandom division petitioned to have CPP-supporter Imoro destooled because he wanted to secede from the Lawra State Council without consulting the sub-divisional chiefs. The NPP-dominated Lawra State Council tried to suspend Imoro from office and pushed ahead with the case. Imoro appealed to the CPP government, but he died before a decision was made. After Imoro's death, Polkuu claimed that Imoro had appointed him chief according to a local tradition in which a dying chief appoints his successor. The CPP ruled in favour of Polkuu against his rival Yuori, who was supported by the pro-NPP land priests and headmen. The decision came after a protracted enquiry during which Yuori claimed legitimacy on the grounds that the land priests had appointed him chief, also supposedly according to tradition. The enquiry thus focused ostensibly on interpretations of tradition and whether chiefs or land priests had the right to appoint chiefs' successors. For clear political reasons, the CPP decided in favour of the chiefs. Local power struggles had been absorbed into party politics, and, as one of Lentz's informants observed, 'Polkuu was able to win through politics'.[121]

Meanwhile, political candidates fought similar battles in the Frafra District, which had been created out of the Frafra Native Authority in 1952 and remained part of the Mamprusi Traditional Area until late 1957.[122] Similar to the north-west, the politicisation of the north-east channelled longstanding rivalries between chiefs into party politics. As noted above, NPP co-founder Mumuni Bawumia was close

[120] Lentz, *Ethnicity and the Making of History in Northern Ghana*, 338, 344, 349.
[121] Ibid., 349–56.
[122] Austin, *Politics in Ghana*, 9.

to the *Nayiri* and served as the clerk of the Mamprusi District Council. Bawumia and the *Nayiri* campaigned among the divisional chiefs of the Mamprusi area, saying that the chiefs and sub-chiefs had to vote for the NPP to show proper loyalty to Mamprusi.[123] The CPP after all had been started in Bolgatanga by a shopkeeper, R.B. Braimah, and had drawn fire from the NPP as an anti-chiefs' party. For its part, the CPP campaigned aggressively against the NPP to recruit candidates in Frafra and Bawku.[124]

The results of the 1954 election in Mamprusi seemed to confirm the NPP as a chiefs' party, since the CPP won only one out of ten seats in the Mamprusi Traditional Area. Beneath the surface, however, the picture was more complicated, and once again political differences reflected lineage and chiefly politics. For instance, the campaign in Bongo pitted the chief's candidate, William Amoro, against the former Regent's candidate and son, Kofi Akumolga. Both the chief and Regent were from the same ruling lineage, the latter having been appointed when the chief was exiled between 1947 and 1952. The chief's return in 1952 thus set up a power struggle, which filtered into party politics in 1954 as each man sought representation in Accra. For their part, the party affiliations of the two candidates were flexible. Both had been early members of the CPP, but Akumolga converted to the NPP because of its northern platform. As a member of a royal lineage, he could mobilise important followers from Bongo's royal families as well as their close kin. Amoro did not have a royal background, and as a former teacher he sympathised with the CPP. However, he chose to run as an independent because he did not trust the "C.P.P. label", and, after all, because he had allied with the chief. Amoro won a narrow victory, perhaps because he was able to mobilise his lineage as well as the educated elite and their lineages. In parliament, Amoro initially supported the NPP, but in 1955 he crossed the floor to join the CPP. The NPP seemed to have the last word, however, because later that year the chief died and the pro-NPP *Nayiri* appointed the Regent as his successor. But the new chief ruled as an autocrat, losing the support of many of his subjects, and Amoro won the 1956 election for the CPP.[125]

---

[123] Ladouceur, 118–19.
[124] Lund, 591.
[125] Austin, *Politics in Ghana*, 9–12.

As in the north-west, the Bongo experience illustrates that, far from simply pitting chiefs against non-chiefs, party politics provided a crucible for deeply rooted local struggles over power and political office. As these struggles became politicised, individual candidates used local struggles for their own end, vying to gain individual power at the national level. In the process, the prospect of a northern consensus on politics or development disintegrated. By the mid-1950s, it was clear that the colonial administration had failed in its attempt to channel the modernisation of politics into the safe vessel of African community.

Conclusion

As Cooper argues, after 1935 the Colonial Office invoked development as a tool to increase production and raise living standards in Britain's African colonies. In the Gold Coast, colonial development aimed squarely at solving the southern problems of labour unrest and unemployment among school leavers. On the one hand Governor Burns embarked upon a political program of Africanisation which resulted in increased African representation under the 1946 constitution. On the other hand, the colonial state turned to developing the Northern Territories on a massive scale through the application of a £1 million land planning and agricultural development scheme. This program sought to produce food surpluses in order to increase living standards in the north itself, but also and perhaps more importantly to provide foodstuffs to the south in an effort to blunt the forces of urban discontent.

Economically, the size of the development allocation and the perceived need for land planning resulted in gradual centralisation, typified by the CLUC. Politically, the colonial administration tried to block the emergence of a nationalist elite in the Northern Territories by channelling development through the chief-based NTC and the Native Authorities. Indirect rule had failed to contain the secularisation of politics and it was jettisoned in favour of local government. However, local government reforms simply produced yet another framework for individual struggles over power and authority. In the 1950s, these struggles became tied in complex ways to party politics and the contests between the NPP and CPP. In the process, neither the educated elite nor the chiefs would adhere to the colonial ideal of African community.

However, the colonial administration continued to privilege community as the focus of economic development in the Northern Territories. As we shall discover in Chapter Eight, the colonial administration attempted to structure its largest development project in the north, a mechanised groundnut scheme in Western Gonja, along traditional, village-based lines. At the same time the government invoked Mass Education and Community Development in order to smooth the transition from "traditional community" to "modern community," based on voluntary association at the village level. The Gonja project and the campaign for Mass Education and Community Development form the core of Chapter Eight.

CHAPTER EIGHT

MECHANISED AGRICULTURE AND COMMUNITY DEVELOPMENT, 1948–1957

Introduction

Chapter Seven discussed the shift in development doctrine from indirect rule and mixed farming to local government and land planning. This chapter traces the implementation of two further components of this plan: mechanised agriculture and community development. Mechanisation focused on Western Gonja, an uninhabited area that the administration believed had been locked up from development by trypanosomiasis and slave raiding. Drawing on past ideas about the Northern Territories, colonial officials constructed Western Gonja as an area of previous social upheaval that could be rehabilitated in the name of development. In this sense the Gonja project mirrored Morris's work in the Kamba and Kulpawn valleys, but on a much larger scale, hoping to resettle eighty thousand peasants from the overcrowded Zuarungu District onto uninhabited land near the village of Damongo (see Map 6). Settlers would be resettled in their original village units to prevent social dislocation and preserve African community. In this manner, the colonial administration believed that it could revolutionise agricultural production in the Northern Territories without triggering social transformation. At the same time, a parallel program of community development would bring enough local benefits to guard against a mass flow of migrants into the project area before the Gonja scheme found its feet.

As with earlier schemes, the Gonja project failed to reconcile economic development with the preservation of African community. In fact, the most successful outcome of the scheme was a construction company that split from the agricultural operations in the early 1950s to become a profitable contractor for soil conservation works. The agricultural company floundered and in 1957 was forced to liquidate its assets to Kwame Nkrumah's new government. Meanwhile, in the rural areas subject to community development, the most successful economic enterprises were transport and soil conservation

Map 6: Northern Ghana
Source: Franz Kröger and Barbara Meier (eds.), *Ghana's North: Research on Culture, Religion, and Politics of Societies in Transition.* Frankfurt am Main: Peter Lang, 2003.

works, neither of which involved community participation at any level. Soil conservation survived as a major project, and by 1958 a wave of American conservationists had descended upon the Northern Territories to usher in a new era of development in the newly independent country of Ghana.[1] By this time, the dream of socially engineering a community of eighty thousand collectivised peasants in the undeveloped northern estates had vanished, to be replaced by large-scale, fully mechanised state farms. The following chapter chronicles the attempt and failure by the colonial state to pursue mechanised agriculture and community development, in an attempt to reconcile economic development and African community.

Developing the Estates: Fabian Colonialism and Agricultural Development

The Gonja development scheme originally sought to produce groundnuts for Britain by mechanising peasant-based agriculture. The project began officially in 1950 with the appointment of J.B. Panton as managing director of the Gonja Development Company (GDC).[2] Governor Alan Burns gave Panton the mandate to develop groundnut production on 30,000 acres of uninhabited land recently acquired from the Damongo Native Authority in lieu of rent and compensation for lost crops.[3] It was a major project, receiving £1,000,000 in government equity capital and an operating budget of £120,000 in the first year and £100,000 per year thereafter.[4] Panton recognised the challenge of attempting such an ambitious scheme on marginal land during Britain's dollar crisis and severe shortages of equipment and hard currency.[5] This difficulty, however, made the project all the more appealing as an experiment in social engineering.

The motivation for the Gonja scheme called up the ghost of Chamberlain's doctrine of developing the colonial estates. As noted

[1] Northern Territories Council Standing Committee, minutes of the 73rd Meeting, 29 May 1958, ADM65/5/4, National Archives of Ghana, Accra (NAGA), 2–3.

[2] *Gold Coast Daily Echo*, 26 Januray 1950, in CO96/554/459, Great Britain, Public Record Office (PRO).

[3] J.B. Panton, *Gonja Development Company, Managing Director's Report, 1950–52*, 2,5, CO96/554/459, PRO.

[4] D.J. Morgan, *Official History of British Colonial Development, Volume Two* (Atlantic Highlands: Humanities Press, 1980), 215.

[5] Panton, *Gonja Development Company, Managing Director's Report, December, 1950–June, 1952*, 32, CO554/459, PRO.

in Chapter Seven, World War Two left Britain with a serious shortage of oils, fats and protein. Facing declining production in East Asia and India and a growing dollar crisis, the Labour Government turned to West Africa as a source of raw materials within the sterling area.[6] As the crisis deepened the British government became more aggressive in promoting production rather than welfare in the West African colonies. The commitment to raw materials production led to the creation of two major development organisations, the Colonial Development Corporation (CDC) and the Overseas Food Corporation (OFC). Operating as a strictly commercial institution, the CDC became involved in the search for oilseeds in West Africa.[7]

However, Attlee's Labour government was influenced by Fabian socialists, and, in contrast to Chamberlain, the Colonial Office wanted to transform West African agriculture without opening it up to private capital. As Cowen and Shenton note, in the absence of free markets in land and labour this project required intensive state intervention into production. In other words, in order to extract raw materials from West Africa under the conditions of post-war Fabian colonialism, colonial states had to take up the "positive side of trusteeship."[8] However, post-war state intervention also had to mesh with the West African policy of satisfying social needs under land nationalisation and peasant production. "Colonial policy in West Africa," stated the Colonial Development Corporation in 1949, "supports native tradition and is opposed to the alienation of land from the Government which holds it on behalf of the people."[9]

In developing the African estates after World War Two, Britain thus faced the problem of reconciling agricultural mechanisation with peasant production. However, by the 1940s most colonial officials had lost faith in individual peasant producers. The challenge thus involved developing an agrarian structure capable of modernising and co-ordinating peasant production for the world market. In 1932,

[6] Morgan, *Official History of British Colonial Development, Volume Two*, 177–79.

[7] Robert Shenton, "Nigerian Agriculture in Historical Perspective: Development and Crisis, 1900–60," in *State, Oil and Agriculture in Nigeria*, ed. Michael Watts, 46–9 (Berkeley: The Regents of the University of California, 1987). On the formation of the CDC, see Mike Cowen, "Early Years of the Colonial Development Corporation: British State Enterprise Overseas During Late Colonialism," *African Affairs* 83, No. 330 (1984): 63–75.

[8] M.P. Cowen and R.W. Shenton, *Doctrines of Development* (London: Routledge, 1996), 296–7.

[9] Shenton, *Nigerian Agriculture*, 50.

H.G. Wells anticipated the way out of this dilemma by advocating the integration of peasant producers into large-scale schemes controlled by the state.[10] Under such a structure the state would mediate between capital and labour to maximise production while minimising social transformation. In the West African context, this model involved combining, co-ordinating and modernising communities of rural producers. This strategy reflected the belief that individual peasants were inherently unproductive but that it was undesirable to transform them into capitalist producers.[11] Resistance to West African capitalism was rooted in the history of African resistance to European exploitation. It was supported, however, by Fabian economic theory, which developed Henry George's ideas about landlordism by arguing that capitalists, skilled workers and bankers, as well as landlords, appropriated "unearned increments" from tenants and local communities.[12] In this way Fabian socialist economics dovetailed with the political climate in West Africa to produce a model of agricultural production designed to develop the estates while simultaneously preserving African community.

Collective agriculture provided the answer to this challenge. Its proponents included Meyer Fortes, who provided an example of a more general consensus, framed within the context of Durkheimian sociology and Fabian Colonial Secretary Rita Hinden's *Plan For Africa*.[13] Politically, Fortes' vision resembled Duncan-Johnstone's project of amalgamating of tribes into a modern nation. Drawing on Durkheim, Fortes described the amalgamation process as a transition from the mechanical solidarity of "primitive society," strengthened by British rule, to the organic solidarity of industrial society, held together by the division of labour.[14] "The central problem of colonial development," wrote Fortes in a collection of Fabian colonial

[10] H.G. Wells, *The Work, Wealth and Happiness of Mankind* (London: William Heinemann Ltd., 1934).

[11] M.P. Cowen and R.W. Shenton, "The Origin and Course of Fabian Colonialism in Africa," *Journal of Historical Sociology* 4, No. 2 (June 1991): 167–8.

[12] On the Fabian rent theory, see A.M. McBriar, *Fabian Socialism and English Politics, 1885–1918* (Cambridge: Cambridge University Press, 1966), 29–47.

[13] Rita Hinden, *Plan for Africa* (London: George Allen and Unwin Ltd., 1941). Fortes' connections to the Fabian Colonial Bureau have been noted by Jack Goody in *The Expansive Moment: Anthropology in Britain and Africa, 1918–1970* (Cambridge: Cambridge University Press, 1995), 54.

[14] On mechanical and organic solidarity, see Emile Durkheim, *The Division of Labour In Society* (London: Collier-Macmillan Limited, 1933), 70–132.

essays, "is, to begin with, the problem of integrating clusters of small-scale primitive societies held together in mechanical juxtaposition by the firm scaffolding of European rule into large-scale organic structures."[15] To achieve this transition Fortes advocated an aggressive program of state-driven collectivised agriculture, fuelled by forced saving through direct taxation, which would provide a foundation for industrialisation.[16] Such a programme, Fortes wrote, would give the African population "a direct and communal (as opposed to individual) interest in their own economic development," which would "foster development more swiftly than if the accumulation of capital is left to the private person."[17] Agricultural collectivisation would overcome the low productivity of peasant farmers and permit the rapid agrarian transformation needed to increase living standards and industrialise the Gold Coast. At the same time, it would guard against the emergence of "a limited class of rentiers and capitalists wedded to the new order by profits and power they get out of it at the community's expense."[18]

Some officials within the Colonial Office echoed Fortes' views, going so far as to suggest Stalinist collectivisation in the West Indies and Africa as a hedge against the growth of individual landholdings. For instance, colonial economist G.L.M. Clauson argued that Britain's colonies shared Russia's "excessive fractionalisation of holdings," which he called the "great curse of agriculture." As a remedy, he continued, "the Russian collective (or, as it would be better to call it, cooperative) farm" provided "a complete cure" for "certain evil consequences" of the individualisation of land tenure. Perhaps Britain should consider "whether the African communal system can with advantage be steered in this direction, instead of the direction of individual holdings towards which it is rapidly moving." As in Russia, African peasants would work cooperatively on communal land, producing cash crops for export, and they would be given "garden plots" for subsistence production. Clauson's ideas were framed by a memorandum on Russian farming by another Colonial Office official,

[15] Meyer Fortes, "An Anthropologist's Point of View," in *Fabian Colonial Essays*, ed. R. Hinden, 232 (London: George Allen and Unwin, 1944).

[16] Meyer Fortes, "Comments on Rita Hinden's *Plan for Africa*," 1942, FCB 81/1, Oxford University, Rhodes House Library (RHL). Fortes, "An Anthropologists Point of View," 228.

[17] Fortes, "Comments on Rita Hinden's *Plan for Africa*," 7.

[18] Fortes, "An Anthropologist's Point of View," 228.

S.S. Murray. In the Russian model, wrote Murray, individual peasants had their own houses, subsistence plots and animal stock, but they were organised into communal settlements with a communal farm nearby. The state owned all the machinery, including tractors, which were hired out to the collective farms. In theory, policy was decided at regular monthly meetings of all farm members, but in practice farm management eventually became the responsibility of a staff of trained professionals. Wages were paid on a piecework basis and each collective farm had to deliver its harvest, with production levels set by the state, to the government at below-market prices. Farmers purchased personal goods at a government store, where supplies were better and prices lower than local market levels. According to Murray, the Soviet government also looked after the peasants' social needs, and the collective farms resembled "a complete Beveridge plan with children's nurseries, medical attention, provision for old age and for education, culture, amusement and social welfare".[19]

This odd sympathy for Russian collevisation reflected Fabian socialist ideals stretching back to Sidney and Beatrice Webb's visit to the Soviet Union in the 1930s.[20] After 1945, mindful but not fully aware of the negative effects of Stalin's programme, Fabian colonialists sought to develop collective agriculture without dissolving existing communities of African peasants.[21] In an effort to domesticate Stalinism, the colonial administration would insert arm's-length development corporations between the state and the peasantry.[22] In the process, the preservation and reproduction of African community would be achieved by co-ordinating peasant production through co-operative marketing and distribution. But the vision entailed more than the

[19] Clauson, minute on S.S. Murray, "The Organisation of Agriculture in the U.S.S.R.," 23 July 1943, CO852/402/1, PRO. I thank Dr. R.W. Shenton for bringing this file to my attention.

[20] Sidney and Beatrice Webb, *Soviet Communism: A New Civilisation?* (Special Limited Edition Printed by the Authors for Subscribing Members of Trade Unions, October, 1935).

[21] Cowen and Shenton, "Origins and Course of Fabian Colonialism in Africa," 143–174. Cowen and Shenton, *Doctrines of Development*, 270. McBriar, 38–41.

[22] On "Webbism" (the belief that Stalinism could be implemented without its political horrors), see Samuel P. Huntington, "Political Development and Political Decay," *World Politics* 17, No. 3 (1965). According to Cowen and Laakso, Webbism led Fabian socialists to praise Stalin's development policies. See Michael Cowen and Liisa Laakso, *An Overview of Election Studies in Africa* (Working Paper 1/97, paper presented at Elections in Africa—workshop, Institute of Development Studies, University of Helsinki, 12–21 December, 1996), 19.

marketing co-operatives of the cocoa belt, because the peasants would work on communal farms.

"Persuasion" was to key to collectivisation, and the colonial administration felt confident that it could be effective. This confidence grew out of what Sutton calls an ideology of tradition,[23] or what may more usefully be called the anthropological idea of African community. By resettling entire villages and substituting a development company for land priests and local markets, the colonial state believed that agricultural collectivisation could be achieved voluntarily without breaking down traditional community. Armed with technical knowledge of mechanisation and anthropological knowledge of "tradition," the colonial administration thus set out to achieve economic development while preserving African community in the vast, uninhabited Western Gonja region of the Northern Territories.

Mechanised Agriculture in the Northern Territories, 1947–1948

Filtered through Fabian socialism, the idea of collective agriculture framed the Gonja agricultural scheme. As noted above, the project began officially in 1950 when Governor Burns appointed J.B. Panton as managing director of the Gonja Development Company (GDC). The project dated to 1947, when the Colonial Office revived the idea of developing the north in response to a claim by Unilever that the Northern Territories could support "an area of not less than one million acres" of groundnut production.[24] Despite an earlier, pessimistic report on this potential in West Africa,[25] and doubts about Unilever's motives,[26] the Colonial Office investigated the claim "for the Northern Territories' sake" and for the sake of Britain's strug-

---

[23] Inez Sutton, "Colonial Agricultural Policy: The Non-Development of the Northern Territories of the Gold Coast," *International Journal of African Historical Studies* 22, No. 4 (1989): 668.

[24] Panton, *Managing Director's Report*, 207.

[25] Morgan, *Official History of British Colonial Development, Volume One* (Atlantic Highlands: Humanities Press, 1980), 180–87, 205.

[26] The Colonial Office doubted the UAC's claim, suspecting that the Company simply wanted a railroad in order to monopolise the West African edible oils market. See Dawson to Hollins (Ministry of Food), 19 March 1947, CO829/8, PRO. Dawson to K.E. Robinson, Clay, Orde-Browne, Monson, 19 February 1947, CO852/915/2, PRO. See also Robinson, 27 February 1947, CO852/915/2, PRO.

gling economy.[27] Preliminary reports convinced the Colonial Office that, "at a guess," the Northern Territories would be "fairly favourable" for groundnuts.[28]

On this hunch the Colonial Office sent out a West African oilseeds mission, under the chairmanship of Colonial Agricultural Advisor G.F. Clay, to investigate the potential for oilseed production in the Gold Coast, Nigeria and the Gambia.[29] The Mission focused on the potential for state-run, partially mechanised groundnut production, paying "due regard . . . to the social and economic effects on the territory concerned."[30] This program of "light scale mechanisation" would eliminate the "bottlenecks" of peasant production without transforming the peasantry into a wage labour force at the hands of private capital.[31] From the outset, private capital was to be excluded, on the grounds that "politically it would be fatal to refer to private concessions in West Africa." The Colonial Office also rejected direct production by the British government, through the Overseas Food Corporation, because this had resulted in disaster in a similar groundnut scheme in Tanganiyika.[32] As a result, the individual colonial governments would be expected to run the projects.

Government control would allow for social as well as economic development, and the Colonial Office instructed the Clay Mission to consider "the interests of the African" rather than treating its investigation "as an occasion for the exploitation of Africa's resources to meet a temporary need elsewhere."[33] This requirement influenced the Mission's choice of potential sites in the Gold Coast, which were confined to three uninhabited regions, where farmers would not have

---

[27] Courtland, 6 March 1947, CO852/915/2, PRO. Gold Coast, Colonial Secretary to Chief Commissioners, 20 March 1947, NRG8/11/13, NAGT.

[28] CO96/829/8: Extract from the Report of the Sorghum Mission: West African Oilseeds Mission Report: Colonial #224, PRO.

[29] Beyond Clay, the mission included transport expert D. McKenna (from the London Passenger Transport Board), mechanisation expert A.F.S. Sykes (mechanisation expert), and W.L. Monson (Assistant Secretary of the Colonial Office's Production Department). Sykes farmed on a large scale himself, and also for "two or three large landowners, whose farming operations he controls." E.W. Bovill to Sydney Caine, 12 May 1947, CO852/915/2, PRO.

[30] Colonial Office, 7 March 1947; Telegram, Secretary of State to Gold Coast and Nigeria, 17 April 1947, CO852/915/2, PRO.

[31] Dawson to Hollins, 19 March 47 CO852/915/2, PRO. Monson, 14 April 1947, CO852/915/2, PRO.

[32] Monson, 8 April 1947, CO852/915/2, PRO.

[33] Clay Mission to Secretary of State, 25 November 1947, CO852/916/1, PRO.

to be evicted. Damongo was the least suitable site, dotted with numerous rock outcrops and lacking continuous strips of cultivable land. However, as the only region in the Northern Territories it could be appropriated most easily because it fell under the Land and Native Rights Ordinance.[34] And, in any case, its problems could be twisted into an advantage, as Mission member W.L. Monson did when he wrote that "it confirms our approach to the problem. The organisation of development by means of a large aggregate of small self-contained units is just right for an area where the suitable soils do not form one continuous stretch."[35] In Monson's opinion, "semi-mechanisation" was perfect for West African conditions, a conclusion supported by the Colonial Committee on Agriculture, Animal Health and Forestry in light of West Africa's "topographical, ecological and political considerations."[36]

Clay accepted the notion of semi-mechanisation, referring to the "final objective" of "group cultivation by families, with assistance from mechanisation rather than maximum replacement of labour."[37] The Damongo project thus emerged as an experiment in social engineering with the goal of establishing "peasant communities" on uninhabited, marginal land, fully employed in semi-mechanised agricultural production. Built on a traditional foundation, the resettled villages would be developed into "new social communities, modernised and made more efficient."[38] The peasants would be able to cultivate more land for subsistence and export crops. Increased foodstuff production would protect families from famine and hunger, and increased cash crop production would provide higher standards of living. Natural and artificial manures would produce better soil fertility and environmental sustainability. The efficiency of cash crop production would be increased through a village-based division of labour, in which all peasants from one village would perform the same function in the

[34] Clay Mission Report, 44, CO852/915/2, PRO. The mission selected 2,400 square miles around Damongo, along with 750,000 acres east of Atebubu-Ejura road near Wenchi, and 90,000 acres north of Kintampo (Mampong) for groundnut trials. Clay Mission Report, Appendix VIII, CO852/915/2, PRO. Clay to Urquhart, 5 November 19/47, CO852/915/2, PRO.

[35] Monson to Clay, 6 November 1947, CO852/915/2, PRO.

[36] Extract from 269th Meeting of the Colonial Advisory Committee of Agriculture, Animal Health and Forestry, 1 August 1947, CO852/915/2, PRO.

[37] Sykes to Clay, 31 July 1947; Clay to Sykes, 7 August 1947, CO852/915/2, PRO.

[38] Clay, *Managing Director's Report*, 22.

production process.[39] Settlers would be trained as tractor drivers, lorry drivers, cattle-keepers and market clerks. Eventually, the division of labour would "establish a tradition which could be carried over into the independent communities already established."[40]

This vision would be achieved by a three-stage process, which Clay referred to as "Socio-Agricultural Planning." In Phase One, which Clay considered "artificial," paid labour gangs would be grouped into villages and work alongside company tractors to clear the land and sow and harvest the first crop. During Phase Two, the workers would be joined by their families, each of whom would be resettled in their "natural village unit."[41] Water supplies would dictate unit sizes, which typically would include twenty tractors and 1,600 people. The production units would need European supervision for a number of years, but eventually each unit would form a self-supporting community complete with health, education and leisure centres.[42] By this point the project would have moved into Phase Three, which would witness the emergence of "permanent peasant communities" organised around the collective farms. Though controlled by the colonial state, the process of development would be "natural" because each stage would contain the "embryo" of the next.[43]

Governor Burns hesitated, citing African resistance to the "reputed design of non-African interests to secure an economic stranglehold" on the colony.[44] Nonetheless, he agreed to apply for funding to the Colonial Development Corporation (CDC) for Clay's £12.75 million proposal. However, selling the idea proved very difficult, and ultimately the process only served to alienate CDC President Lord Trefgarne from the Gold Coast's development plans. Trefgarne not only disliked the politics of the venture, but he also was irritated by the repeated failure of the administration to demonstrate its economic potential. In the summer of 1948, Gorell Barnes of the Colonial office wrote that the Gonja project was

> most unlikely to go through . . . I cannot help feeling firstly, that the right bodies to put up the capital are the C.D.C. and the Gold Coast

[39] Clay to Duckham and Stewart, 28 January 1948, CO852/916/2, PRO.
[40] Clay, *Managing Director's Report*, 22.
[41] Ibid., 23.
[42] Notes of a meeting in Nigeria, 9 July 1947, CO852/915/2, 2, 3.
[43] Ibid.
[44] Morgan, *Official History of British Colonial Development, Volume Two*, 209.

> Government, and secondly, that no C.D.C. scheme will be successfully launched in the Gold Coast as long as it is considered necessary, on political grounds, to have a financial arrangement which really takes away from the Corporation any real incentive to make the business a success.[45]

At a mere three percent, the scheme's return was too low for the CDC, and in early 1949, the Corporation rejected the Gonja scheme in favour of a more lucrative proposal from Nigeria.[46] However, by this time, Colonial Secretary Gerald Creasy already had publicised the project as a *fait accompli*[47] and the government set it in motion by creating an Agricultural Development Corporation (ADC) and appropriating the land.[48] Burns was forced into launching the Gonja project with his own money.

The Gonja Development Company (GDC), 1948–57

The GDC Begins

With his hand forced, Governor Burns established the Gonja Development Company (GDC) in 1950, as a subsidiary of the ADC.[49] At the Colonial Office's request to "revamp" the project around the domestic market, Burns shifted its focus from groundnut exports to foodstuff production for the Colony and Ashanti. The motivation for the shift was political. A decade earlier, the Nowell Commission had warned against mechanised groundnut exports in favour of local food crops. Remembering the disturbances that gave rise to the Nowell report, one CO officer advised Burns that "it would be very nice indeed, from a political point of view, if it were possible to re-vamp the scheme so that it turned itself into an experiment in group cultivation by semi-mechanised means of something for local consumption."[50] Having been reborn as a foodstuff project, the Colonial

---

[45] Gorell Barnes to Sir Thomas Lloyd (through Cohen), 12 August 1948, C0852/916/3, PRO.

[46] Shenton, *Nigerian Agriculture*, 50.

[47] In May, 1947, Creasy issued a press release giving the project cost as £30 million and stating that the CDC would be needed to finance the scheme. Extracts, *West Africa*, 15 May 1948, *Manchester Guardian*, 21 July 1948, C0852/916/3, PRO.

[48] Creasy to Sir Thomas Lloyd, 17 December 1948, C0852/916/3, PRO.

[49] Gorell Barnes to Eastwood, CO96/829/8, PRO.

[50] Melville, 8 July 1948; Eastwood, 9 July 1948, C0852/916/3, PRO.

Office permitted the GDC to appropriate 30,000 acres of uninhabited land from the Gonja Native Authority under the Land and Native Rights Ordinance.[51]

As a major element in Burns' ten-year development plan, the GDC received £1,000,000 in government equity capital and an operating budget of around £100,000 per year. To support the project, Burns also approved the extension of tsetse eradication to Damongo, and he proposed the construction of a railway between Kumasi and Navrongo.[52] This was a risky commitment, especially considering Burns' own admission that Damongo had been chosen primarily because "(n)o previous rights of occupancy have been granted," unlike Northern Ashanti where "land tenure difficulties" had precluded the choice of a better site than Damongo.[53]

Echoing his predecessors, Panton rationalised Damongo by emphasising the social engineering aspect of the project. Beyond its economic objectives, wrote Panton, the GDC scheme was designed to "establish village settlements, accommodating in tribal groups, settlers from the more densely populated areas of the Northern districts where the increase in population, soil erosion, and a falling soil fertility are creating a social and economic problem."[54] The anthropological notion of African community, which we have seen most obviously in Eyre-Smith and Rattray, deeply informed Panton's development vision. He repeatedly emphasised that traditional structure of the GDC's farm units, which would be organised according to settlers' original communities.[55] With an eye towards authentic development and modernisation, the GDC would take the place of the village market and the Company's Unit Manager would assume the role of the land priest by allocating land to the settlers. Within each farm unit, the GDC would provide settlers with thirty-six acre

---

[51] The GDC paid compensation to the Gonja Native Authority for the loss of fishing, hunting, firewood, shea-nut and grazing rights, as well as rent of £5 per square mile on the fifty square mile concession. Gonja Development Company, Managing Director's Report (Panton), December, 1950–June, 1952. CO554/459: Damongo, PRO. See also CO96/829/8, PRO.

[52] Gold Coast, *The Development Plan, 1951* (Accra: Government Printing Department, 1951), 14–15. Gold Coast Chief Secretary, circular memo, 15 January 1951, NRG8/7/2, NAGT. Morgan, *Official History of British Colonial Development, Volume Two,* 215.

[53] CO96/829/8: Governor's Request for Damongo Land, PRO.

[54] Panton, *Managing Director's Report,* 2.

[55] Piet Konings, *The State and Rural Class Formation in Ghana* (London: KPI Limited, 1986), 252–3.

leasehold plots for subsistence production.[56] The settlers would be encouraged to form a Farmers' Co-operative Society and lease individual plots from the Society.

The units, or "village groups," would have a "tribal basis" but would also be "absorbed into the new local government system". Panton thus proclaimed the development area "Essalikawu" (ward) under the Local Government Ordinance and planned to send one elected member to the Gonja District Council. Eventually, the settlers would buy out the GDC's shares and establish their own local council, representing some four hundred and fifty families organised into village-units, with a representative on the District Council.[57] As a modernised form of traditional community, Panton's vision inherited past ideas about "proper" African development. Indeed, the reports by such figures as Eyre-Smith, Rattray, Kerr and Fortes contributed directly to the doctrine of development which determined the structure of the Damongo project. Clinging to the notion of African community, Panton repeatedly emphasised the need to resettle tribal villages intact, in order to preserve their social structures on the project site.

The GDC Unravels

It quickly became apparent that the project would not unfold as Panton had hoped. Indeed, within two years the Company experienced major problems in every stage of production, marketing and distribution. Arguably, most of trouble grew out of the requirement to preserve community during the process of development. First, as Burns and Panton admitted, West African politics forced the colonial state to locate the scheme on uninhabited, and thus marginal, land, to avoid expropriation. This requirement produced a host of problems, including everything from clearing land and constructing soil conservation works to attracting settlers, producing crops and maintaining acceptable breakage rates on machinery. Second, resettling the peasants proved to be extraordinarily difficult. Third, there were major labour problems. Skilled labourers were difficult to attract and keep, and unskilled peasant labourers were inefficient under the model of partial mechanisation. Finally, Panton struggled to find

[56] Panton, *Managing Director's Report*, 28.
[57] Ibid., 28–30.

marketable foodstuff crops that could be produced efficiently enough to yield profits in the face of extremely high transportation costs. Each of these problems shall be discussed below.

(a) *Land Clearing, Production and Marketing*

The choice of Damongo produced major problems of land clearance, soil erosion and mechanisation. In 1952, Panton concluded that only fourteen thousand acres of the Damongo site could be cultivated and that even this land was far from ideal.[58] Water courses and rock outcrops rendered the contour strips unsuitable for "maximum efficiency in the operation of mechanical equipment."[59] Ploughing against the contour, however, posed the risk of serious erosion. Panton thus was forced to adopt an inferior buffer strip method, leaving natural buffer strips to conserve the soil. This method, while (barely) acceptable from an environmental perspective, posed problems for mechanisation because the buffer strips broke up the farm units into disconnected blocks.[60]

Worse yet, semi-mechanisation could not produce crops efficiently enough to make the venture profitable. Panton experimented with groundnuts for local markets, but they were poorly suited for mechanised production. During the planning phase this fact could be applauded as perfectly suitable for the peasant-friendly dream of "semi-mechanisation." On the ground, however, the GDC's reliance on hand labour rendered production inefficient. Moreover, where groundnuts found markets at all, the prices offered by local traders were well below the GDC's expectations.[61] As a result Panton quickly abandoned groundnut production as infeasible and concentrated on other crops. Some of the alternative crops would grow reasonably well, but they also faced difficulties finding markets at prices sufficient to offset the high costs of production and transport. The project site was located far from the major market centre, Kumasi, with poor roads and no access to railways. George Rees, who managed the GDC's agricultural operations after 1954, estimated that the cost of transport equalled the cost of production.[62]

---

[58] Panton, *Managing Director's Report*, 4, 5.

[59] Ibid., 23.

[60] Ibid., 24, 25, 28.

[61] See for example the letter to Panton, 11 November 1952, NRG8/11/40, NAGT.

[62] Interview, George Rees and D.W. Parry, 30 August 1995.

Given the high cost of transport, most GDC crops failed to find sufficient markets to justify their production. In fact, some of the crops most suitable for mechanisation failed to find markets at all. For instance, the main crop after groundnuts, hegari (dwarf sorghum), could be mechanised efficiently but failed to find a local market because the local population preferred other varieties. This problem forced Rees to remove hegari from the crop rotation in 1955.[63] For different reasons, the GDC rejected the large-scale production of tobacco, another crop suited to the GDC site. Though tobacco could be grown and marketed, once again the high cost of transportation rendered the crop unprofitable. In this case, however, an expatriate firm (the Pioneer Tobacco Company) offered to buy the crop at its source and cover the cost of transport to Kumasi. Wary of capital, Panton rejected the firm's offer and confined tobacco production to a small portion of the GDC's acreage. Ultimately, none of the GDC's major crops found profitable markets and few crops were planted.[64] By 1955 the project had two thousand acres of guinea corn and one hundred and fifty acres of groundnuts under cultivation.[65]

(b) *Labour*

The labour question also plagued the GDC project from the beginning, on several fronts. Panton found it difficult to attract unskilled labour at any stage of the process, including gang labourers for clearing and settlers for weeding and harvesting. During the clearing phase, unskilled labourers defected at alarming rates, if they could be enticed to Damongo's inhospitable location at all. Sixty per cent of the unskilled labour force deserted in the first nine months, leaving only fifteen workers available for clearing. More commonly, workers avoided Damongo altogether, because of its poor reputation for food and water supplies.[66] The clearing gangs who stayed performed very poorly, partly because they were too scattered to be controlled effectively by the GDC. As a result of poor clearing caused high rates of breakage among Caterpillars, Massey-Harris tractors and

[63] Ibid.

[64] See for example the letter to Panton, 11 November 1952, NRG8/11/40, NAGT.

[65] "The Gonja Development Company Limited, Report from 1st November, 1954–31st March, 1955," in *Annual Report of the Agricultural Development Corporation, 1954–55* (Accra: Government Printer, 1956), 12.

[66] Northern Territories Employment Officer, 22 June 1950, NRG8/37/2, NAGT.

combine seeders. This was a serious issue because equipment and parts were in very short supply after the war.[67]

As for the settlers, they were difficult to attract and Panton complained bitterly that the Gold Coast had saddled the GDC with the task of recruitment. In 1952 he wrote that "the administrative problems of the resettlement scheme are now sufficiently to the fore to merit serious study" and the appointment of "specialist administrative officers." On this score, Panton complained that the Gold Coast expected the GDC "to undertake the functions of local government and to deal with the administrative problems of resettlement."[68] To make matters worse, once settled the peasants did not adapt well to their supposedly natural roles as communal farmers. According to Panton, "(m)eetings have been held and an effort has been made to get the "settlers to operate certain farming activities on a communal basis; some difficulty was experienced in securing agreement regarding this activities of this kind."[69] Panton thus faced a major challenge in teaching the settlers to behave "communally". Even more difficult was the task of educating the settlers on modern agricultural methods. "Many social, educational and economic problems arise," he wrote, "in connection with re-settlement of people accustomed to a tribal organisation and traditional agricultural methods. Not the least of these is the ability of the settler to adapt himself to the new environment and to modern mechanised agriculture."[70] In order to modernise the resettled peasant farmers, the Company, it seemed, first would have to teach them to become "traditional."

Beyond the gang labourers and settlers, Panton experienced problems with the skilled labour force. First, he was forced out of necessity to recruit skilled labourers from the south, a policy which contradicted the GDC's mandate to preserve tradition during the process of development.[71] Second, the skilled workers tended to defect to the more lucrative southern labour market after receiving their training at Damongo. Those who stayed organised walkouts if Panton asked them to work at other tasks during the off-season.[72] Finally, he found

[67] Panton, *Managing Director's Report*, 24, 25, 28.
[68] Ibid., 30/31.
[69] Ibid., 30.
[70] Ibid.
[71] *Glasgow Herald*, 27 January 1950, in CO96/829/8, PRO.
[72] "The Gonja Development Company Limited, Annual Report", in Gold Coast, *Report of the Agricultural Development Corporation, 1953–54*, Appendix, 11–12. See also Panton, *Managing Director's Report*, 19, 23, 30–32, 41.

it difficult to attract peasant settlers to the project in the first place, much less to use them profitably in the production of cash crops.

Problems with labour and production pushed Panton into a secret plan to transform the Damongo project into a plantation based on full mechanisation and wage labour. The peasant ideal, it seems, did not last long when confronted with reality on the ground. When Colonial Office representative Maurice Smith visited Panton in 1952 he was shocked to discover a plan to convert Damongo into a full-fledged plantation using settlers as skilled labourers "on the English model rather than as small scale individual farmers."[73] The Colonial Office reacted with horror at the idea of a Damongo plantation, maintaining a resolute commitment to mechanising agriculture while preserving the peasantry. As one CO officer put it,

> I think we have all been looking to Damongo as a pilot scheme to produce basic information for a future pattern of peasant agricultural development. I see no reason why the high degree of mechanisation should be incompatible with individual farmers provided its layout of farms and terms of tenure are such as to facilitate mechanisation, and proper soil conservation measures.[74]

Under no circumstances did the Colonial Office wish to develop capitalist agriculture in the Northern Territories.

The controversy over Panton's ideas prompted the Colonial Office to meet with him in England in early 1953. By this time, the question of future plans had become crucial as the project acreage was expanding rapidly. Panton received permission from the Colonial Office to form a Committee of Enquiry to investigate the Damongo project and make recommendations for its future.[75] At issue was the form which production would take over the next few years. The Colonial Office argued against converting the scheme into a plantation rather than a settlement scheme. Panton, however, emphasised the need to find the most profitable means to increase export production. Should the GDC plan to export crops to the southern Gold Coast, Panton asked, "where, with an increasing concentration of cash crops and industrialisation including the Volta River scheme, more homegrown foodstuffs would be urgently needed in the next

[73] M.G. Smith, 31 November 1952, CO96/554/459, PRO.
[74] P. Nye, minute, n.d but 1952, CO554/459, PRO.
[75] M.G. Smith, minute, n.d. but 1953, CO554/459, PRO.

few years if the country was not to become a large net importer of foodstuffs?"[76] As the process of urbanisation proceeded, the need for "homegrown foodstuffs" became ever more urgent.

Adding urgency to the GDC question was the spectacular failure of a £50 million British groundnut project in East Africa. The project began in 1947, when Britain attempted to mechanise groundnut production on a vast tract of uninhabited, marginal land in Tanganyika. According to one eyewitness, Alan Wood, the land proved extremely difficult to clear and the soil on the cleared land resembled "a sheet of concrete." To make matters worse, the African settlers refused to live in their supposedly traditional, communal housing units. "Detribalisation" occurred, disputes arose along class lines—including a strike in the second year—wage rates rose and the project failed to produce groundnuts in any significant numbers. Wood summarised the embarrassment as follows:

> ... those who saw it ... may wonder if it really happened, or whether they merely dreamt, in some idle moment, that a timber mill was sited before anyone really counted the trees for the wood; that a pipeline costing £500 000 or more was built to take fuel, at a huge operating expense, to tanks set miles away from anywhere in the African bush; that a railway was begun without anyone knowing where it was going in the end; and that inspiring everything was a faith that you could grow groundnuts when you had not even bothered to inspect the ground.[77]

After the downfall of the Labour Government in 1951, the new Conservative leaders wished to avoid a repeat of the Tanganyika experience. The Gold Coast and GDC shared this concern. Despite the positive assessment by Panton and the GDC, as of late January, 1953, both the Gold Coast government and the GDC were "anxious to avoid premature publicity" in the wake of the East African experience.[78]

In 1953, the urgency of the situation in Damongo prompted the Colonial Office to create an Advisory Committee on the Gonja scheme. Reporting at the end of March, the Committee made more than twenty-five recommendations for the future of the Company.

[76] J.B. Panton, n.d., but 1953, quoted by M.G. Smith, minute, CO554/459, PRO.

[77] Alan Wood, *The Groundnut Affair* (London: The Bodley Head, 1950), 151.

[78] M.G. Smith, 23 January 1953, CO554/459, PRO.

The report asked the government to stop any further clearing, planting and resettlement until detailed studies were performed on the economics of crop production and marketing. No additional settlers were to be brought to Damongo until the GDC determined exactly which crops they could grow profitably.[79]

The GDC Splits

By the time of the Advisory Committee's recommendations, Panton had turned to road construction and soil conservation in search of profits. In 1955 the Gold Coast government broke the two sections into separate Companies. Panton moved to Kintampo to head the construction business and left the agricultural operation to a new Managing Director, George Rees.[80] In 1956, a Second Advisory Committee recommended the retention of the profitable GDC construction company, to support resettlement schemes in other regions.[81] On the agricultural side, on the advice of the Committee the GDC reduced its acreage to 1,500 acres and concentrated on tobacco, the only consistently profitable crop.[82] In 1957, after failing to improve its performance, the Company entered into voluntary liquidation and sold its assets to Nkrumah's government.[83] In a fate similar to the CDC-sponsored Nigerian project, which collapsed by 1953/4, the historical and political need to preserve and reproduce African community rendered mechanised agriculture hopelessly infeasible in Western Gonja.[84]

---

[79] *Gonja Development Company: Report of the First Advisory Committee, 1953*, 32–33, NRG8/3/91, NAGT.

[80] According to Rees, Panton rarely if ever ventured onto the Damongo site after 1954. Interview, George Rees and D.W. Parry, 3 August 1995.

[81] "Memorandum for the Standing Development Committee by the Minister of Agriculture: The Future of the Gonja Development Company, Limited, December, 1956," 1–2, NRG8/3/192, NAGT.

[82] See for example the letter to Panton, 11 November 1952, NRG8/11/40, NAGT.

[83] S.T. Quansah, "The Gonja Settlement and Development Scheme-Ghana." *Economic Bulletin of Ghana* 2, No. 1 (1972): 18–19. T.E. Hilton, "Land Planning and Resettlement in Northern Ghana," *Geography* 44 (1959): 240. Konings, 253.

[84] For a similar case in Northern Nigeria, see Cowen and Shenton, *Doctrines of Development*, 297, Shenton, *Nigerian Agriculture*, 49, and W.B. Morgan and J.C. Pugh, *West Africa* (London: Metheun and Co. Ltd., 1969), 645.

Community Development in the Northern Territories

While the GDC scheme unfolded, the Northern Territories administration gained international acclaim for an innovative program of community development, aimed at village-level projects in the areas of education, health and agriculture.[85] These projects involved everything from the construction of buildings for schools and clinics to adult literacy classes. The communities themselves were responsible for submitting ideas for projects to local development committees, which were established in every District under the chairmanship of the District Commissioners. In the spirit of self-help, labour for the projects, when needed, was provided by community volunteers.[86] At first glance, this focus on small, locally initiated rural projects seems at odds with the large-scale development efforts normally associated with the second colonial occupation. As we shall discover, however, the simultaneous appearance of these two very different approaches to development was no mere coincidence.

The Idea of Community Development

The idea of community development, present in latent form during the making of the British West African policy of the WALC, underwent a transformation in the 1920s. Responding to the Phelps-Stokes Commission of 1921–23, the Colonial Office issued a White Paper 1925, *Education Policy in British Tropical Africa*, which stressed the importance of protecting "good tribal conditions" by educating "the whole community."[87] In 1935, a *Memorandum on the Education of African Communities* tied this strategy to the need for developing raw materials production without producing "de-nationalisation." In 1944, this

---

[85] Robert Scott, "Community Development and Local Development Committees," Accra: Colonial Secretary's Office, 19 September 1949, NRG8/1/49, NAGT. By 1958 the program had gained an international reputation. See *Annual Report of the Department of Social Welfare and Community Development, 1958* (Accra: Government Printer, 1959), 27.

[86] See for example the *Report of the Department of Social Welfare and Community Development, 1946–51* (Accra: Government Printer, 1953), 57. *Annual Report of the Department of Social Welfare and Community Development, 1952* (Accra: Government Printer, 1953), 22.

[87] L.J. Lewis, "Theory and Practice of Mass Education and Community Development," in *Perspectives in Mass Education and Community Development*, ed. F.H. Hilliard in L.J. Lewis, 1, (London: Thomas Nelson and Sons, 1955).

approach emerged as "mass education," which the 1948 Cambridge Conference of African Governors equated with community development,[88] and which the Labour Government adopted as its official colonial policy in 1949. According to the British government, mass education sought to "promote better living for the whole community" and was to be achieved through local initiative and participation wherever possible.[89]

In the Gold Coast, the administration began to send mass education officers into rural areas in the 1950s, as part of the programme "to help fit the individual to live the fullest possible life in a particular society.[90] In the words of Professor L.J. Lewis, mass education and community development sought three goals: "(1) the improvement of health and living conditions; (2) the improvement of (community) well-being in the economic sphere; (3) the development of political institutions and political power until the day arrives when the people can become self-governing."[91] Lewis emphasised that this program was "not concerned only with the development and application of means by which the peoples as a whole can be equipped with the basic tools of modern living, but that we must be intimately concerned with the end points, the application of those tools to effective living by the whole community."[92] Mass education and community development thus sought to develop the potential of "the individual in society."[93]

Since communities implied social or geographical boundaries, however, community development inevitably involved the protection and containment of local social cultures against the uncontrolled forces of progress. In other words, community development workers believed that they were protecting African communities from the evils of westernisation. In this project, mass education officers consciously sought to protect African communities from the disintegration which Britain had experienced during the industrial revolution. Lewis, for instance, referred to the example of British Registrar-General William Farr II

---

[88] Ibid.; F.H. Hilliard, "Community Development—Its Problems and Possibilities," in *Perspectives in Mass Education and Community Development*, ed. F.H. Hilliard and L.J. Lewis, 27 (London: Thomas Nelson and Sons, 1955).

[89] Cowen and Shenton, *Doctrines of Development*, 309–10.

[90] Hilliard, "Community Development," 28–9.

[91] Lewis, 2.

[92] Ibid., 3.

[93] Hilliard, "Community Development," 29.

(1807–83) and the development of education in England. "Schools were coming into being," he wrote,

> as part of a formal system of education, in part as a result of a genuine concern for building up an intelligent educated community, but to a considerable extent as a measure of self-defence, the urbanisation of the industrial revolution having created serious social problems in clashes between various elements of society.[94]

Without mass education and community development, argued another author in the same volume, the rapid westernisation of Africa would erode the Africans' capacity for "self-defence" and produce uncertainty, insecurity and the breakdown of community.[95] Applying the lessons of Europe would allow the British "to ensure that West Africa avoids being embroiled in the kind of soul-destroying, monotonous, prideless work which Charles Chaplin so vividly portrayed in one of his great pre-war films, *City Lights*."[96] On the ground, this approach involved creating a buffer zone of rural regions between the villages and the towns, protecting communities from cultural extinction at the hands of urbanisation and ushering in "real West African progress."[97]

Community Development and Large-Scale Projects

Community development programs were closely connected to the larger agricultural development schemes. On the one hand, mass education sought to insulate African communities from potential social upheaval in the wake of the big projects.[98] Beyond the social protection of village communities, however, community development also carried the more practical goal of buying time while colonial governments waited for the large-scale schemes to pay off. In the Gold Coast, Colonial Secretary Robert Scott stressed the *necessity* of community development in the wake of the larger projects:

---

[94] Lewis, 7.

[95] A. Taylor, "Fundamental Motives in Community Living," in *Perspectives in Mass Education and Community Development*, ed. F.H. Hilliard and L.J. Lewis, 14 (London: Thomas Nelson and Sons, 1955).

[96] Hilliard, "Community Development," 32.

[97] Ibid., 34; F.H. Hilliard, "The Need for Roots," in *Perspectives in Mass Education and Community Development*, ed. F.H. Hilliard and L.J. Lewis, 40 (London: Thomas Nelson and Sons, 1955).

[98] Hilliard, "The Need for Roots," 36.

> Major proposals, such as the Volta River Development plan and the mechanised agricultural schemes in the Northern Territories and Northern Ashanti, have entailed a great deal of planning extending over many months. A large number of detailed investigations have been made into a variety of agricultural plans concerning the production of new crops or the expansion of existing ones . . . but all this planning had been on too broad a scale to comprise the minor needs or the rural areas, and too technical in character to permit of much participation by the people themselves in the preparation of the plans. Although the benefits of this major reorganisation will eventually be felt throughout the country, it is inevitable that, for some time to come, the direct advantages must be localised.[99]

Community development thus provided the means to bring short-term benefits to northern villages during the development of the larger projects. Otherwise, rural areas in the African colonies would suffer from the same problem that plagued Britain in the nineteenth century: the uncontrolled movement of the population from rural to urban areas. In the words of Mass Education expert F.H. Hilliard,

> in planning the work of mass education in terms of the ultimate goal of community development, we may hope to avoid the mistakes made in the rural life of England and other countries following the industrial revolution. No real plan to provide a full rural life for the English villages was thought out or even considered. The result has been a continual drift away from villages to towns . . . something of unique value disappears from the life of a people when its rural life is neglected and decays. The sturdy independence and self-reliance, the quiet reflection and, of course, the simple provision of food—all these things go if rural life decays. And yet, rural life must offer a full life or it is bound to decay; people want to live a full life and will go where they think it can be found.[100]

According to Hilliard, these problems could have been avoided in Britain if rural development had been planned properly. In the Gold Coast, mass education and community development provided the means for such proper planning processes, which would develop a "well-ordered rural life" in which each rural region would be developed as a "cultural and social unit" between the villages and the towns.[101]

---

[99] Robert Scott (Gold Coast Colonial Secretary), "Community Development and Local Development Committees," 19 September 1949, Annexure II, NRG8/1/49, NAGT.

[100] Hilliard, "Community Development," 33–4.

[101] Ibid., 34. Hilliard borrowed this idea from Henry Morris' report to the Educational Committee of the Cambridge County Council in 1925.

The threat of rural-urban drift had plagued the Gold Coast administration since the early 1930s.[102] By the late 1940s, the colonial administration recognised that its plans for mechanised agriculture threatened to disrupt the social structure of the northern countryside. Most dangerously, the projects threatened to transform subsistence farmers into wage labourers. "The systematic development of agriculture and industrial projects," wrote Hilliard,

> inevitably affects and will continue to affect, the whole social structure. The old tradition by which a man works on land belonging to his people in order to provide himself and his dependants with food, clothing and shelter, is forced to give way increasingly to a new method of work—to the system of employer and employees, in which one man receives a wage in return for work done for others. I was told that in one West African territory the Government was faced with the dilemma that if it pushed ahead with plans for large-scale agricultural development on scientific lines, it could do so only at the cost of a major upheaval in the whole social structure of that area; very naturally it hesitated before making such a difficult choice.[103]

Along with the stagnation of rural life came landlessness, unemployment and social dislocation caused by the transformation of the peasantry into wage labourers. But social upheaval was an inevitable corollary of progress. The key for Hilliard was not to balk at large-scale projects but rather to manage their negative effects by preserving the cultural core of traditional African societies during their implementation. "No nation has ever made progress," he wrote,

> without economic, social and spiritual upheaval, and it is the price to be paid in all worthwhile human betterment. But we must try to see that the progress is real West African progress; that is, to see that the best of the past is carried on into the future, and that the old is combined with the new wherever the old is valuable and needs preserving."[104]

Combining the old with the new implied that development had to be organic if it was to be legitimate. It had to come from within, it had to be "real West African progress," or else it would be corruption. Mass education and community development provided the tools for this vision, the foundation for achieving economic development without triggering harmful social change.

---

[102] A.W. Cardinall, *The Gold Coast, 1931* (Accra: Government Printer, 1931), 4.
[103] Hilliard, "The Need For Roots," 36–7.
[104] Ibid., 40.

Planning was central to this project. In the words of W.L. Shirer, the official responsible for community development in the Northern Territories,

> The success of projects may well depend upon the thoroughness of the planning. Neglect of some important phase of a community's social, religious, political or economic structure, or its relation to the larger community of which it is a part, may well lead to failure . . . lack of planning and integrating a project to the moral and social needs of a community can do a great deal of harm.[105]

In Shirer's comments we can see Guggisberg's emphasis on planning filtered through the moral and social organicism of the colonial anthropologists.

Shirer's innovation was to wed this vision to village participation. "Progress," he wrote, "cannot be imposed upon a people. Those concerned must be partners in planning as well as in executing projects for community improvement."[106] As Hughes had done for the tsetse schemes, Shirer invoked the Tennessee Valley Authority (TVA) as an example of good development planning, which had been a "genuine effort to develop a social structure in harmony with natural conditions and local potentialities." Significantly, the TVA had emerged as a response to an uncontrolled development process which had produced massive soil degradation during a period of rapid population growth. Development had not been planned with "regard for future welfare," and the result had been "poverty, illness, poor diet, primitive housing, ignorance and limited social and cultural interests."[107] For Shirer, the moral was clear:

> Planning must be with the people from the beginning, giving every consideration to their social, political, religious and economic needs. It must not impose anything from above upon the people, and must be related and co-ordinated to other development plans. It must have at its core the aim of developing the moral and social structure of society and enlightening the people, so the advance will be steady within the community.[108]

---

[105] W.L.L. Shirer, "Planning Community Development," in *Perspectives in Mass Education and Community Development*, ed. F.H. Hilliard and L.J. Lewis, 69 (London: Thomas Nelson and Sons, 1955).
[106] Ibid., 70.
[107] Ibid., 72.
[108] Ibid., 73.

The colonial state attempted to implement this programme through the establishment of local development committees. Operating from the grassroots, colonial officials believed, community development carried the potential to control the chaos associated with development while retaining all that was best in African tradition.

Retaining the best of African tradition meant preserving community in the midst of agricultural revolution and industrialisation. This was the main intention of community development, and it was to be achieved on several levels. First, mass education would prevent unemployment by stemming the drift of school leavers and unskilled workers into the larger project sites before jobs were available. Second, community development would block individual accumulation in rural areas by channelling individuals into communal projects. Ultimately, in contributing to the preservation of rural communities, community development would prevent the growth of civil society, or at least its darker side, in the Northern Territories.

Conclusion

The colonial administration chose the Damongo site for its groundnut scheme because of its location near a vast tract of unoccupied land. Colonial officials rationalised the site and the structure of the project on the grounds that European technology and planning techniques would allow the state to develop mechanised agricultural production on marginal land. At a more general level, the administration drew on the familiar discourse of African evolution and its interruption by the slave raiding and trypanosomiasis. Technocratic development planning would open up Western Gonja, which had been locked up from development by the slave raiders and tsetse flies. In this sense, the Gonja project was framed by a certain discourse of development. But discourse alone does not explain fully why the Damongo scheme was organised along peasant lines, with the intention of preserving village communities. As with earlier development programs, the colonial concern with African social cohesion came in response to previous periods of development which had failed to contain the forces of individual accumulation. Underlying this aspect of the agrarian doctrine of development was a very real concern rooted in the material world. In the post-war period, several colonial governments in British West Africa had balked at implementing similar large-scale development projects out of the fear of social disorder. In the Gold Coast, colonial officials believed that they could guard against social dislocation by transplanting villages and incorporating them *as communities* into the groundnut project. In the meantime, African community would be preserved outside the project area through the careful application of mass education and community development. The point here is that colonial officials recognised that economic development necessarily implied social upheaval, but they also believed that it could be managed in order to guide the process along communal lines.

As Peter Worsley argues, this response was generalised across the colonial world after World War Two, as colonial governments invoked community development in response to peasant resistance to the development of capitalism. Worsley's comments are worth quoting at length:

> Ideologically, (community development) drew upon a de-politicised version of Mid-West populism mixed with a vulgarised North American psychology in which any vestige of conflict theory had been removed. The central theoretical notion was that farmers' problems were basically problems of knowledge (i.e. ignorance) and of communication, and could be solved via education and by discussing their difficulties with other members of the local community and with the local representatives of government. The wider vision, and class militancy, of traditional Western populism . . . were thus expunged, and group therapy put in its place. If the blockages to the spontaneous expression of the peasants' basic needs could be overcome, it was assumed, popular energies would be released on a gigantic scale. And the whole thing would be democratic.[109]

Cast in this light, community development appeared as one element in a package through which colonial officials tried to achieve large-scale economic development without transforming peasants into wage labourers. Community development and Fabian colonialism thus acted as post-war tools in the continuing struggle to promote economic development without social transformation. On the one hand, agricultural projects such as the Damongo groundnut scheme sought to generate large-scale cash crop production while preserving peasant community organisation. On the other hand, mass education and community development sought to provide opportunities for

[109] Peter Worsley, *The Three Worlds: Culture and World Development* (Chicago: University of Chicago Press, 1984), 145–147.

work at the village level without permitting enough individual accumulation to produce the growth of a middle class. In both programmes, the British tried to achieve development without triggering the rise of civil society.

Put more provocatively, collectivised agriculture and community development sought to guard against the social problems associated with the development of agrarian capitalism. As such, the program represented a continuation of the state's attempt to block the growth of class formation in the African countryside. As a hedge against civil society, the colonial state invoked co-operatives and community development, the very measures which the governance literature praises for strengthening the "civil public realm."[110] Rather than supporting and nurturing community, the growth of civil society threatened to disrupt the ordering of progress. The last phrase is key in that it points to what must have been the biggest failure of the Damongo scheme for the colonial state. The GDC project and the community development program were designed to be economically progressive and socially conservative. The colonial state believed that it could develop agricultural productivity while preserving traditional social structures in the Northern Territories. In this goal the state failed completely, and the Damongo scheme thus provides one of the clearest examples of the intractable contradiction between the twin intentions of the British colonial doctrine of development.

[110] See for example Aili Mari Tripp, "Local Organisations, Participation, and the State in Urban Tanzania," in *Governance and Politics in Africa*, ed. Goran Hyden and Michael Bratton, 237–8 (Boulder: Lynne Reinner Publishers, 1992).

CHAPTER NINE

CONCLUSION

In many ways, the history of colonial development in Northern Ghana confirms Mamdani's argument that "the African colonial experience produced "a one-sided opposition between the individual and the group, civil society and community, rights and tradition."[1] Colonial officers worried about individualism, as chiefs and the educated elite vied for economic and political power. These kinds of struggles had a long history in the south, and by the 1950s they had appeared on northern soil. As more opportunities presented themselves, space opened up for the development of civil society in the form of a northern elite. Although civil society did not develop very far in the north, it had a long history in the south, where the elite had resisted colonial rule since the late nineteenth century. Many colonial officials worried about a similar process occurring in the Northern Territories, which they associated with the breakdown of tribal authority. In response, colonial officials turned to community as a hedge against the destruction of tradition ("detribalisation") and the potential development of civil society. This policy contrasts with the recommendations of many present-day development scholars who equate the two ideas, seeking to develop civil society by nurturing the development of community associations. In contrast, colonial officials supported African community in Northern Ghana to guard against civil society rather than to encourage its development. Indirect rule formed the basis of this policy, seeking to support the chiefs as trustees over the preservation of African community. In this sense, Mamdani is correct in arguing that the doctrine sought to build decentralised despotism as a basis for colonial hegemony.

Our story has shown, however, that this colonial project was less successful than Mamdani would have us believe. Berry's work shows us that indirect rule established a terrain of struggle and conflict rather than simply imposing British hegemony on African societies

[1] Mamood Mamdani, *Citizen and Subject: Contemporary Africa and the Legacy of Late Colonialism* (Princeton: Princeton University Press, 1996), 22.

based on the European notion of "tribe."[2] This argument is supported by my evidence, as well as the work of other Ghana scholars such as Lentz and Allman and Parker. As Lentz argues for the north-west, the imposition of tribal hierarchies laid the groundwork for new conflicts, because "the model of unambiguous territorial-political ties ran counter to local practices of mobility and multilocality."[3] The same can be said of the north-east, as Allman and Parker demonstrate, where indirect rule laid the foundation for "locally authored scripts." In the process, new terrain was established for struggles over resources, as Africans absorbed colonial policies into "local configurations of power," beyond the intentions of colonial policy.[4] These struggles were rooted in precolonial social networks and power relations, but they took advantage of colonial institutions as African actors exerted their agency within the colonial system. They threatened the basis of indirect rule because they promoted rivalries which cut across colonial tribal categories and intersected with the growth of market forces. The failure of indirect rule to contain individual accumulation is borne out by the experience of the Northern Territories.

Just as importantly, and this is my main contribution to the literature, the administration implemented indirect rule in response to an earlier period of development. This is significant because it helps us to unravel the deeper roots of the agrarian doctrine of development in British West Africa. On one level, the doctrine was rooted in a particular discourse of the corruption of African evolution by slave raiding, and the consequent need for colonial interventions to nurture the authentic development of African tribes into modern nation-states. However, an exclusive focus on discourse does not explain the agrarian doctrine of development, which sought to extract resources from the Northern Territories while simultaneously preserving African community. As Cowen and Shenton observe, the turn towards community occurred not simply because the discourse precluded alternatives, but also (and more importantly) as a reaction

[2] Sara Berry, *No Condition is Permanent: the Social Dynamics of Agrarian Change in sub-Saharan Africa* (Madison: University of Wisconsin Press, 1993), 24–30.

[3] Carola Lentz, *Ethnicity and the Making of History in Northern Ghana*, manuscript, forthcoming as *Ethnicity and the Making of History in Northern Ghana* (Edinburgh: Edinburgh University Press, 2006), 174.

[4] Jean Allman and Jonathan Parker, *Tongnaab: The History of a West African God* (Bloomington: Indiana University Press, 2005), 91.

to the material forces produced by a previous period of development. Specifically, the colonial commitment to African community in the Gold Coast appeared after Joseph Chamberlain's initial attempt to bring the creative destruction of capitalism to bear on the undeveloped estates of West Africa. Between 1895 and 1900, Chamberlain attempted to force through an agrarian transformation in British West Africa. By 1900, however, Chamberlain had started to retreat from aggressive development in the face of British and African resistance.[5] The Liberal victory of 1906 completed the shift away from forceful agrarian transformation. Influenced by the ideas of Henry George, the Liberal West African policy consciously sought to block the development of landlordism on African soil. Instead, development doctrine focused on protecting African community from the disorder associated with capitalism. Setting themselves up as the most capable trustees, colonial officials turned to land nationalisation as the best means towards this end.[6] This vision worked itself out first through the Northern Nigerian Lands Committee (NNLC) of 1908 and the West African Lands Committee (WALC) of 1912–17.[7] As we have seen, the NNLC/WALC recommendations were implemented in the Northern Territories between 1927 and 1932.

During this period the colonial state turned away from exploiting the north's resources in favour of establishing a hierarchy of chiefs as labour contractors. For a brief period, the colonial administration actively constructed the Northern Territories as a labour pool for the industries of the south.[8] After 1908, the idea of the north as a labour pool gave way to the notion of the region as a clean slate for African development. Politically, this period witnessed an attempt to put African community on a sure footing, based on the peasant option advocated by Morel and the NNLC/WALC. However, before the 1920s the full WALC program was considered too dangerous

---

[5] Two Gold Coast Lands Bills (1894 and 1897) had failed to pass through the legislature and Accra had to settle for a weaker Concessions Ordinance in 1911. See O. Omosini, "The Gold Coast Land Question, 1894–1900: Some Issues Raised on West Africa's Economic Development," *International Journal of African Historical Studies* 5, No. 3 (1972): 465–468.

[6] Anne Phillips, *The Enigma of Colonialism: British Policy in West Africa* (London: James Currey, 1989), 66–7, 113.

[7] Phillips, 76. R.W. Shenton, *The Development of Capitalism In Northern Nigeria* (Toronto: University of Toronto Press, 1986), 46–7.

[8] See Jeff Crisp, *The Story of an African Working Class: Ghanaian Miners' Struggles, 1870–1980* (London: Zed Books, 1984), 35–53.

politically to implement in the West African colonies.[9] Still, Governors such as Sir Hugh Clifford accepted the need to preserve African community. Clifford in particular considered the Northern Territories an ideal site for development along peasant lines because of its comparative lack of development.[10] As we have seen, Clifford argued that the region had been saved from both the "horrors of inter-tribal conflicts"[11] and the scourge of rapid and uncontrolled westernisation. With the important exception of land nationalisation, Clifford thus committed the Northern Territories to the WALC vision of community-based African development. In so doing, Clifford set the Northern Territories on the track towards the peasant road analysed so admirably by Anne Phillips.[12]

Governor Guggisberg brought the full spirit of Henry George to the Northern Territories through the Land and Native Rights Ordinance (LNRO). The LNRO was to provide the basis for Guggisberg's plan to develop the north as a world producer of groundnuts and shea butter, the profits from which could be ploughed into infrastructure, health care and education. The ultimate goal—Guggisberg's Cities of Final Development—would be the emergence of a modern nation-state stitched together out of modernised native states, which would be developed without "denationalising" the traditional societies. To achieve this plan, however, Guggisberg was forced to encourage the expansion of cocoa and mineral production, which facilitated labour migration and social change, and thus worked against Guggisberg's vision of engineering development without undermining African community. If Guggisberg brought Henry George a step closer to the Gold Coast, therefore, his development plan also facilitated the growth of westernisation in the south through the development of cocoa production and mining. As a result, corruption appeared to worsen in the Gold Coast between 1919 and 1927. In the Northern Territories, the problem appeared in the form of increased labour migration and chiefly despotism. The Eyre-Smith/Rattray solution was to reinstate the land priests, considered the

[9] Phillips, 77–8.

[10] Sir Hugh Clifford, "Recent Developments on the Gold Coast," *Journal of the Royal African Society* 18, No. 72 (July, 1919): 244.

[11] Clifford's speech to the Legislative Council, 13 October 1913, quoted in G.E. Metcalfe, *Great Britain and Ghana: Documents of Ghana History, 1807–1957* (London: Thomas Nelson and Sons, Ltd., 1964), 546.

[12] Phillips, 74–79.

rightful leaders under "primitive" relations of status. By realigning political and religious power along traditional lines, Eyre-Smith and Rattray believed that development would right itself along a natural historical path. The administration disagreed, supporting the chiefs against the land priests and attempting to integrate them into the administration through a formal system of indirect rule.

In the mid-1930s, the administration thus implemented a system of Native Administration along the lines of the Northern Nigerian legislation of 1910. Native Authorities were created as discrete political and economic units with chiefs responsible for local administration, justice and finance. Echoing Lugard, Governor Slater proudly referred to the chiefs as "a living part of the machinery of Government."[13] For Slater, indirect rule was a moral as well as a political project, integrating the spirit of tradition into British colonial rule.[14] At the same time, Slater hoped that Native Administration would act as a barrier against the corruption of authentic development.[15] The notion of natural African development drew on the ideas of Charles Temple, and, through Temple, on the single-tax theories of Henry George. As such, indirect rule was connected to the ongoing debate over landlordism in British West Africa. In the Gold Coast, W.J.A. Jones equated taxation with land rent, thus completing the Georgeist thread running through the implementation of Native Administration.[16] Combined with the LNRO, the imposition of indirect rule brought the full Georgeist West African policy to the Northern Territories.[17] The preservation of African community became the cornerstone of development in the north.

With indirect rule as an institutional base, the colonial state turned to tsetse eradication and mixed farming as the main pillars of development in the Northern Territories before 1940. This program was tied to the development of mining and cocoa farming in the south, since foodstuffs, meat and a disease-free population were needed to maintain the labour force on the southern mines and cocoa farms. Northern integration into the Gold Coast economy, however, was

---

[13] Slater's emphasis. A.R. Slater, *Native Administration in the Gold Coast and Its Dependencies* (Accra: Government Printer, 1930), 3, CO96/700/14, PRO.

[14] Sir Donald Cameron, *My Tanganyika Service and Some Nigeria* (London: George Allen and Unwin Ltd., 1939), 94–5.

[15] Slater, *Native Administration in the Gold Coast and its Dependencies*, 4.

[16] W.J.A. Jones, 31 September 1931, CO96/700/14, PRO.

[17] Phillips, 114, 123.

to be reconciled with the preservation of community and the protection of the north from the problems of labour unrest and unemployment, both of which had appeared in the south in the 1930s. In the opinion of most colonial officials, these problems could be avoided because they had not yet appeared in the Northern Territories, despite the fact that many northern peasants were integrated into regional markets by the 1930s. Colonial development policy sought to prevent these processes from taking root on northern soil and spiralling out of the control the colonial state. Filtered through indirect rule, tsetse eradication and mixed farming were organised to foster economic development without undermining African community.

The outbreak of World War Two intensified the need to develop the Northern Territories and prompted colonial officials to challenge the wisdom of the slow road to development through indirect rule. Britain's wartime need for raw materials and the spread of resistance to colonial rule contributed greatly to the perceived need for rapid development in the north. By this time, indirect rule had failed as a development policy. Neither mixed farming nor tsetse eradication had demonstrated that the chiefs could be harnessed adequately as trustees of their communities. More significantly, the African population did not simply settle into their respective communities after the implementation of indirect rule. On the contrary, the Native Authority system provoked individual struggles over economic, political and social accumulation. As noted above, recent studies of Northern Ghana have shown that these struggles were rooted in the local politics of chieftaincy and lineage, which did not necessarily follow colonial tribal divisions. In the 1940s, faced with failure, the administration began to search for alternatives to indirect rule.

These alternatives consisted of large-scale development projects, centralised control and the secularisation of local administration. Politically, Governor Burns began to Africanise the political service with his constitution of 1946. Over the next few years, Africanisation was extended to the regional and village level through local government. In the Northern Territories, local government was implemented in part to fend off the threat of unemployment by channelling young school leavers into community development projects administered by local authorities. Economically, the colonial state set its sights on developing the Northern Territories as a major producer of oilseeds and foodstuffs. Initially geared towards the British market, this program eventually sought to make food surpluses available to southern markets within the Gold Coast. In the process, the administration jettisoned indirect rule. The sheer size of the northern oilseed project and projected land planning areas required a more centralised approach. Meanwhile, at the political level indirect rule could not make room for educated commoners, who were absorbed into the institutions of local government.

Despite these changes, the doctrine of community continued to frame colonial development doctrine in the Northern Territories, although it took on a secular hue. Rejecting Land Commissioner R.C. Stacpoole's plea to reinstate the land priests,[18] the colonial administration opted for the chiefs, many of whom by now were connected to the educated elite. By the late 1940s, therefore, it was clear that the Native Authorities, though retaining their supposedly traditional base, would be opened up to the emerging northern elite.[19] This trend became reality with the implementation of local government in the 1950s.

During the transition to local government, the administration developed the Gonja groundnut project. Choosing Damongo because it was unoccupied, the colonial state attempted to engineer a massive collectivised farming scheme to produce foodstuffs for the growing markets of the south. Recognising the potential for social and political upheaval, colonial officials turned to mass education to bring immediate benefits to northern villages while waiting for the big scheme to pay off. This approach was part of a more general invocation of community development in the post-war colonial world, invoked as a hedge against peasant resistance to the social dislocation triggered by rapid economic transformation. In fact, community development represented a strategy to pursue rural development without "undoing the peasantry", in Peter Worsley's phrase, by triggering the growth of wage labour.[20] In other words, post-war development doctrine invoked community in order to achieve development without producing the social disorder of capitalism.

Similar to indirect rule, however, post-war community development schemes failed to contain individual accumulation in the Northern

---

[18] R.C. Stacpoole, May, 1948, 159, NRG8/1/51, NAGT.

[19] "Conference on African Governors, 1947, Local Government in Africa," Confidential AGC #12, Enclosure to the Secretary of State's Confidential Despatch dates the 13 January, 1948, NRG8/2/96, NAGT.

[20] Peter Worsley, *The Three Worlds: Culture and World Development* (Chicago: University of Chicago Press, 1984), 145–147.

Territories. As in the past, economic growth revolved around local social networks and the linkage between the north and south through trade and labour migrancy.[21] Two prominent examples included the commercialization of sacred shrines and the development of trading and transport businesses. In many cases these activities had an underlying political purpose. For example, the Gandah family used its trading ventures to buttress the power of Birifu against the chiefs of the Lawra Confederacy.[22] In response, the colonial administration tried to prevent these types of conflicts from connecting up with nationalist politics by creating the Northern Territories Council and shutting the chiefs out of national political participation.[23] However, after 1954 local political cleavages—rooted in the era of indirect rule—worked their way into national party politics. Nkrumah's CPP penetrated Tamale between 1949 and 1950, drawing northern chiefs as well as educated commoners into its orbit.[24] The NPP emerged in response. As we have seen, the split between the CPP and NPP, though complex, reflected the lines of power established during the colonial period.[25] More importantly for my purposes, by the mid-1950s the northern chiefs were very much part of civil society, educated, and involved in business and regional politics.

For many colonial officers, these trends represented the breakdown of African community and the rise of a politically dangerous educated elite. In other words, previous periods of development fed into the growth of civil society, which represented the breakdown of community, not a space for its development. We must not exaggerate the actual development of a middle class in Northern Ghana,

[21] The trends themselves were very real. By the 1940s it appears that migrant labourers to the mines and cocoa farms comprised a significant percentage of the populations of both Lawra and Zuarungu. Although Sutton questions the extent of migration from the Northern Territories, it was significant enough to draw the attention of District Officials, Meyer Fortes and the Gold Coast government. Inez Sutton, "The Non-Development of the Northern Territories of the Gold Coast," *International Journal of African Historical Studies* 22, No. 4 (1989): 637–669. For the full story of mining in the Gold Coast, see Crisp, *The Story of an African Working Class*.

[22] Jack Goody, *Cooking, Cuisine and Class* (Cambridge: Cambridge University Press, 1982), 68. Goody's observations lend support to the account of chief Gandah's generosity found in S.W.D.K. Gandah,'s historical biography of his father. See S.W.D.K. Gandah, *Gandah-Yir (The House of the Brave)* (unpublished manuscript, n.d.), 147–149.

[23] The Birifu chief did not succeed in this quest. See the correspondence in NRG8/2/10: Lawra Native Affairs, NAGT 4–8.

[24] Ladouceur, 81–2.

[25] Dennis Austin, *Politics in Ghana, 1946–1960* (London: Oxford University Press, 1964), 184–6.

which was very small in the 1950s. However, colonial officers feared its development, and they responded to the threat of civil society with an agrarian doctrine of development based on the preservation of African community. In the end, however, the project failed. Civil society could not be contained by the doctrine of African community. Whether this experience holds any lessons for current development practitioners might be debated, but at the very least it raises questions about any attempt to reconcile economic development with social changelessness.

BIBLIOGRAPHY

Archival Sources

Ghana

National Archives of Ghana—Accra (NAGA)
ADM11/824: Report on Wa, 1908.
ADM56/1/87: Hut/Poll Tax, 1909–1927.
ADM56/1/290: Lawra-Tumu Chiefs, 1927–31.
ADM56/1/301: Lawra-Tumu: District Native Affairs, 1921–41.
ADM56/1/309: Tumu Native Affairs, 1913–31.
ADM56/1/335: Political Conference, 1921–29.
ADM56/1/336: North Mamprusi Native Affairs, 1935.
ADM61/5/11: Lawra-Tumu District Record Book, 1927–38.
ADM61/5/16: Lawra District Informal Diary, 1937–45.
ADM68/5/4: Zuarungu District Record Book, 1922–29.
ADM68/5/5: Zuarungu District Record Book, 1935–52.

National Archives of Ghana—Tamale (NAGT)
NRG3/2/11: Zuarungu Native Affairs, 1934–5.
NRG3/13/1: Northern Territories Welfare Committee, First Meeting, 1944.
NRG3/15/4: Trypanosomiasis: Mamprusi, 1947–49.
NRG8/1/49: Land Planning and Utilisation Policy, 1949–50.
NRG8/1/51: Land and Native Rights Ordinance, 1947.
NRG8/1/57: Land and Native Rights Ordinance, 1948–58.
NRG8/1/68: Land Planning and Utilisation Policy, 1950–52.
NRG8/1/70: Land Utilisation and Soil Conservation, 1950.
NRG8/1/85: Land and the Land and Native Rights Ordinance, 1947–48.
NRG8/1/93: Land Planning, 1952–53.
NRG8/1/113: Land Utilisation Policy.
NRG8/2/14: Tugu Native Affairs, 1927–30.
NRG8/2/52: Native Administration, Lawra-Tumu, 1932–39.
NRG8/2/65: Native Authorities, Tumu, 1932–39.
NRG8/2/96: Native Administration and Local Government, 1947–49.
NRG8/3/91: Mamprusi District Annual Report, 1939–40.
NRG8/2/110: Birifu Petition, 1951.
NRG8/3/192: Gonja Development Company, First Advisory Committee Correspondence. NRG8/5/36: Northwestern Land Planning Committee, 1949–56.
NRG8/28/23: Local Government Correspondence, 1951–52.
NRG10/6/2: Mass Education, Northern Territories.
NRG16/4/7: Trypanosomiasis, 1925.

Great Britain

National Archives (Public Record Office), Kew
CO96/674/5: Gold Coast Land and Native Rights Ordinance.
CO96/693/2: Native Administration Ordinance, 1930.
CO96/693/17: Land Tenure, 1931.

CO96/694/7: Land and Native Rights Ordinance, 1930.
CO96/697/8: Northern Territories Administration Ordinance Amendment, 1931.
CO96/700/8: Land Tenure, 1931.
CO96/700/14: Indirect Rule, 1931.
CO96/702/4: Land and Native Rights Ordinance, 1932.
CO96/704/6: Indirect Rule, 1932.
CO96/715/8: Forest Policy: Report by Mr. H.W. Moor, 1934.
CO96/721/6: Forestry Department, Staff, 1937.
CO96/722/15: Native Administration/Taxation, Northern Territories, 1935.
CO96/723/7: Sleeping Sickness, 1935.
CO96/727/12: Northern Territories: Direct Taxation, 1936.
CO96/727/13: Medical Department, Staff, 1936.
CO96/729/11: Higher Agricultural Education/Development of the Fishing Industry, 1936.
CO96/731/6: Visit of Sir F.A. Stockdale to West Africa, 1936.
CO96/732/5: Livestock, 1936.
CO96/735/2: Forestry Department, Staff, 1937.
CO96/739/1: Higher Agricultural Education/Development of the Fishing Industry, 1937.
CO96/740/11: Livestock, 1937.
CO96/741/8: Tsetse Eradication, 1937.
CO96/747/1: Sleeping Sickness, 1938.
CO96/746/3: Direct Taxation, 1938.
CO96/750/1: Livestock, 1938.
CO96/767/5: Medical Department Reports, 1938.
CO96/773/19: Agricultural Reports, 1941–43.
CO96/829/8: Extract, Report of the Sorghum Mission, Colonial #224.
CO98/50: Administration Reports, 1927–8
CO554/459: Gonja Development Company, Report of J.B. Panton, 1950–52.
CO852/19/14: Relations Between Nutrition, Health and Agricultural Production.
CO852/59/2: Nutrition, Health and Agricultural Production.
CO852/59/5: Nutrition, 1937.
CO852/61/2: Nutrition: Economic Advisory Council Papers, 1936.
CO852/402/1: The Organization of Agriculture in the USSR, 1947.
CO852/915/2: Clay Mission Papers, Part 1: 1947.
CO852/916/1: Groundnuts, West Africa: Clay Mission Report, 1947.
CO852/916/2: Groundnuts, West Africa: Clay Mission Report, 1948.
CO852/916/3: Groundnuts, Gold Coast, CDC Project, 1948.
CO879/58: Confidential Print, African (West).

Oxford University, Rhodes House Library
FCB81/1: Fabian Colonial Bureau Papers.
Mss.Afr.s.141: Mark H. Hughes Papers.
Mss.Afr.s.593: Angus Colin Duncan-Johnstone Papers.
Mss.Afr.s.977: J. Gordon and H.B. Daniel, "Notes on Gold Coast Crops/Agriculture."
Mss.Afr.s.979: Andrew Jones Papers.
Mss.Afr.s.1207: Humphrey Amherst District Diaries, Gold Coast.
Mss.Afr.s.1824, KM: K.R.S. Morris Papers.
Mss.Brit.Emp.s.332, 44/1: Arthur Creech-Jones Papers.
Mss.Perham.390/5: Marjory Perham Papers, 1938–43.

Other Documents

Gold Coast, Northern Territories Council. *Record of the Tenth Session of the Territorial Council*, Tamale, 31 October–2 November, 1951 (Balme Library Collection, University of Ghana).
Kerr, Alan F. "Frafra Constitutional Development." n.d. but c.1937/8. I thank Mr. Kerr for providing access to his personal copy of the report.
——. "Handing-over Notes to I.S. Warren," 22/1/40, p. 13, personal papers, A.F. Kerr.

Official Reports

Eyre-Smith, E.S. *A Brief Review of the History and Social Organisation of the Peoples of the Northern Territories of the Gold Coast.* Gold Coast: Government Printer, 1932.
Gold Coast. *Department of Agriculture Annual Reports, 1932–33, 1934–35,1935–36, 1936–37, 1947–8, 1948–9.* Accra: Government Printer.
——. *Department of Agriculture, Ten-Year Plan, 1949/50–1959/60.* Accra: Government Printer.
——. *Department of Tsetse Control Annual Reports, 1949, 1950–1* Accra: Government Printer.
——. *Forestry Department Annual Report, 1947–8.* Accra: Government Printer.
——. *Gonja Development Company: Report of the First Advisory Committee.* Accra: Government Printer, 1953.
——. *Report of the Agricultural Development Corporation, 1953–54.* Accra: Government Printer, 1954.
——. *Report on the Northern Territories of the Gold Coast, 1920.* London: HMSO, 1921.
——. *General Plan for Development.* Accra: Government Printer, 1944.
——. *Mamprusi District Annual Report, 1939/40.* Accra: Government Printer.
——. *Medical Department Annual Reports, 1933/4, 1934/5, 1935/6.* Accra: Government Printer.
——. *Northern Territories, Tumu District Annual Report, 1946.* Accra: Government Printer.
——. *Veterinary Department Annual Reports, 1937–8, 1938–9, 1940–1, 1942–3.* Accra: Government Printer.
Great Britain. *Report of the Commission on the Marketing of West African Cocoa.* London, HMSO, Cmd.5845, 1938.
Great Britain, Colonial Office. *Report of the West African Oilseed Mission, 1948.*
Lynn, C.W. *Agriculture in North Mamprusi.* Gold Coast: Department of Agriculture, Bulletin #34, 1937.
——. *Report on a Visit to Northern Nigeria to Study Mixed Farming.* Accra: Department of Agriculture, Gold Coast, Bulletin #33, 1936.
Marshall, R.C. *Report on the Gold Coast Forest Problem.* Accra: Government Printer, 1936.
Moor, H.W. *Report on Gold Coast Forests.* Accra: Government Printer, 1934.
Northcott, H.P. "Further Correspondence of the Northern Territories," CO879/58, Great Britain, Public Record Office (PRO), p. 178.
——. *Report on the Northern Territories of the Gold Coast.* London: HMSO, 1899.
Rattray, R.S. *Report by the Anthropology Commissioner.* Accra: Government Printer, 1930.
Shephard, C.Y. *Report on the Economics of Peasant Agriculture in the Gold Coast.* Gold Coast: Sessional Paper I of 1936.

Published Primary Sources

Bagehot, Walter. *Physics and Politics, or, Thoughts on the Application of the Principles of 'Natural Selection' and 'Inheritance' to Political Society*. New York: D. Appleton and Company, 1873.

Buell, R. *The Native Problem in Africa*. London: Frank Cass and Company, 1965, originally published, 1928.

Cameron, Sir Donald. *My Tanganyika Service and Some Nigeria*. London: George Allen and Unwin Ltd., 1939.

Cardinall, A.W. *The Gold Coast, 1931*. Accra, Government Printer, 1931.

Clifford Sir Hugh. "The Gold Coast." *Blackwood's*, 1918 (January): 51–68.

——. "The Gold Coast and Its Dependencies." *United Empire*, 1915 (August): 622–46.

——. "Recent Developments on the Gold Coast." *Journal of the African Society*, 18(72) (July, 1919): 241–53.

——. "Some Facts Concerning the Gold Coast." *Journal of the African Society*, 14(53) (October, 1914): 15–23.

Collins, W. "Extension Work in Kusasi, 1932–1959." *The Ghana Farmer*, 4(2) (May, 1960).

Durkheim, Emile. *The Division of Labour in Society*. London: Collier-Macmillan Limited, 1933.

Faulkner, O.T. and J.R. Mackie. *West African Agriculture*. Cambridge: Cambridge University Press, 1933.

Fortes, M. "An Anthropologist's Point of View," in R. Hinden (ed), *Fabian Colonial Essays*. London: George Allen and Unwin, 1944.

——. *The Dynamics of Clanship among the Tallensi*. London: Oxford University Press, 1945.

——. *The Web of Kinship among the Tallensi*. London: Oxford University Press, 1949.

Fortes, M. and S.L. Fortes. "Food in the Domestic Economy of the Tallensi." *Africa*, (9)(2) (April, 1936): 237–76.

Guggisberg, Sir F.G. "The Goal of the Gold Coast." *Journal of the African Society*, 21(82) (January, 1922): 81–91.

——. *The Gold Coast: A Review of the Events of 1920–1926 and the Prospects of 1927*. Accra: Government Printer, 1927.

Guggisberg Sir F. and A.G. Fraser. *The Future of the Negro: Some Chapters in the Development of a Race*. London: Student Christian Movement, 1929.

Hailey, William Malcolm. *Native Administration in the British African Territories*. London: HM Stationary Office, 1950.

Hinden, Rita. *Plan for Africa*. London: George Allen and Unwin Ltd., 1941.

Lugard, Sir F.D. *The Dual Mandate in British Tropical Africa (3rd Ed.)*. Edinburgh: William Blackwood and Sons Ltd., 1926, originally published 1922.

McPhee, Allan. *The Economic Revolution in West Africa*. London: Frank Cass and Company, originally published, 1926.

Metcalfe, G.E. *Great Britain and Ghana: Documents of Ghana History, 1807–1957*. London: Thomas Nelson and Sons Ltd., 1964.

Mordi, C.C., "The African Groundnut Scheme: Where Do Africans Benefit?" *The West African Review*, (December, 1947): 1425–7.

Morel E.D. *Affairs of West Africa*. London: Heinemann Press, 1902.

——. *The Black Man's Burden*. Manchester: National Labour Press, 1920.

Rattray, R.S. *Ashanti Law and Constitution*. Oxford: The Clarendon Press, 1929.

——. *Tribes of the Ashanti Hinterland, Volume One*. Oxford: The Clarendon Press, 1969 (originally published 1932).

——. *Tribes of the Ashanti Hinterland, Volume Two*. Oxford: The Clarendon Press, 1969 (originally published 1932).

Ricardo, David. *The Principles of Political Economy and Taxation*. London: J.M. Dent & Sons Ltd., 1911, originally published, 1817.
Rodger, Sir John "The Gold Coast of Today." *Journal of the Royal African Society*, 9(33) (October, 1909): 1–19.
Strickland, C.F. *Co-operation for Africa*. London: Oxford University Press, 1933.
——. *Cooperation in the Colonies*. London: George Allen and Unwin, 1945.
Watherston, Lt.-Col. A.E. "Northern Territories of the Gold Coast." *Journal of the African Society*, 7(28) (July, 1908): 344–69.
Webb, Sidney and Beatrice Webb. *Soviet Communism: A New Civilisation?* Special Limited Edition Printed by the Authors for Subscribing Members of Trade Unions, October, 1935.
Wells, H.G. *The Work, Wealth and Happiness of Mankind*. London: Heinemann, 1934.
Wood, Alan. *The Groundnut Affair*. London: The Bodley Head, 1950.
N/A. "Land Tenure and Political Evolution in West Africa." *American Review of Reviews*, 47 (January–June, 1913): 617–619.

Interviews

Hinds, John and Betty. Prestwick, Scotland, 5 October 1995.
Kerr, A.F. Tynron, Scotland, 3 October 1994.
Rees, George and Parry, Denzil. Newport, Wales, 30 August 1995.

Secondary Works

Adjaye, Joseph K. "Agyeman Prempe I and British Colonization of Asante: A Reassessment." *International Journal of African Historical Studies*, 22(2) (1989): 225–6.
Agbodeka, F. "Sir Gordon Guggisberg's Contribution to the Development of the Gold Coast, 1919–1927." *Transactions of the Historical Society of Ghana*, 13(1) (June 1972): 51–64.
Alence, Rod, "Colonial Government, Social Conflict and State Involvement in Africa's Open Economies: The Origins of the Ghana Cocoa Marketing Board, 1939–46," *Journal of African History*, 42 (2001): 397–416.
Allman, Jean, *The Quills of the Porcupine: Asante Nationalism in an Emergent Ghana*. Madison: University of Wisconsin Press, 1993.
Allman, Jean and Jonathan Parker. *Tongnaab: The History of a West African God*. Bloomington: Indiana University Press, 2005
Anafu, M. "The Impact of Colonial Rule on Tallensi Political Institutions, 1898–1967." *Transactions of the Historical Society of Ghana*, 14(1) (June 1973): 17–37.
Anim, Robert Kwaku. *Agricultural Activities and the Role of Extension in the Adoption of New Farming Activities in Kusasi Region of Ghana*. Ph.D. Dissertation, Ohio State University, 1978.
Anyane, S. *Ghana Agriculture*. London: Oxford University Press, 1963.
Apter, David. *Ghana in Transition*. Princeton: Princeton University Press, 1972.
Arden Hoppe, Kirk. "Lords of the Fly: Colonial Visions and Revisions of African Sleeping Sickness Environments on Ugandan Lake Victoria, 1906–61." *Africa*, 67(1) (1997): 86–105.
Arhin, Kwame (ed). *The Papers of George Ekem Ferguson: A Fanti Official of the Gold Coast Government, 1890–1897*. African Social Research Documents, 7, Leiden and Cambridge: Afrika-Studiecentrum, 1974.
——. *West African Traders in the Nineteenth and Twentieth Centuries*. London: Longman Group Limited, 1979.

Arhin, K. and J. Ki-Zerbo. "States and Peoples of the Niger Bend and the Volta." In J.F. Ade Ajayi (ed.), *UNESCO General History of Africa, Volume VI: Africa in the Nineteenth Century Until the 1880s.* Oxford: Heinemann, 1989, pp. 662–698.

Austin, Dennis. "Elections in a Rural African Area," in William John Hanna (ed.), *Independent Black Africa: The Politics of Freedom.* Chicago: Rand McNally and Company, 1964, pp. 341–63.

——. *Politics in Ghana, 1946–1960.* London: Oxford University Press, 1964.

Austin, Gareth. *Labour, Land and Capital in Ghana: From Slavery to Free Labour in Asante, 1907–1956,* Rochester: University of Rochester Press, 2005.

——. "The Emergence of Capitalist Relations in South Asante Cocoa-Farming, c. 1916–33," *Journal of African History,* 28 (1987): 259–79.

Barker, Jonathan. *Rural Communities Under Stress.* Cambridge: Cambridge University Press, 1989.

Bauer, P.T. *West African Trade.* Cambridge: Cambridge University Press, 1954.

Bening, R.B. "Administration and Development in Northern Ghana, 1898–1931." *Ghana Social Science Journal,* 4(2) (1977): 58–76.

——. "Colonial Development Policy in Northern Ghana, 1898–1950." *Bulletin of Ghana Geographical Association,* 17 (1975): 65–79.

——. "The Definition of the International Boundaries of Northern Ghana, 1888–1904." *Transactions of the Historical Society of Ghana,* 14(2) (December 1973): 229–61.

——. "The Development of Education in Northern Ghana, 1908–1957." *Ghana Social Science Journal,* 1(2) (November 1971): 21–41.

——. "Foundations of the Modern Native States of Northern Ghana." *Universitas,* 5(1) (November 1975): 116–38.

——. *A History of Education in Northern Ghana, 1907–1976.* Accra: Ghana Universities Press, 1990.

——. "Indigenous Concepts of Boundaries and Significance of Administrative Stations and Boundaries in Northern Ghana." *Bulletin of the Ghana Geographical Association,* 15 (1973): 7–20.

——. "Land Policy and Administration in Northern Ghana, 1898–1976," *Transactions of the Historical Society of Ghana,* 16(2) (1995): 227–66.

——. "Land Tenure Systems and Traditional Agriculture of the Sissala." *Bulletin of the Ghana Geographical Association,* 18 (1976): 15–34.

Berman, Bruce. *Control and Crisis in Colonial Kenya: The Dialectic of Domination.* London: James Currey, 1990.

Bobbio, Noberto, "Gramsci and the Concept of Civil Society," in John Keane. *Civil Society and the State: New European Perspectives,* London: Verso, 1988, pp. 73–99.

Bratton, Michael. "Civil Society and Political Transitions in Africa," in *Civil Society and the State in Africa,* edited by John W. Harbeson, Donald Rothchild and Naomi Chazan. Boulder: Lynne Rienner Publishers, Inc., 1994.

Bourret, F.M. *Ghana: The Road to Independence, 1919–1957.* Stanford: Stanford University Press, 1960.

Chalfin, Brenda, *Shea Butter Republic: State Power, Global Markets, and the Making of an Indigenous Commodity.* New York: Routledge, 2004.

——. "Centering the Margin: The Border Zone Economies of Northeast Ghana," paper presented to the African Studies Association Annual Meetings, Columbus, Ohio, Nov. 13–16, 1997.

Chambas, Mohamed Ibn. *The Politics of Agricultural and Rural Development in the Upper Region of Ghana: Implications of Technocratic Ideology and Non-Participatory Development.* Ph.D. Dissertation, Cornell University, 1980.

Cline, Catherine Ann. *E.D. Morel, 1873–1924: The Strategies of Protest.* Belfast: Blackstaff Press, 1980.

Collins, Robert O. *Historical Problems of Imperial Africa.* New York: Markus Wiener Publishers, 1994.

Constantine, Stephen. *The Making of Colonial Development Policy, 1914–1940*. London: Frank Cass And Company, 1984.
Cooper, Federick. *Decolonization and African Society: The Labor Question in French and British Africa*. Cambridge: Cambridge University Press, 1996.
Cooper, Frederick and Randall Packard. *International Development and the Social Sciences: Essays on the History and Politics of Knowledge*. Berkeley: University of California Press, 1997.
Cowen, M. and R. Shenton. "Bankers, Peasants and Land in West Africa, 1905–37." *Journal of Peasant Studies*, 19(1) (October 1991): 26–58.
——. *Doctrines of Development*. London: Routledge, 1996.
——. "Imagining Development," in Crush, Jonathan, *Power of Development*. London: Routledge, 1995.
——. "The Origin and Course of Fabian Colonialism in Africa." *Journal of Historical Sociology* 4, no 22 (June 1991): 143–174.
Cowen, Michael. "The Early Years of the Colonial Development Corporation: British State Enterprise Overseas During Late Colonialism." *African Affairs*, 83, no. 330 (1984): 63–75.
Cox-George, N.A. *Studies in Finance and Development: The Gold Coast (Ghana)Experience, 1914–1950*. London: Dennis Dobson, 1973.
Crisp, Jeff, *The Story of an African Working Class: Ghanaian Miners' Struggles, 1870–1980*. London: Zed Books, 1984.
Crowder, Michael. *Colonial West Africa: Collected Essays*. London: Frank Cass and Company Limited, 1978.
Curtin, Phillip, Steven Feierman, Leonard Thompson and Jan Vansina, Jan. *African History: From Earliest Times to Independence*. London: Addison Wesley Longman Limited, 1996.
Davidson, Basil. *Black Man's Burden: Africa and the Curse of the Nation-State*. New York: Times Books, 1992.
Der, B.G. "Colonial Land Policies in the Northern Territories in the Gold Coast, 1900–1975." *Universitas (New Series)* 4, No. 2 (1975): 127–142.
——. "Agricultural Policy in Northern Ghana During the Colonial Era." *Universitas (New Series)* 8 (1979): 3–18.
Deutsch, Jan-Georg, *Educating the Middlemen: A Political and Economic History of Statutory Cocoa Marketing in Nigeria, 1936–1947*. Berlin: Das Arabische Buch, 1995.
Dike-Nworah, K.O. "The West African Operations of the British Cotton Growing Association, 1904–1914." *African Historical Studies*, 4, No. 2 (1971): 315–331.
Eades, J.S. *Strangers and Traders: Yoruba Migrants, Markets and the State in Northern Ghana*. Edinburgh: Edinburgh University Press, 1993.
Edsman, Bjorn. *Lawyers in Gold Coast Politics c. 1900–1945: From Mensah Sarbah to J.B. Danquah*. Stockholm: Almqvist & Wiksell International, 1979.
Edwards, Michael. *Civil Society*. Cambridge: Polity Press, 2004.
Fage, J.D. and Roland Oliver. *The Cambridge History of Africa: Volume VI, 1870–1905*. Cambridge: Cambridge University Press, 1985.
Ferguson, James, "Anthropology and Its Evil Twin: 'Development' in the Constitution of a Discipline," in *International Development and the Social Sciences: Essays on the History and Politics of Knowledge*, edited by Frederick Cooper and Randall Packard, Berkeley: University of California Press, 1997, pp. 150–75.
Ferguson, James. *The Anti-politics Machine: 'Development,' Depoliticization and Bureaucratic Power in Lesotho*. Cambridge: Cambridge University Press, 1990.
Ferguson, P. and I. Wilks, "Chiefs, Constitutions and the British in Northern Ghana," in *West African Chiefs*, edited by M. Crowder and O. Ikeme. New York: Africana Publishing Corporation, 1970, pp. 326–369.
Fine, Robert. "Civil Society Theory, Enlightenment and Critique." *Democratization* 4, No. 1 (Spring, 1997): 7–28.

Ford, John. "Ideas Which Have Influenced Attempts to Solve the Problems of African Trypanosomiasis." *Social Science and Medicine*, Vol. 13B, 1979.

——. *The Role of Trypanosomiasis in African Ecology: A Study of the Tsetse Fly Problem.* Oxford: Oxford University Press, 1971.

Frimpong-Ansah. Jonathan H. *The Vampire State in Africa: The Political Economy of Decline in Ghana.* London: James Currey, 1991.

Gailey, Harry A. *Clifford: Imperial Proconsul.* London: Rex Collings, 1982.

Gibbon, Peter. "Civil society and political change, with special reference to 'developmentalist' states," paper presented to the Nordic Conference on "Social Movements in the Third World," University of Lund, 1993.

Giblin, James. "Trypanosomiasis Control in African History: An Evaded Issue," *Journal of African History* 31 (1990): 59–70.

Goody, Jack. *Cooking, Cuisine and Class.* Cambridge: Cambridge University Press, 1982.

——. *Death, Property and the Ancestors.* Stanford: Stanford University Press, 1962.

——. *The Expansive Moment: Anthropology in Britain and Africa, 1918–1970.* Cambridge: Cambridge University Press, 1995.

——. "The Political Systems of the Tallensi and Their Neighbours, 1888–1915." *Cambridge Anthropology*, 14, No. 2 (1990): 1–25.

——. *Social Organisation of the LoWiili.* London: Oxford University Press, 1967.

Greenstreet, D.K. "The Guggisberg Ten-Year Development Plan." *Economic Bulletin of Ghana* 8, No. 1 (1964): 18–26.

Haight, B.M. *Bole and Gonja: Contributions to the History of Northern Ghana.* Ph.D. Dissertation, Northwestern University, 1981.

Harbeson, John W. "Civil Society and Political Renaissance in Africa," in *Civil Society and the State in Africa*, edited by John W. Harbeson, Donald Rothchild and Naomi Chazan. Boulder: Lynne Rienner Publishers, Inc., 1994.

Hargreaves, J.D. *Decolonization in Africa.* London: Addison Wesley Longman Limited, 1995.

——. *Prelude to the Partition of West Africa.* London: Macmillan and Company Ltd., 1963.

——. *West Africa Partitioned, Volume 1: The Loaded Pause.* London: The Macmillan Press, 1974.

——. "Western Africa, 1886–1905," in J.D. Fage and Roland Oliver, *The Cambridge History of Africa: Volume VI, 1870–1905.* Cambridge: Cambridge University Press, 1985, pp. 259–75

Hart, Keith. "The Economic Basis of Tallensi Social History in the Early Twentieth Century." in *Research in Economic Anthropology, Volume One*, edited by George Dalton. Greenwich: IAI Press, 1978, pp. 185–216.

Hawkins, Sean. "Disguising Chiefs and God As History: Questions on the Acephalousness of LoDagaa Politics and Religion." *Africa* 66, No. 2 (1996)

——. *Writing and Colonialism in Northern Ghana: The Encounter Between the LoDagaa and the "World on Paper."* Toronto: University of Toronto Press, 2002.

Hayden, Anthony P. *Sir Matthew Nathan: British Colonial Governor and Civil Servant.* St. Lucia: University of Queensland Press, 1976.

Hicks, Ursula K. *Development From Below: Local Government and Finance in Developing Countries of the Commonwealth.* Oxford: The Clarendon Press, 1961.

Hill, Polly. *The Gold Coast Cocoa Farmer: A Preliminary Survey.* Oxford: Oxford University Press, 1956.

——. *The Migrant Cocoa Farmers of Southern Ghana: A Study in Rural Capitalism.* Cambridge: Cambridge University Press, 1963

Hilton T.E. "Land Planning and Resettlement in Northern Ghana." *Geography* 44 (1959): 227–240.

Holden, J.J. "The Zabarima Conquest of North-West Ghana." *Transactions of the Historical Society of Ghana* 8 (1965): 60–86.

Howard, Rhoda. *Colonialism and Underdevelopment in Ghana.* London: Croom Helm, 1978.

——. "Formation and Stratification of the Peasantry in Colonial Ghana." *Journal of Peasant Studies* 8, No. 4 (1981): 62–80.

Hunwick, John and Nancy Lawlor (eds.). *The Cloth of Many Colored Silks: Papers on History and Society Ghanaian and Islamic in Honor of Ivor Wilks.* Evanston: Northwestern University Press, 1996.

Hutchful, Eboe. "The Civil Society Debate in Africa." *International Journal* 51, No. 1 (1995–6): 54–77.

Hyden, Goran. "Civil Society, Social Capital, and Development: Dissection of a Complex Discourse," *Studies in Comparative and International Development* 32, No. 1 (Spring, 1997): 3–30.

Hyden, Goran. "Governance and the Study of Politics," in *Governance and Politics in Africa*, edited by Goran Hyden and Michael Bratton. Boulder: Lynne Rienner Publishers, 1992.

Hyden, Goran and Michael Bratton (eds.). *Governance and Politics in Africa.* Boulder: Lynne Rienner Publishers, 1992.

Iliffe, John. *A Modern History of Tanganyika.* Cambridge: Cambridge University Press, 1979.

Illiasu, A.A. "The Establishment of British Administration in Mampurugu, 1898–1937." *Transactions of the Historical Society of Ghana* 16, No. 1 (1975): 1–28.

——. "Rex v. Yagbongwura and Six Others." *Universitas*, 5, No. 1 (1975): 139–151.

Johnson, Marion. "Cotton Imperialism in West Africa." *African Affairs* 73, No. 291 (April, 1974): 178–187.

Judd, Denis. *Radical Joe: A Life of Joseph Chamberlain.* London: Hamish Hamilton, 1977.

Kay, Geoffrey. *The Political Economy of Colonialism in Ghana: A Collection of Documents and Statistics, 1900–1960.* Cambridge: Cambridge University Press, 1972.

Keane, John. "Despotism and Democracy," in *Civil Society and the State: New European Perspectives*, edited by John Keane. London: Verso, 1988, pp. 35–71.

Kimble, David. *A Political History of Ghana: The Rise of Gold Coast Nationalism, 1850–1928.* London: Oxford University Press, 1965.

Killing ray, David. "Repercussions of World War One in the Gold Coast," *Journal of African History* 19, No. 1 (1978): 39–59.

Kjekshus, Helge. *Ecology Control and Economic Development.* London: Heinemann, 1977.

Konings, Piet. *The State and Rural Class Formation in Ghana.* London: KPI Ltd., 1986.

Kössler, Reinhart and Henning Melber. *The Concept of Civil Society and the Process of Nation-Building in African States.* NEPRU WORKING PAPER 44, Windhoek, The Namibian Economic Policy Research Unit, 1994.

Kuklick, Henrika. *The Savage Within: The Social History of British Anthropology, 1885–1945.* Cambridge: Cambridge University Press, 1995.

Kuper, Adam. *The Invention of Primitive Society: Transformations of an Illusion.* London: Routledge, 1988.

Ladouceur, Paul Andre. *Chiefs and Politicians: The Politics of Regionalism in Northern Ghana.* London: Longman Group Limited, 1979.

Lance, James Merriman. *Seeking the Political Kingdom: British Colonial Impositions and African Manipulations in the Northern Territories of the Gold Coast Colony.* Ph.D. dissertation, Stanford University, 1995.

Legassick, Martin. "Firearms, Horses and Samorian Army Organization, 1870–1898." *Journal of African History* 7, No. 1 (1966): 95–115.

Lentz, Carola, "Stateless Societies or Chiefdoms: A Debate Among Dagara Intellectuals," in *Ghana's North: Research on Culture, Religion, and Politics of Societies in Transition*, edited by Franz Kroger and Barbara Meier. Frankfurt am Main: Peter Lang, 2003.

——. "Colonial Constructions and African Initiatives: The History of Ethnicity in Northwestern Ghana," *Ethnos* 65, No. 1 (2000): 107–136.
——. "'The Time When Politics Came': Ghana's Decolonisation from the Perspective of a Rural Periphery." *Journal of Contemporary African Studies* 20, No. 2 (2002): 245–74.
——. "Colonial Ethnography and Political Reform: the Works of A.C. Duncan-Johnstone, R.S. Rattray, J. Eyre-Smith and J. Guiness on Northern Ghana." *Ghana Studies* 2 (1999): 119–69.
——. *Die Konstruktion von Ethnizität. Eine politische Geschichte Nord-West Ghanas, 1870–1990.* Köln: Köppe, 1998.
——. "A Dagara Rebellion Against Dagomba Rule? Contested Stories of Origin in North-Western Ghana." *Journal of African History* 35 (1994): 457–92.
——. "Histories and Political Conflict: A Case Study of Chieftaincy in Nandom, Northwestern Ghana." *Paideuma* 39 (1993).
Lively, Jack and Andrew Reeve, "The Emergence of the Idea of Civil Society: the Artificial Political Order and Natural Social Orders." *Democratization* 4, No. 1 (Spring, 1997): 63–75.
Louis, Wm. Roger and Robinson, Ronald. "The Imperialism of Decolonization." *Journal of Imperial and Commonwealth History* 22, No. 3 (1994): 462–511.
Lovejoy, P. *Caravans of Kola: The Hausa Kola Trade, 1700–1900.* Zaria: Ahmadu Bello University Press, 1980.
——. "The Internal Trade of West Africa to 1800," in *History of West Africa, Volume One (3rd edition)*, edited by J.F.A. Ajayi and M. Crowder. Harlow: Longman Group Limited, 1985.
Lyons, Marinez. "From 'Death Camps' to *Cordon Sanitaire*: The Development of Sleeping Sickness Policy in the Uele District of the Belgian Congo, 1903–1914." *Journal of African History* 26 (1985): 69–91.
Mamdani, Mahmood. *Citizen and Subject: Contemporary Africa and the Legacy of Late Colonialism.* Princeton: Princeton University Press, 1996.
——. "The Social Basis of Constitutionalism in Africa." *Journal of Modern African Studies* 28, No. 3 (1990): 359–74.
——. "State and Civil Society in Contemporary Africa: Reconceptualizing the Birth of State Nationalism and the Defeat of Popular Movements." *Africa Development* 15, Nos. 3/4 (1990): 47–70.
Markovitz, Irving Leonard. "Uncivil Society, Capitalism and the State in Africa," *Commonwealth and Comparative Politics* 36, No. 2 (July, 1998): 21–53.
McBriar, A.M. *Fabian Socialism and English Politics, 1884–1918.* London: Cambridge University Press, 1966.
McCaskie, T.C. "Empire State: Asante and the Historians." *Journal of African History* 33 (1992): 467–76
——. "R.S.Rattray and the Construction of Asante History: An Appraisal." *History in Africa* 10 (1983): 187–206.
——. *State and Society in Precolonial Asante.* Cambridge: Cambridge University Press, 1995.
Meredith, David, "State Controlled Marketing Boards and Economic Development: the Case of West African Produce During the Second World War," *Economic History Review* 34, No. 1 (1986): 77–91.
Mikell, Gwendolyn. *Cocoa and Chaos in Ghana.* New York: Paragon House, 1989.
Milburn, Josephine, "The 1938 Gold Coast Cocoa Crisis: British Business and the Colonial Office," *African Historical Studies* 3, No. 1 (1970): 57–74.
Mohan, Giles. "The Disappointments of Civil Society: the Politics of NGO Intervention in Northern Ghana," *Political Geography* 21 (2002): 125–54.
Moore, Henrietta L. and Megan Vaughan. *Cutting Down Trees: Gender, Nutrition and Agricultural Change in the Northern Province of Zambia, 1890–1990.* Portsmouth: Heinemann, 1994.

Morgan D.J. *The Official History of British Colonial Development, Volume One: The Origins of British Aid Policy, 1924–1945.* London: The MacMillan Press Ltd., 1980.
Morgan, D.J. *The Official History of British Colonial Development, Volume Two: Developing British Colonial Resources, 1945–51.* Atlantic Highlands: Humanities Press Ltd., 1980.
Omosini, O. "The Gold Coast Land Question, 1894–1900: Some Issues Raised on West Africa's Economic Development." *International Journal of African Historical Studies* 5, No. 3 (1972): 453–69.
Patterson, K. David. *Health in Colonial Ghana: Disease, Medicine and Socio-Economic Change, 1900–1955.* Waltham: Crossroads Press, 1981.
Pelczynski, Z.A. "Solidarity and the 'Rebirth of Civil Society'" in *Civil Society and the State: New European Perspectives*, edited by John Keane. London: Verso, 1988, pp. 361–80.
Person, Yves. "Samori and Resistance to the French." in *Protest and Power in Black Africa*, edited by Robert Rotberg and Ali A. Mazrui. New York: Oxford University Press, 1970, pp. 80–112
——. "Samori and Islam," in *Studies in West African Islamic History, Volume 1: The Cultivators of Islam*, edited by John Ralph Willis. London: Frank Cass and Company Limited, 1979, pp. 259–77.
——. "States and peoples of Senegambia and Upper Guinea, in *UNESCO General History of Africa, Volume VI: Africa in the Nineteenth Century until the 1880s*, edited by J.F. Ade Ajayi. London: Heinemann, 1989, pp. 636–61.
——. "Western Africa, 1870–1886," in *The Cambridge History of Africa, Volume VI: from 1870 to 1905*, edited by J.D. Fage and Roland Oliver. Cambridge: Cambridge University Press, 1985, pp. 208–256.
Phillips, Anne. *The Enigma of Colonialism: British Policy in West Africa.* London: James Currey, 1989.
Plange, Nii-K. *Colonialism and Underdevelopment in Northern Ghana: The Political Sociology of the Colonial Situation, 1900–1950.* Ph.D. Dissertation, University of Toronto, 1976.
——. "Opportunity Cost and Labour Migration: A Misinterpretation of Proletarianization in Northern Ghana." *Journal of Modern African Studies* 17 (1979): 655–676.
——. "Underdevelopment in Northern Ghana: Natural Causes or Colonial Capitalism?" *Review of African Political Economy* 15/16 (1979): 4–14.
Quansah, S.T. "The Gonja Settlement and Development Scheme-Ghana." *Economic Bulletin of Ghana* 2, No. 1 (1972): 14–24.
Rathbone, Richard, *Murder and Politics in Colonial Ghana.* New Haven: Yale University Press, 1993.
——. *Nkrumah and the Chiefs: The Politics of Chieftaincy in Ghana, 1951–60.* Athens: Ohio University Press, 2000.
Rothchild, Donald (ed.). *Ghana: The Political Economy of Recovery.* Boulder: Lynne Rienner Publishers, 1991.
Shenton, R. *The Development of Capitalism in Northern Nigeria.* Toronto: University of Toronto Press, 1986.
——. "Nigerian Agriculture in Historical Perspective: Development and Crisis, 1900–60." in *State, Oil and Agriculture in Nigeria*, edited by Michael Watts. Berkeley: The Regents of the University of California, 1987.
Sheperd, A. *The Development of Capitalist Rice Farming in Northern Ghana.* Ph.D. Dissertation, Cambridge University, UMI, 1979.
Southall, Roger J. "Farmers, Traders and Brokers in the Gold Coast Cocoa Economy." *Canadian Journal of African Studies* 12, no. 2 (1978): 185–211.
St. John-Stevas, Norman. *Bagehot's Historical Essays.* New York, Anchor Books, 1965.
Staniland, Martin. *The Lions of Dagbon: Political Change in Northern Ghana.* Cambridge, Cambridge University Press, 1975.
Sutton, I. "The Non-Development of the Northern Territories of the Gold Coast." *International Journal of African Historical Studies* 22, No. 4 (1989): 637–669.

Tashijan, Victoria B., "The diaries of A.C. Duncan-Johnstone: a preliminary analysis of British involvement in the "native courts" of colonial Asante", *Ghana Studies* 1 (1998): 135–50.

Thomas, R.G. "Forced Labour in British West Africa: The Northern Territories of the Gold Coast." *Journal of African History* 14, No. 1 (1973): 79–103.

——. "Military Recruitment in the Gold Coast during the First World War." *Cahiers d'etudes Africaines* 15, No. 1 (1975): 57–83.

Waller, Richard D. "Tsetse Fly in Western Narok, Kenya." *Journal of African History* 31 (1990): 81–101.

Webster J.B. and A.A. Boahen. *History of West Africa: The Revolutionary Years, 1815 to Independence.* New York: Praeger Publishers, 1970.

White, Luise. "Tsetse Visions: Narratives of Blood and Bugs in Colonial Northern Rhodesia, 1931–9." *Journal of African History* 36 (1995): 219–245.

Whitehead, Laurence, "Bowling in the Bronx: The Uncivil Interstices Between Civil and Political Society," *Democratization* 4, No. 1 (Spring, 1997): 94–114.

Wight, Martin. *The Gold Coast Legislative Council.* London: Faber and Faber, 1947.

Wilks Ivor. *Asante in the Nineteenth Century: The Structure and Evolution of a Political Order.* Cambridge: Cambridge University Press, 1975.

——. *Forests of Gold: Essays on the Akan and the Kingdom of Asante.* Athens: Ohio University Press, 1993.

——. *Wa and the Wala: Islam and Polity in Northern Ghana.* Cambridge: Cambridge University Press, 1989.

Wolf, Eric. *Europe and the People Without History.* Berkeley: University of California Press, 1982.

Wood, Alan. *The Groundnut Affair.* London: The Bodley Head, 1950.

Wood, Ellen Meiksins. *Democracy Against Capitalism: Renewing Historical Materialism.* Cambridge: Cambridge University Press, 1995.

Worboys, Michael. "The Discovery of Colonial Malnutrition Between the Wars." In *Imperial Medicine and Indigenous Societies*, edited by David Arnold. Manchester: Manchester University Press, 1988, pp. 208–225.

Worsley, P.M. "The Kinship System of the Tallensi: A Revaluation." *Journal of the Royal Anthropological Institute of Great Britain and Ireland* 86 (1956): 37–75.

Worster, Donald. *Dust Bowl: The Southern Plains in the 1930s.* Oxford: Oxford University Press, 1979.

Wraith, R.E. *Guggisberg.* London: Oxford University Press, 1967.

Yarak, Larry, "Slavery and the State in Asante History," in *The Cloth of Many Colored Silks: Papers on History and Society Ghanaian and Islamic in Honor of Ivor Wilks*, edited by John Hunwick and Nancy Lawlor. Evanston: Northwestern University Press, 1996, pp. 223–40.

Unpublished Manuscripts

Gandah, J. *Gandah Yir (House of the Brave).* Unpublished manuscript. I thank Mr. S.W.D.K. Gandah for providing a copy of this personal account of the life of his father.

INDEX

Page numbers in italics refer to maps

AFRICAN SOCIAL STUDIES SERIES

1. Saskia Brand, *Mediating Means and Fate.* A Socio-Political Analysis of Fertility and Demographic Change in Bamako, Mali.
2001. ISBN 90 04 12033 5

2. Axel Harneit-Sievers, *A Place in the World.* Local Historiographies in Africa and South Asia.
2002. ISBN 90 04 12303 2

3. John O. Oucho, *Undercurrents of Ethnic Conflict in Kenya.*
2002. ISBN 90 04 12459 4

4. Sandra J.T.M. Evers, *Constructing History, Culture and Inequality.* The Betsileo in the Extreme Southern Highlands of Madagascar.
2002. ISBN 90 04 12460 8

5. Kempe Ronald Hope, Sr., *From Crisis to Renewal.* Development Policy and Management in Africa.
2002. ISBN 90 04 12531 0

6. Wisdom J. Tettey, Korbla P. Puplampu, and Bruce J. Berman (eds.), *Critical Perspectives on Politics and Socio-Economic Development in Ghana.*
2003. ISBN 90 04 13013 6

7. Janet Andrewes, *Bodywork: Dress as a Cultural Tool.* Dress and Demeanor in the South of Senegal.
2004. ISBN 90 04 14107 3

8. Allen M. Howard and Richard M. Shain (eds.), *The Spatial Factor in African History.* The Relationship of the Social, Material, and Perceptual.
2005. ISBN-13: 978 90 04 13913 8 ISBN-10: 90 04 13913 3

9. Richard Kuba and Carola Lentz (eds.), *Land and the Politics of Belonging in West Africa.*
2006. ISBN-13: 978 90 04 14817 8 ISBN-10: 90 04 14817 5

10. Maghan Keita, *A Political Economy of Health Care in Senegal.*
2006.ISBN-13: 978 90 04 15065 2 ISBN-10: 90 04 15065 X

11. Dzodzi Tsikata, *Living in the Shadow of the Large Dams.* Long Term Responses of Downstream and Lakeside Communities of Ghana's Volta River Project.
2006. ISBN-13: 978 90 04 14144 5 ISBN-10: 90 04 14144 8

12. Kenneth Swindell and Alieu Jeng, *Migrants, Credit and Climate.* The Gambian Groundnut Trade, 1834-1934.
2006. ISBN-13: 978 90 04 14059 2 ISBN-10: 90 04 14059 X

13. Gerhard Seibert, *Comrades, Clients and Cousins*. Colonialism, Socialism and Democratization in São Tomé and Príncipe.
2006. ISBN-13: 978 90 04 14736 2 ISBN-10: 90 04 14736 5

14. Jeff D. Grischow. *Shaping Tradition*. Civil Society, Community and Development in Colonial Northern Ghana, 1899-1957.
2006. ISBN-13: 978 90 04 15243 4 ISBN-10: 90 04 15243 1